MY AFRICAN JOURNAL

A Personal Memoir of Four Years as an Englishwoman
Abroad

ANNE SHIRLEY

This book is dedicated to Keith, who only read a small part of it, but who was the whole part of it.

Contents

Foreword

I started life living with my parents and brother in two rooms
with no bathroom or inside toilet, but I still thought we were
fairly well off because most people I knew were in the same situation. Some friends were even poorer than us and I felt sorry for
them. Did I have ambition? No. I never thought I should be or
ever would be better off than I was at that time. Yet 'someone
up there' has always looked after me.

No, I wasn't ambitious. In this, I was more like my father
than my mother. My father thought everyone should stay within
their own social class, as they would be happier doing so, but my
mother always wanted the better things in life, though these
better things continued to elude her no matter how hard she
worked.

I left school in 1956 at the age of fifteen, as was the norm
for children who didn't go to a grammar school, and went to
work in the office of my local hospital as a junior clerk,
progressing to shorthand-typist after a year or so of night
school. Most of the girls in my class had gone to work in the
mills of Yorkshire, which were still thriving in the 1950s, and I
expected I would follow my parents into that employment. It

was my mother's ambition that nudged me along a different route, though this path had only been opened to me when, in my final year at school, we got a new teacher, or I should say, we got a fully qualified teacher. I had spent the previous two years of schooling being taught by student teachers, merely biding my time.

My new teacher was a wonderful nun whose name, sadly, I have forgotten. She must have seen potential in four of us girls because, while the rest of the class were doing art, she began to teach us the basics of Pitman's shorthand.

I loved writing the cartouches, though I made only slow progress – my memory has never been particularly wonderful. My mother was thrilled to see my interest in shorthand and by the time I was due to leave school, just after my fifteenth birthday, in her mind she already had me working as private secretary to the British prime minister! Strangely, I never knew what my father thought about me as he was a man of very few words.

At that time, I could never have imagined how wonderful my life was going to be. Within three years of starting work, and at the age of eighteen, I met Keith, the man who was to be my future husband, though it took another three years for him to realise that! This good looking young man stepped into my life when he began working as a hospital porter during his Easter vacation while studying at Imperial College, a London university.

From the time I was married in 1963 at the tender age of twenty-two, and for the next ten years, I was on skis soaring up the precipitous hills and freewheeling down the gentle slopes of life.

ONE

Beginnings

Keith's eldest brother and family had moved to Gwelo, Rhodesia, a number of years before I met him, but I was often present when the 8mm home movies from Gwelo were showing at his parents' home. Life coming through the screen seemed idyllic and Keith often talked about living and working overseas like his brother. I too would be transported to faraway places but thought that with my lack of qualifications it was just a pipedream for me. All that changed when Keith decided to abandon the course he was taking at Imperial College and move back to Yorkshire. For a while, he was lost, unsure what he wanted to do, but by the time we decided to marry in 1963, he had made up his mind to be a teacher like his brother, knowing that this would enable him to follow his dream. My dream, too. We knew that one day soon we would be going to Africa!

From the 1950s onwards, Africa had been gaining independence from colonial rule and the bells had already begun to toll for the Federation of Rhodesia and Nyasaland. In December 1960, Northern Rhodesia became Zambia and in 1964, Nyasaland became Malawi. Southern Rhodesia, however, refused to hand political control over to its African majority and in 1965 the white government unilaterally proclaimed independence from Britain. The first-ever serving British premier to visit South Africa was the Conservative prime minister, Harold Macmillan, who had made his famous 'Wind of Change' speech on 3 February 1960 to the South African parliament and which caused outrage:

"The wind of change is blowing through this continent, and whether we like it or not, this growth of national consciousness is a political fact. And we must all accept it as a fact, and our national policies must take account of it.

Of course, you understand this better than anyone, you are sprung from Europe, the home of nationalism, and here in Africa you have yourselves created a free nation. A new nation. Indeed, in the history of our times, yours will be recorded as the first of the African nationalists. And this tide of national consciousness which is now rising in Africa is a fact, for which you and we, and the other nations of the Western world are ultimately responsible. For its causes are to be found in the achievements of Western civilisation, in the pushing forward of the frontiers of knowledge, in the applying of science to the service of human needs, in the expanding of food production, in the speeding and multiplying of the means of communication, and perhaps above all and more than anything else in the spread of education.

As I have said, this growth of national consciousness in Africa is a political fact, and we must accept it as such. That means, I would judge, that we've got to come to terms with it. I sincerely believe that if we cannot do so, we may imperil the precarious balance between East and West on which the peace of the world depends.

The world today is divided into three main groups. First, what we call the Western Powers. You in South Africa, we in Britain, belong to this group, together with our friends and allies in other parts of the Common- wealth. In the United States of America and in Europe we call it the Free World. Secondly, there are the Communists – Russia, her satellites in Europe, China, whose population will rise by the end of the next ten years to the staggering total of 800 million. And then thirdly, those parts of the

2

world whose people are at present uncommitted either to Communism or to our Western ideas.

In this context, we think first of Asia and then of Africa. As I see it the great issue in this second half of the twentieth century is whether the uncommitted peoples of Asia and Africa will swing to the East or to the West. Will they be drawn into the Communist camp? Or will the great experiments in self-government that are now being made in Asia and Africa, especially within the Commonwealth, prove so successful, and by their example so compelling, that the balance will come down in favour of freedom and order and justice?

The struggle is joined, and it is a struggle for the minds of men. What is now on trial is much more than our military strength or our diplomatic and administrative skill. It is our way of life. The uncommitted nations want to see before they choose." (Extracted from a copy of the original speech).

There is some indication that Harold Macmillan had declined to present his Wind of Change speech to Verwoerd before addressing the whites-only Parliament that day, only briefly summing up the main content to him. However, this was not the first time Macmillan had made the speech as he was repeating the address he had made on 10th January 1960 during his visit to Ghana (a British colony on the Gold Coast before Independence in 1957).

When the speech was over, there was visible shock on Verwoerd's face and he quickly jumped to his feet. He was furious and, it has been said, his reply was completely 'off the cuff'.

Hendrik Verwoerd's response to the 'Winds of Change' speech made to the South African Parliament on 3 February 1960:

"The tendency in Africa for nations to become independent, and at the same time to do justice to all, does not only mean being just to the black man of Africa, but also to be just to the white man of Africa.

We call ourselves European, but actually we represent the white men of

Africa. They are the people not only in the Union but through major portions of Africa who brought civilisation here, who made the present developments of black nationalists possible. By bringing them education, by showing them this way of life, by bringing in industrial development, by bringing in the ideals which Western civilisation has developed itself.

And the white man came to Africa, perhaps to trade, in some cases, perhaps to bring the gospel, has remained to stay. And particularly we in this southernmost portion of Africa, have such a stake here that this is our only motherland, we have nowhere else to go. We set up a country bare, and the Bantu came in this country and settled certain portions for themselves, and it is in line with the thinking of Africa, to grant those fullest rights which we also with you admit all people should have and believe providing those rights for those people in the fullest degree in that part of southern Africa which their forefathers found for themselves and settled in. But similarly, we believe in balance, we believe in allowing exactly those same full opportunities to remain within the grasp of the white man who has made all this possible."

TWO

Leaving England

On a warm August day in 1966, as Keith and I boarded the train at Leeds City Station at the commencement of a trail-blazing journey to Africa, I had no idea then I was setting the scene for some amazing memories to recall in my old age. For two young people, by then aged twenty-five, who had never been out of England before, it was a huge step to take and I know I would never have had the courage to do it alone. I could only have done it with my husband.

From the moment I arrived in Africa, I loved the feel of it, just like a pair of soft leather shoes nicely worn in. The excitement of the future overcame any fears I may have had. There were a number of shocks to come but we took those in our stride, as most young people do. To us, dying and old age were things that happened to other people and were far into the future.

There were many incidences not recorded in my letters home, but re-reading the letters has reminded me of some of those missing occasions. In particular, I will never forget the final part of our journey by train from Cape Town up into Malawi...

IT WAS MONDAY, 12 September 1966. Our train had arrived at Dondo Junction near Beira early that morning. The previous evening we had been advised we would need to vacate the Pullman carriage that had been our home for five days and nights by 9 a.m. on the twelfth, which would give us time to perform our ablutions and enjoy a leisurely breakfast. Keith and I were happy to be nearing the end of our long journey from England and were very keen to board the railcar which would take us into Malawi. The railcar we joined was part of the Portuguese/Malawi public transport system and it was busy, there being many Africans already on board. We took our seats with the rest of the passengers, stowing our luggage beneath the seats and up on the inadequate roof rack. With no time to spare, the train quickly started moving but we hadn't been travelling very long when there was a sound of grinding metal and we were astonished to see steel shutters lowering to cover the windows. Eventually, the whole coach was in darkness except for a small number of dim light fittings at each end of the coach. We looked around to see if anyone else looked nervous, but the Africans didn't appear to be taking any notice. Then we saw the signs affixed to the partition between the windows, written in both English and Chinyanja (which is a Bantu language spoken in Mozambique and parts of Malawi where it is an official national language, along with English), advising passengers that the section of railway between Mozambique and Malawi was bandit country and that on the outskirts of Lourenco Marques, en route to Blantyre, the windows would have metal coverings added to prevent possible heavy machine-gun fire from the FRELIMO (the Mozambique Liberation Front) guerrillas' AK-47 rifles smashing the glass. My husband and I were quiet for a long time, coming to terms with our individual thoughts. Fortunately, no such event occurred; however, the incident remained in our memories.

Once settled in Malawi, we quickly fell into the congruent

existence of the many old colonialists who arrived all those years before and, in some cases, were still demonstrating those pioneering views. It was likely that we were going to be the last of the founding spirits to live and work in this part of Africa.

The Malawians were kind, respectful, shy, honest, and any number of adjectives I care to interpose here. I always felt safe in their company. My husband and I got the same impression of the Rhodesian Africans we met on our first visit to that beautiful country in December 1966. However, we wondered if those people would remain the same once Rhodesia gained its independence, as we knew it surely would in the end. Now, fifty years later, we know the answer to that uncertainty. I've had a wonderful life. It's been a great party and I wouldn't change a second of it, neither the sorrow nor the joy.

I knew then that in my old age I would have tremendous memories of my earlier life because I lived those days to the full. Yet, I could never have foreseen that my wonderful mother would ensure those memories survived for my daughter and granddaughters by keeping almost every one of the letters I sent from Africa all those years ago, and which I found only after she died, carefully wrapped and numbered one to 120. Apart from a few letters, which presumably were never returned after having done the rounds of relatives, I have almost my entire life in Africa recorded for posterity.

I sincerely hope I have come near to fulfilling my mother's ambition for me all those years ago.

On re-reading my letters, both Keith and I were startled at the impression they must have given because the letters often seem to show two disgruntled people. Yet, we knew we loved those four years in Africa, even though there were occasional problems. Perhaps we are forgetting the bad times and only remembering the good.

However, I still think that Africa (not Yorkshire?) is God's own country and I will be very happy if Paradise is half as nice, as the song goes. I also hope my family will remember what I told them when we were on top of Table Mountain together in 2013.

THREE

Letters From 1966

As a family, we had never been demonstrative. The very first time I ever remember kissing my parents was on my wedding day, and it was such an emotional experience that I still remember with perfect clarity that moment, standing outside the pub in my wedding dress, wondering if I was being soppy.

Many, many years later, I managed to say the words 'I love you' to my father only weeks before he died. This quiet, lovely man had been ravaged by cancer, and as he rested in my bed in my old bedroom, I lay down beside him. Putting my arms around his thin, bony body, I felt an overwhelming desire to keep him safe. I told him that I loved him and he said he knew. He loved me too. Sadly, my mother developed Alzheimer's. By the time she was eighty years of age, she didn't even know me, though to this day I still regret that I never got the opportunity to say those three little words to her before she died.

But I digress. It is 1966, I'm young and I have the excitement of my whole life ahead of me.

WEDNESDAY, 24 August 1966

I HAD ARRANGED to visit my parents the day before Keith and I were to leave on our big adventure. I had been dreading saying this final goodbye which, when the time came, I had found to be totally devastating. My mother, as usual, was stoical, and as soon as I had hugged and kissed her, she walked towards the kitchen door with her back to me. My father, on the other hand, clung to me, sobbing. It nearly broke my heart. They both managed to say goodbye through their tears and as I walked to the door for the last time for a while, I remember thinking: 'Will one of them be missing when I return?' I walked down the path to the car and opened the door, keeping my back to my parents who I knew would be behind me, heading for the gate. My tears nearly devoured me. I managed to smile when I turned to them and told them not to worry, that I would write often and that I would see them very soon. That would have been a good time to tell my parents I loved them.

As soon as I sat down in the driver's seat, I wound down the window (no electric windows in those days) and started the engine. I drove down the street for the last time in what would be nearly three years. I put my arm through the open window, and waving to my father and mother, watched them in my side mirror wave back to me. We continued waving until I turned into the main road and was out of sight. I was driving off into the sunset of my past life. The sunrise of my new life beckoned.

LEEDS. Thursday, 25 August 1966

KEITH and I awoke in our tiny terrace house in Leeds. We prepared our breakfast as usual, washing up our mugs and dishes, leaving them to dry on the draining board, and then went back upstairs to finish packing. A taxi had been booked to take us to the railway station but we had requested that no family member see us off. We felt it would have been too savage to cut the ties so dramatically, leaving them to sadly make their way homeward while we were excited, anticipating our new life. Instead, we had insisted we say our goodbyes individually in the days before our departure. We were not worldly-wise creatures.

As we waited for the arrival of the taxi, there was a nervousness in the room. We both gave a sigh of relief when at last our transport drew up outside and, collecting our suitcases and bags we had left in the hallway, we headed out to the waiting taxi and quietly began loading our things into the boot.

Having already discussed our need to say farewell to the house once our suitcases had been loaded, we walked back up the drive. My heart unexpectedly felt heavy at the thought that I was leaving our first real home, the home that had been newly built when we moved in at the beginning of our marriage.

Before closing and locking the door on the first three years of our life together, I took one last look inside the house, etching the memory onto my mind. So much so, after all these years, I can still visualise the low black, grey and fawn tiled fireplace with the shiny, black tiled hearth; the chimney breast wall we had decorated black and was where we displayed a print of Edouard Mandon's *The Song of the Surf* in a white picture frame. The picture was the room's centrepiece. The rest of the sitting room had been painted either a very pale green or decorated with pale green, black and white wallpaper. The three-piece suite, a wedding present from my parents, was upholstered in a speckled red and black uncut moquette material. Though I didn't think of it at the time, the three-piece suite was probably still being paid for on hire-purchase as my parents didn't have spare cash to buy such an expensive item. The curtains were mainly grey but contained red and black squares (OMG) and the sideboard and dining room furniture was all teak wood, G Plan, a very popular style in the 1960s. Being a through lounge to dining area, we had zoned the room with a vertical divider made of floorboards cut to the correct width and stained to match the dining area flooring. Each piece of wood was fixed at its ends to the one below it with two large brass screws and the whole unit hung from ceiling to floor. It became an airy way of dividing the room, allowing light to penetrate through the windows at each end of the house. We had found horse brasses from somewhere and used these to provide further decoration to the hanging unit. It all sounds so ghastly now, but we thought it was the bee's knees at the time.

The staircase was wallpapered in a multi-coloured paper and we had grown used to the fact that it didn't match halfway down. This was because Keith and I, knowing very little about paper-hanging at the beginning of our marriage, had started decorating the same staircase wall, me from the top and Keith from the bottom. When we met in the middle, we discovered there was only a half-width of wall left upon which to apply a whole width of paper. I thought I knew a bit more about wallpapering than Keith – I used to help my father decorate our home, and at the age of sixteen, I had papered the whole of my bedroom, my father having hung the first length – but apparently not. My excuse was that I knew nothing about decorating long, high staircases! On remembering our mistake, I smile once more.

After finally leaving the house, we put the spare house keys through the letterbox, retraced our steps down the garden path and climbed into the waiting taxi. As the car moved off, I took one last look back at the house and waved goodbye, knowing I had left some part of my soul there forever.

Driving over the familiar roads for the last time, reality suddenly hit us and we began to laugh with excitement, our anticipation of what was to come by then exceeding any sorrow we might have felt. Yes! At last, we were en route to a new life. I get goose bumps as I type this because that new life was to be such a happy time.

In the excitement, I don't remember alighting the taxi nor walking to the train, but I do remember, as the train drew away from Leeds City Station, that I looked at the old brown buildings with a new clarity, realising I might never see them again. Nor do I remember much of the conversation Keith and I had during the journey from Leeds, although we must have had lots to talk about. However, I do remember arriving at Southampton and looking for accommodation. We stayed overnight in a small boarding house and the following morning took a taxi-ride the short distance to the port.

The Edinburgh Castle

The *Edinburgh Castle*, a P&O liner, was already berthed and it only remained for us to check in our luggage. Some months before we had sent on ahead of us everything we thought we would need during our three-year stay in Malawi; therefore, our check-in at Southampton didn't take very long. We only had our personal possessions on us, which left time to spare to look around the docks. There was a lot of hustle and bustle further along the quayside. We could see that the *Castel Felice* was being loaded both with goods and passengers, so we meandered along to see what was happening. We asked someone about the ship and passengers and were told that the ship was being prepared for a journey to Australia. Most passengers were travelling on the Australian government's Assisted Passage Migration Scheme, under which British subjects were being accepted to live permanently in that country for a charge of ten pounds. The policy was intended to substantially increase the Australian population, which had fallen after World War II, and supply workers for the country's booming industries.

As people boarded, they moved to the port side of the ship, frantically searching the crowds on the quayside for the faces of friends and families; once located, they waved wildly, shouting silent farewells, their voices fading in the wind. I was so over-whelmed by this that I sat on a bollard on the dockside, looking at the tableau unfolding before me, and sobbed my heart out, realising that the majority of passengers would probably never return to England. Future generations would never know what the country of their descendants had been like.

But our turn to embark came quickly and we were whisked aboard an amazingly beautiful ship, for the time, at least. Wandering around the upper deck, we mingled with the other passengers and familiarised ourselves with its layout. We also availed ourselves of the refreshments that had kindly been laid out for passengers awaiting departure.

When the ship finally set sail at 13:00 hours on Friday, 26 August 1966, Keith and I also found ourselves standing at the port side rails, waving wildly to anyone who would wave back, though by then we weren't crying, we were laughing with excitement.

We waited until we had passed The Needles before venturing down from the deck and into the cavern of the ship to look for the cabin that was to be our home for the next eleven days.

Our journey was to be 6,000 miles long, with one stop at Las Palmas, before we would eventually arrive at Cape Town.

FINALLY, ON BOARD.

SUNDAY, 28 August 1966 at 3.40 p.m. – my first letter.

DEAR MAM, Dad and All,

Well, we are now well and truly on our way. We make our first stop tomorrow noon at Las Palmas, one of the Canary Islands. We have booked to go on a tour which will last a couple of hours. My writing is a bit jittery because the ship has a slight tremble.

We got off to a good start on Thursday morning! We left behind some presents which we had been given on Wednesday. We didn't realise until we were nearly at Doncaster and by then we were too late to do anything immediately. When we reached King's Cross we phoned Margaret, at her office in Leeds, and asked if Jack could go to see the couple who had bought our house to arrange to collect the presents and send them on to us. From Kings Cross, we took a taxi to Waterloo Station and from there caught the train to Southampton. That was when we realised we had made a second mistake. While we were assembling all our luggage at the docks we noticed that a bag was missing and immediately realised we must have left this on the Waterloo train, which was going on to Bournemouth after Southampton. After twenty phone calls and a cost of 10/= which we could ill afford, we were able to get the bag back. But now we have mislaid Keith's briefcase with all his books in. There is a search of the ship going on at present and I'll tell you how this turns out later.

Despite the encouraging start to our journey on the Friday afternoon, when we hardly knew we were moving, by Friday evening there was a terrific roll on the ship and it had become so ghastly we found we couldn't stand up very easily. At first, it was quite funny, but on Saturday morning I felt so ill I wasn't able to get up for breakfast. By this time, we had sailed into the Bay of Biscay, which has a reputation for being rough. For the next two meals, about a quarter of the passengers were missing, although I managed to eat something each time, but as soon as I could after the meal, I went up onto the deck, in spite of the wind and spray, and the fresh air seemed to help. This morning, thank goodness, we are out of the Bay of Biscay and heading for Spain. I was thinking about you while I was at 8.15 a.m. Mass (9.15 a.m. your time – we put our clocks back one hour last night). There is Mass every morning – 7.15 a.m. and 8.15 a.m. – but it was the first time I felt well enough to attend. There were quite a number of people there, too, though I was surprised to note that there were very few English people and I guessed the congregation consisted of mostly German or Dutch people, judging by their dialect.

We are settling into the routine now and beginning to enjoy ourselves. There is plenty of organised entertainment, sport, etc. going on each evening. Last night, we went to see the film The Wrong Box, a very recent one which we had seen in Leeds only two weeks ago. We decided to go anyway as there wasn't much else to do but we were so tired we fell asleep nearly as soon as it started, so it was a good job we had seen it before. We spent the morning today sunbathing – you should see Keith's face!

The meals are fabulous – for breakfast, three courses with cheese and biscuits to finish off if desired; the same for lunch. Tea is at 4.15 p.m. (it is now 4.10 p.m.) and evening meal at eight o'clock. Again, three courses.

I shall be posting this letter tomorrow at Las Palmas – you should get it by next weekend. One of the Castle liners will bring it when it calls at Las Palmas on the way back to England.

Cheerio for now. I'll write again very soon. Give my love to everyone, including Auntie Mary and Uncle John.

Lots of love,

Keith and Anne xx

JACK, who I mention above, was Keith's brother, and Margaret was Jack's wife and also my best friend.

At the time of our departure, they were comparatively newly married. Sadly, I wasn't present on the occasion the family first met Margaret as I had had words with Keith, which was only the second time we had had a disagreement during our marriage, or in the preceding years when we were courting but, strangely, both occasions had, directly or indirectly, a connection with Jack. Though, on reflection, it probably had more to do with me and my insecurity than with this lovely man.

I had expected to feel sick immediately we embarked from Southampton on the Friday afternoon but found this was not the case as the sea was very calm. Unfortunately, we discovered soon enough that this was not the prelude to what was to come as, by the following day, the seas were dancing like wild horses, the sea spray wetting the wooden benches that were laid out around the deck It was nearly impossible to walk in a straight line and the force of the wind took your breath away. Though I didn't feel too well that first morning, I managed to devour some toast and tea, which seemed to help. By evening, I was feeling hungry, so Keith and I risked going down to the dining room but were surprised to see that it was very quiet. Presumably, the absentees could have been found lying in their bunks, visualising land with flowers and trees!

The seas were rough for a few more days but gradually diminished, and by the time we were nearing the equator, the weather had improved greatly.

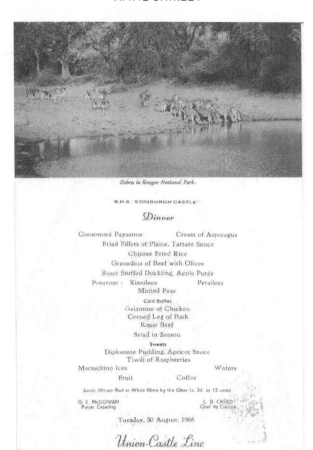

Zebra in Kruger National Park.

R.M.S. "EDINBURGH CASTLE"

Dinner

Consommé Paysanne   Cream of Asparagus
Fried Fillets of Plaice, Tartare Sauce
Chinese Fried Rice
Grenadins of Beef with Olives
Roast Stuffed Duckling, Apple Purée
Potatoes :   Rissolees   Persilees
Minted Peas

Cold Buffet
Galantine of Chicken
Corned Leg of Pork
Roast Beef
Salad in Season

Sweets
Diplomate Pudding, Apricot Sauce
Tivoli of Raspberries
Maraschino Ices   Wafers
Fruit   Coffee

South African Red or White Wine by the Glass 1s. 3d. or 13 cents

G. E. McGOWAN   L. D. CREED
Purser Catering   Chef de Cuisine

Tuesday, 30 August, 1966

Union-Castle Line

Second Day Evening Menu

18

WEDNESDAY, 31 August 1966

DEAR MAM, Dad and All,

Although I am writing to you now, I know you won't get this letter until after we arrive in Cape Town because we don't make any more calls to enable me to post it. The temperature at noon today was 80°F on deck and 82°F the sea water. It's absolutely smothering, but that is because we are practically on the equator. There is the 'Crossing the Equator' ceremony on Friday, but officially we cross it before then – probably tomorrow. I am getting nicely brown now, but Keith has burnt his legs from sitting in the sun too long and is now trying to keep out of it as much as possible.

For something to do, he put his name down for the 'Crossing the Equator' contest, but unfortunately he and his partner, a South African girl living in Rhodesia, lost in the knockout competition this afternoon.

We have met some brilliant people. They are all very friendly, especially the Afrikaners. Last night, we had cocktails with the captain – oh, very posh I can hear you say! At the event, we met a young Irish couple who are going on to Zambia and we spent most of the evening chatting with them.

On Monday, we docked at Las Palmas, Canary Islands, and went on a coach tour of the town. The whole island seems to have been formed by a volcanic eruption millions of years ago, and the land outside the coastal town is mostly grey ash. We took some film of the tour so eventually, you will be able to see for yourselves. We think that maybe the bus driver could have taken us to a better part of the area, as I understand the island is becoming popular for tourists to fly to so there must be a better view than the one we had.

Another day, another view. I'm looking out of the window

just now – I wish you could see the sea. It's beautiful and calm and blue. There is a slight breeze blowing but it's a warm breeze. The deck is too warm to put bare feet upon, but the kiddies seem to like it. There is a swimming pool on deck. If you sit in a deck chair and close your eyes, the sounds are exactly the same as those of Blackpool or Scarborough, the children screaming and splashing about in the water. The only thing missing is the cacophony of excited dogs barking as they race along the sands.

When we boarded the ship at Southampton there was a telegram from Auntie Mary and Uncle John wishing us a pleasant voyage and then, after we had been sailing for about an hour, a letter from them was pushed under our door. It was lovely. I was really touched. Please tell Auntie Mary and Uncle John that I'll write to them very soon and thank them for their lovely letter and telegram. It was a great surprise and I should have mentioned this in my first letter to you but I didn't have the room.

We have overcome the upset at leaving everybody, as I do so hope you have, too. We are now really looking forward to arriving in Malawi, having met some people who lived there and say it is a fabulous place.

We saw the dolphins following the ship a short time ago and have seen lots of flying fish – they are tiny things, only about six inches long.

There is a boy from Newcastle at our table and he has us all in stitches. Keith and I can hardly understand a word he's saying so you can imagine the problem the rest of the passengers have, especially the South Africans. It's hilarious to see the puzzled expressions on the faces of people speaking with him, as they strain to pick out a few recognisable words that they can then put into a sentence, as we have to do.

Sorry, but I'm finding it very difficult to write. There is a slight tremble from the engines, so you will have to excuse the scrawl. We are very nearly halfway there now and are on a level with Cape Verde, somewhere in Northwest Africa. I spend my days in shorts and a blouse – I needn't be embarrassed about my big bum either. Oh, Mam, I wish you could see the sights of some of the women in swimsuits! I'm embarrassed just at the thought.

We arrive in Cape Town next Wednesday, so I'll post this letter then. I'll number it in case I write again before we dock.

Cheerio for now and lots of love to you and everyone. I'll write to Michael soon, too.

Love

Keith and Anne xx

Crossing the Equator antics

THE 'CROSSING THE EQUATOR' ceremony was brilliant. It had started the previous night, though Keith and I were not aware of this as I believe we had gone to the cinema. On the day, we gathered around the pool with the other passengers to watch what was to be a rousing ceremony, taking in the crew and passengers alike. We all laughed as King Neptune and his attendants, who were Davy Jones and Princess Amphitrite, proceeded to put the 'volunteer suckers' through the most appalling capers, from being cut in half and their stomach contents of sausages, kidneys, spaghetti and raw tripe being tossed into the crowd of onlookers, to being plastered in grease and tossed into the pool. Then came the pillow fight where the two contestants, gripping pillow cases filled with inflated balloons and straddling a greasy pole over the swimming pool, vied to knock each other off the pole, the contest continuing until the last man 'standing' or rather sitting was the winner. We had a great day but I personally wouldn't have been on the 'suckers' side for anything.

Aerial view of Johannesburg.

R.M.S. "EDINBURGH CASTLE"

Dinner

Sherry Consommé   Velouté Camélia

Fried Fillet of King Klip à la Juive

Braised Sheeps' Tongues, Forestière

Devilled Ham Slice, Glazed Pineapple

Roast Sirloin of Beef

Potatoes : Anna   Parsley Boiled

Broccoli Spears

Cold Buffet

Galantine of Chicken

Corned Leg of Pork

Roast Beef

Salad in Season

Sweets

Strawberry Soufflé

Gelée Suedoise

Vanilla Ices, Butterscotch Sauce   Wafers

Fruit   Coffee

South African Red or White Wine by the Glass 1s. 3d. or 13 cents

G. E. McGOWAN   L. D. CREED
Purser Catering   Chef du Cuisine

Wednesday, 31 August, 1966

Union-Castle Line

MONDAY, 5 September 1966

DEAR MAM AND DAD,

This will be my last letter before we dock at Cape Town. We have decided that twelve days at sea is quite enough. The trouble is, after a time, everything is just repetitious and very boring.

You could hardly believe how the weather has changed. For the past two days, it has been too cold even to go for a short walk on deck. We have been told we are in the monsoon season, so the wind and cold are to be expected. According to the daily paper sheet, it is snowing on the mountains in Cape Town. However, by the time we arrive on Wednesday morning (at about 6 a.m.), the winter season should be nearly over. One can tell exactly when each season starts and finishes here, unlike in England when we can have all four seasons in one day.

Every day there is a competition to try and guess the number of nautical miles covered from noon to noon. The captain gives his guess and the passengers usually base their guesses around this figure. The captain doesn't always win.

On Friday evening, there was a dance on the sports deck, and afterwards a fish and chip supper – out of newspaper, just like back home. We found it so funny watching the first-class lady passengers, dressed in their mink stoles, eating fish and chips with their fingers. It would have been a brilliant sight for others to see had there been any ships passing close by. The evening was lovely; the sides of the deck had been raised, and there were coloured lights decorating everything. Prior to the dance, there had been a fancy-dress parade and, of course, the men dressed as ballet dancers won. It was hilarious.

However, everyone seems subdued at the moment. I think they are probably as cheesed off as we are. We have seen nothing but water, water, water since we left Southampton, except for the few hours we spent in Las Palmas on Monday. I certainly don't envy the people going to Australia on the Castel Felice, having to cope with six-weeks' of sailing.

We have reached the dreaded Cape Rollers, the name given to the very choppy sea near Cape Town, and have been told we will have two days of this. I wish you could hear the ship creaking. It's terrifying. But we were told it's when the ship stops creaking that we should worry – it would split down the middle!

We were too tired to get up for breakfast this morning. Everyone else seems the same. The clocks have been messed with so much we don't ever seem to know the correct time. The first day on board we put them back an hour, then on Saturday, Sunday and tonight we have to put them on half an hour each night, if we remember!

On Sunday at afternoon tea I was talking to a priest. He was dressed in a checked shirt and khaki shorts, not a bit like a priest. He is only a young man, about three years older than me. We just talked normally as two ordinary passengers would which seems off when I think about it as, for years, we have been taught to revere priests as they are God's representatives. So strange, as it's difficult to imagine they are ordinary people, really.

Every day seems the same now and they are very short days. Keith keeps himself occupied playing bridge with three other passengers. They are such a mixture: there is a South African girl, a Dutch woman, a Polish man and Keith an Englishman. The South African girl – Betty – has had her purse containing about £50 stolen. She left it on a table and when she remembered it, it was too late. She is with her mother, which is a good thing because she doesn't have a cent now. As for myself, I spend most of my time reading and talking to the other passengers.

I'll write again very soon. Look after yourselves! Love to everyone.

Keith and Anne xx

ON WEDNESDAY, 7 September 1966, we finally docked in Cape Town.

From Cape Town, the *Edinburgh Castle* was to turn south along the coast towards the Cape of Good Hope, then east to Port Elizabeth, East London and Durban, from there doing a turnaround retracing its route which, we were not to know then, would be the route we would take nearly three years later on our return home.

We'd been excitedly told by an Afrikaner lady passenger that we should get up very early, before dawn, on the day the ship docked, in order to see the 'tablecloth' on top of Table Mountain. Having done this, we were rewarded by the sight of what, to us, must surely be the eighth wonder of the world!

Table Mountain

While on deck that morning, we began to hear a rumour that Dr Hendrik Verwoerd had been assassinated the previous day and so were not certain what we would meet when we eventually left the ship after breakfast.

*The Verwoerd Assassination - a crime that shocked the world.

On 6 September 1966, South African Prime Minister Hendrik Frensch Verwoerd entered the House of Assembly and prepared to take his seat. A parliamentary page named Dimitri Tsafendas quickly crossed the floor and approached him. As the prime minister looked up for the expected message, Tsafendas drew out a large knife and stabbed the politician four times in the chest. A mob of nearby MPs quickly restrained Tsafendas while four others (who happened to be medical doctors) tried to help the prime minister. Despite their best efforts, Hendrik Verwoerd was declared dead on arrival at a nearby hospital.

As one of the prime architects of apartheid (separate development) and prime minister during one of the most racially charged eras in South Africa's history, Hendrik Verwoerd continues to be a controversial figure. A trained psychologist, Verwoerd was a professor at the University of Stellenbosch until entering politics. An outspoken advocate of Afrikaner nationalism, he helped draft and implement the various Apartheid Acts after becoming prime minister in 1958 and also led the country to independence in 1961. Verwoerd strengthened his hold on the black majority of the country by enacting various 'pass laws' limiting educational and employment opportunities for non-whites, outlawing political organisations such as the African National Congress, jailing Nelson Mandela and other anti-apartheid activists, and banning interracial relationships to prevent miscegenation.

It was the anti-miscegenation statutes that likely sparked Dmitri Tsafendas' murder plan. Born of a Greek father and Mozambique mother, Dimitri Tsafendas was legally classed as white despite his mixed-race heritage. Shunned by most South Africans due to his dark complexion, which made him either 'too white' for some or 'not white enough' for others, he spent most of his life abroad. Tsafendas drifted from country to country and spent considerable time in psychiatric hospitals in Germany, the UK and the United States.

After returning to South Africa in 1964, he fell in love with a 'coloured' woman but the anti-miscegenation laws drafted by Verwoerd's party made this relationship impossible. Tsafendas even tried to have himself reclassified as 'coloured' only to be refused by the bureaucracy. It was unheard of for a white to have himself declared non-white.

Not only was Tsafendas unable to marry his girlfriend but being seen in public with her would have earned him a prison sentence. She eventually married someone else and he was never again the same man. As his mental health continued to deteriorate, he formed a plan to kill Verwoerd. He gained a job as a parliamentary messenger (a job that was only open to whites at the time) and spent two years planning the assassination.

Tsafendas cooperated fully with police and prosecutors after his arrest. His rationale for killing Verwoerd was certainly unique. He claimed that he was acting on orders from a giant tapeworm living in his stomach. Whether this was a genuine delusion or an attempt to save himself from execution, the government was faced with a problem. Putting a white man on trial for killing the prime minister might have had unintended political consequences. Verwoerd was already being portrayed as a martyr by his party and there were fears that public sympathy for Tsafendas might have undermined the government's apartheid policies.

Dmitri Tsafendas was declared not guilty by reason of insanity without ever going on trial. He was ordered to be detained "at the pleasure of the State President" and sent to Pretoria Central Prison. Tsafendas was placed in a segregation cell on death row, right next to the gallows. For the next twenty-eight years of his life, he saw every prisoner facing execution being led past his cell. Since he was not serving a formal sentence, only an order from the prime minister could ever release him.

And there he stayed until 1993 when Verwoerd's National Party handed over power to the country's first multiracial government. Dmitri Tsafendas was then transferred to Sterkfontein Mental Hospital, where he spent the rest of his life. While he was technically free to leave at any time (the detention order had been lifted by the new government), Tsafendas resisted any attempt to release him. His decades of incarceration had left him so institutionalised that he was unable to function in the community.

He had few visitors during his final years in the hospital and, following his death from pneumonia in 1999 at the age of eighty-one, Tsafendas was buried by members of the Greek community in Krugersdorp. It's debatable whether he was even considered a mental patient, given that he wasn't on psychiatric medication at the time of his death, although he still mentioned his tapeworm at times (and requested a post-mortem to verify that it was in his stomach).

Although Dmitri Tsafendas is considered a martyr in some circles, his impact on South Africa's history is debatable. Verwoerd may have been a major force in apartheid but his death did little to change his racial policies. None of Verwoerd's political foes had any kind words for the 'mad Greek' who killed the politician, and Tsafendas was largely forgotten even before his death. Hendrik Verwoerd's legacy still haunts the country (one of Nelson Mandela's first official acts as prime minister was to make a formal visit to Verwoerd's widow) but the assassin who killed him remains an enigma.

*Providentia, A biased look at psychology in the world.

WE DISEMBARKED from the *Edinburgh Castle* mid-morning and followed the lines of people making their way to the Customs shed.

From there, after having picked up our luggage and gone through Customs regulations, we made our way to the railway station close by, where we deposited our cases etc., in a locker to be collected later in the afternoon. Our train to Malawi was due to leave Cape Town early evening, so we had a few hours to spare for sightseeing. Our journey from Cape Town to Malawi would take five days and nights, so we felt we needed the exercise after the lazy ocean trip.

Walking around the waterfront, we saw that one of the tall buildings was displaying a scrolling message announcing to the world that their prime minister was dead, and this confirmed the rumour on board that morning.

Having made sure we had all the information needed for the next part of our trip, we took some cine film recordings of our surroundings and then headed over to the bus stop indicated to us by the railway guard. We knew that we simply must visit Table Mountain before we left Cape Town – the Afrikaner lady on board had instilled this into our minds so many times that, on occasion, we began to be suspicious that maybe she was a plant, put on the ship by the South African Tourist Board!

There were several Africans waiting with us at the bus stop and when the green single-decker bus finally arrived, we boarded and sat three-quarters of the way down. Immediately the bus started, the conductor made his way towards us but instead of taking our money, he sternly and silently pointed to a sign above the windows on both side of the bus sited halfway down. He waited for us to move to seats towards the front of the bus before taking our fares. We complied without at first fully realising what was wrong, but it soon became clear that we, 'whites', should not have been in the 'Non-Europeans Only' (in Afrikaans 'Slegs vit nie-Blankes') bus at all, and we had clearly upset the black bus conductor. While we felt embarrassed for the black Africans on the bus who had witnessed this scenario and ashamed of our fellow whites, there was nothing we could do but hang onto our dignity.

Segregation Sign

On exiting the bus, we had quite a long walk to the cable car stop and hoped it was going to be worth the effort. It was! We had never seen a cable car before and it looked scary. It was just a small metal box with waist-high doors, the top half being open to the wind and rain and attached to the cable by means of a few nuts and bolts. We joined the small queue waiting to board. Once inside the car, we were whisked into the air, the box gently swinging backwards and forwards, gaining momentum as it gained height. When we enquired if it was safe, we were told that the swing was probably because of the wind but that it was perfectly safe.

Cable car

The view was stunning, and we had found a good viewing spot so soon forgot about the dangers as we watched the ground slowly fall away from our feet until we were no longer looking at the ground but at the mountains on one side and the sea on the other. As we ascended, the air began to feel cooler and by the time we reached the top, I was glad I was wearing my pale green woollen M&S dress with its turtleneck collar, the last thing I bought before departing England. I note now that on my postcard to my parents I say I'm sweltering in my dress, but I must have written the card after being on the mountain and once more down in Cape Town proper.

It was exciting to make this first trip by the cable car to the top of Table Mountain and I still, fifty years later, remember that first gaze from the top, looking down on the world.

As we walked around the unfamiliar terrain, seeing for the first time the unusual flowers growing wild, particularly the stunning king Protea flower with its large pink and green head, I wished for all the world that my family could be seeing these things through my eyes at that very moment. I was almost overcome by the euphoria of the occasion; every blade of grass, every piece of rock, every animal, every person… everything was pure, unseen before by my eyes. It was overwhelming.

I was so glad we had a cine camera that day and we probably used it to excess, filming every conceivable thing as we wanted our families to see the awesome sights we were seeing. Even though August was the South African winter, we found it almost as warm at the top of the Mountain in the sun as some of our English summer days. We took more film at the cafeteria, where we also fed the rock hyrax (common name Dassies) with leftover food. Dassies are cute, small furry animals resembling rabbits but which are actually hoofed mammals related to the elephant.

Dassies (rock hyrax) on Table Mountain

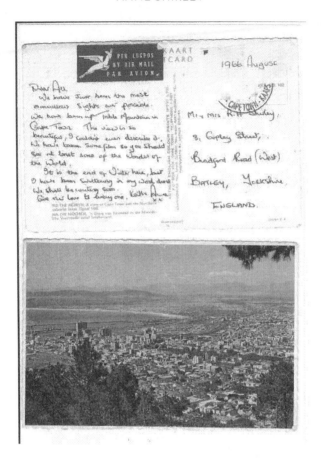

August 1966. My mother removed the stamp

BACK ON TERRA firma and nearly there…

We ate our meal on the move that evening as, once the passengers were settled on board, the train commenced its long journey. The train moved slowly at first, leaving the city and its wealth, moving past the townships with their shacks and on to the dusty plains. The train was long and heavy and there were many hills to climb and we noticed, leaning out of the window, that there was a steam engine at both ends of the train to assist this journey.

Our two-berth sleeper consisted of a long leatherette bench that converted into two bunk beds by pulling down the luggage rack and using the padded backrest as a second mattress. There was a very small sink in the compartment near the window with a mirror overhead, but the toilet and shower rooms were at the end of the corridor en route to the dining car.

Not used to being waited on, we were pleasantly surprised to find that a member of staff had made up the beds while we were in the dining car having our evening meal, which was also a relief as we had been puzzled as to how to set up the second bed!

We made our first stop late that evening, staying for a few hours on a station platform, somewhere in the backwoods, to collect passengers and mail for onward depositing. We travelled slowly through the night, the gentle rocking of the carriages on the narrow-gauge tracks lulling us to sleep. The quicker movement of the train woke us early the following morning and, looking through the window, saw we were rapidly winding our way through the scrubland of the desert. We took cine film at Kimberley Station where the African women, slowly walking alongside the train, tried to sell passengers their wares, carrying the goods in large aluminium dishes on top of their heads, their backs as straight as arrows. Unfortunately, we couldn't buy anything from them as we only had English money.

The scenery for the following few days was that of very dry grassland. We assumed we were in the Kalahari Basin in the Northern Cape. Soon, we began to notice a pattern in our travel: the train would always stop in the evening, and at this time the front and rear engines would be changed. We deduced from this that we were travelling over the border from one country into another and that the engines were only on loan.

Occasionally, we would take our evening meal at a platform restaurant, and it was on one of these occasions that we first saw a cockroach, though at the time we thought it was a mouse because of its size. We had alighted the train and decided to take a short walk outside the station before our evening meal. The road led uphill from the exit and we marvelled at the height of the pavement and the huge drains every few yards, indicating that this part of Africa was used to heavy rains. The width of the roads was unusual too, but then we remembered we had been told that in South Africa and Rhodesia, the roads had been constructed wide enough to enable a coach and horses to turn around in one swing.

There were no street lights but because it was a clear night we could see very well. Looking up into the sky, I saw that the stars were different but my lack of education hadn't prepared me for this anomaly. I hadn't realised that, in the southern hemisphere, the stars would not be the same as in the northern hemisphere. I learned a lot in those few years.

As we walked along, something ran quickly across the road in front of us and towards a drain, where it stopped. We were intrigued as we gingerly walked over to see if it was a mouse as, even though it didn't have the shape of a mouse, it was quite large. Bending to get a better look, we saw it was a huge beetle-type creature with large closed wings, hairy legs and long antennae, the overall colour of the creature being shiny chestnut, glinting in the moonlight. It was unlike anything we had ever seen before. What we didn't know, and could not have envisaged then, was that in a few weeks' time, we would be inundated with these creatures, sharing our allotted house and furniture with them. We continued our walk, eventually returning to the train. We mentioned what we had seen to a number of people – the seasoned African travellers – who told us they were probably cockroaches, but the visitors to Africa, like ourselves, could only ponder.

At our concluding stop on the border between Rhodesia and Mozambique, we alighted the train as it was travelling on to Zambia. We bade goodbye to the people we had chanced to meet on the journey, feeling sadness as, like ships passing in the night, we had shared new experiences with them but never expected to meet again. The final part of our journey to Malawi was to be an anxious one.

The train taking us from Dondo Junction into Malawi was at the station when we arrived, its engine already smoking impatiently. From the outside, we noticed that the train carriages looked different, having long metal boxes affixed to the top of every window. Ah well, this was Africa.

Everything was different!

We boarded the train and found empty seats in what seemed like a busy carriage. There were small groups of well-dressed Africans talking quietly amongst themselves. Having stored our luggage, we settled down to the final part of our journey, window-gazing to see if this part of Africa would look any different to the previous views we had had over the last five days. We had only been travelling for a short time when suddenly there was an almighty noise of machinery grinding metal. To our horror, we saw that metal shutters were slowly being lowered down the outside of the windows. Looking around at the other passengers, we were surprised to note that they seemed to be unaware of what was happening and were continuing to talk normally but, on noticing our bewilderment, one of the African men pointed to a sign on the woodwork between each window. There we saw a notice warning that the outside of the train would be armed while travelling through Portuguese territory to evade possible attacks by FRELIMO rebels, the Mozambique Liberation Front [Frente de Libertação de Moçambique]. FRELIMO was the dominant political party in Mozambique and were the people fighting for independence from Portugal, which they did not get until 1975. On speaking further with our co-passengers, we were told it was not unusual for the train to be fired upon as it travelled along the route through Mozambique, but that we shouldn't worry. Of course, we did worry!

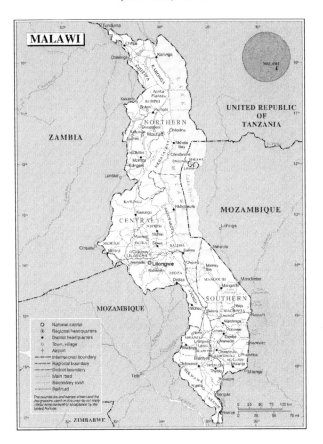

Map of Malawi

MONDAY, 19 September 1966

DEAR MAM AND DAD,

I imagine you've been wondering what has happened as I haven't written for so long. Well, it's a long story.

We arrived safely last Monday and were booked into a hotel in Blantyre for the night. On the Tuesday, the principal (of the college where Keith will be teaching) and his wife met us at the hotel and took us back to Domasi – about fifty-two miles. The scenery is as beautiful as everyone said, really fabulous. Our house was still occupied, we were to learn, by an African teacher, so we were 'put up' by an American teacher, Mrs Turrell, an extremely likeable American lady of about sixty.

On Wednesday, we were taken to see our house. Gosh, what a shock! It was exactly the same as Mrs Turrell's with the same furniture (rather old but strong, which it has to be to weather the white ants), but it was absolutely full of cockroaches. Not like the English ones; these ones have at least two-inch long bodies and are one-inch wide. They are big, brown, horrible things! The person who had been living in this house had been given one day's notice to quit, but the roaches probably needed a bit longer! The horrible insects were in all the wickerwork of the dining chairs, the two lounge chairs, and in every drawer and cupboard. There were also eggs in all the crevices of the tables. And then came the bedroom furniture (beds, wardrobes etc!) We were later to learn that African teachers were not paid the same amount as their European counterparts. In this instance the African, being unable to afford electricity, had been reduced to using candles for lighting. Unfortunately, he had glued the candles onto the wooden furniture with melted candle fat; hence, every piece of furniture, polished and unpolished, was damaged either from runs of melted candle fat or from burns when the candles had burnt themselves out.

We felt quite distressed about the whole thing. We had not expected to travel thousands of miles to end up in what we considered to be grubby accommodation that we wouldn't accept in England. Maybe our expectations have been too high.

Anyway, on Wednesday night Keith and I talked it over and decided to quit and go down to either Salisbury or Natal in South Africa. With trepidation, on Thursday we went to see Mr Jones, the principal and told him of our decision. We were with him for about two hours and really discussed the whole thing. He sympathised with us and said, of course, it was our decision but pointed out it would cost us about £800 with the compensation we would have to pay, as well as the return of fares. During our long conversation, he told us that, from experience, he knew if we stayed six months we would never want to leave. This we could not believe. Anyway, the crux of the matter is we have decided to give it a try – Keith doesn't have to start teaching until November.

The principal's wife has been amazing, so too has the principal himself. They came back down to the house with us, armed with all kinds of powders and sprays and we really went to town. They also found two 'boys' to work for us. John is about thirty and will work in the house, and Cassiano is about twenty-five and will work in the garden. Both men are Africans. I wish you could see John pick the cockroaches up by their one-inch long feelers and kill them. When I see one, I only have to call him and he deals with it as if it was a tiny moth.

We moved into the house on Saturday with a bit of apprehension, but are only finding the recently hatched cockroaches now and these are fairly small. I have put DDT powder in every drawer and the boys have scrubbed every chair, table, cupboard and wardrobe, but tonight I found one in the electric cooker, so I switched it on. Two more came crawling out. I'll have the boys take the inside of the oven out tomorrow and deal with them properly.

We are fairly settled now. Today, Mr and Mrs Jones took us into Blantyre to buy a new refrigerator and we have nearly bought a car, that is, we have chosen a car – a 1965 Morris Oxford saloon for £624 (Registration No. BB 513) – and it is just a matter for the government to approve our loan now, which is merely a formality.

We haven't had time to see any of the country yet, but we are surrounded on two sides by mountains – very lovely. We have a massive house and gardens. I'll count the trees for the next time I write – more than twenty at the very least – and our 'boys' and their wives will live at the bottom of the garden. We have wonderful neighbours – a Canadian family on one side (Doug and Anne) and an American family on the other (Dick and Jane).

Bye for now.

Lots of love to you all,

Keith and Anne xx

WE CONTINUED to find the roaches for many more weeks because we couldn't always get the eggs, and I remember on numerous occasions sitting in a wicker chair, seeing the long hairy feelers extend from the wickerwork beside me, searching the air for foes! On those occasions, Roger Bannister didn't get a look-in; I was up on my feet and moving faster than any four-minute miler.

It was also fascinating to watch the roach eggs hatch and to observe that one egg contained many babies, which would immediately disperse if not stopped in their tracks. It's not surprising that the roach has been on earth for millions of years as, on a number of occasions, we watched the dying female, having been either sprayed or hit, fight for life to deliver her egg before she died in order to continue the existence of this repellent but interesting insect.

SATURDAY, 24 September 1966

DEAR MAM AND DAD,

Hope you received my last letter okay. I still haven't written to anyone else in the family, but life is pretty hectic just at present, though I'm happy to say that things are settling down nicely. I haven't seen many more cockroaches since I last saw one crawling out of the oven. But I don't know what I saw today. It was underneath the food safe and I spied it there after the painters had moved the safe to get to the skirting board – it was a big black thing, like a giant beetle. Not to worry. It's dead now.

Keith has gone into Blantyre today to collect our new car – the Morris Oxford I told you about in my last letter. Maybe now I'll be able to get to church on Sunday. I haven't been able to go for the past two Sundays because it is eleven miles away. I'm going to learn to drive as soon as I can and will then try to get a job. Life is very easy. Our 'boys' are very good, they do all the cleaning and we found out yesterday that John was a cook-houseboy for a European family for fourteen years. His ironing is a thing to behold! I've never seen anything so beautiful in all my life. His washing is also spotless – no electric washers here, though. He merely pounds our clothes in the bath using soap and his hands.

John is extremely shy and I took to him immediately. Cassiano cannot speak very much English so John has to do the translating. Every house has 'servant's quarters' housing, and our servant's quarters accommodation is at the bottom of our garden, which is part of the complex provided to the training college by the local government. The other day, when John had finished all the work necessary in our house, Keith told him he could take Cassiano and spend the rest of the day cleaning out his and Cassiano's own rooms, ready for them moving into. They had been living in the village until that day, and John had come running in to tell us this same morning that his wife had given birth to their first baby – a boy. Thinking that they should clean their rooms before they brought their wives and families over (Cassiano has two babies), Keith and I went with them to see what their rooms were like and my goodness, I could have cried. The walls were very clean but they were just four walls with a door and a window. John had brought with him all his worldly possessions: a wooden box, an overcoat probably given to him by his previous employer, an old blanket which was laid out on the bare floor to sleep upon, a tin box for his flour or whatever the white mealy stuff is that they eat, a comb with half the teeth missing and a piece of mirror. I felt heartbroken. Their standard rate of pay doesn't help very much, either. John, being head boy, gets four shillings per day – twenty-eight shillings per week – plus five shillings Posho (food money). Cassiano gets twenty shillings per week, plus five shillings Posho. How can they possibly live on that money? The trouble is we can't afford to give them any more; we pay them nearly £3 per week, which is quite a chunk of Keith's salary.

However, unknown to Keith, I keep giving them things such as old vests and jumpers. They have neither light nor heat in those houses and the nights are very cold. But the sad instance came the day after John had told us about his new baby. He reported for work duty at eight o'clock that morning as instructed, and waited until I was by myself before telling me that his baby had died – twenty-four hours after birth. I don't think John had been to bed at all because the hospital staff had sent for him at one o'clock that morning.

I told him he could go after he had helped move some furniture because I could see he was very upset. The baby was being buried that same day. Both our 'boys' are Muslims and according to Islamic tradition, the dead are buried before sunset on the same day as death wherever possible, or at the very least before sunset on the following day if the circumstances make same-day burial impossible. Apparently, a speedy burial is important to them. He told me the hospital had sent his wife back to the village twenty-four hours after giving birth. Is that fair?

I think John must have stayed with his wife in the village that night because the following day he came in a bit late and handed me something; his hands were like pieces of ice. He was only wearing a pair of shorts and a torn shirt, plus the nylon stocking he always wears over his hair. Pitiful, really. I asked him if he had had any breakfast and he said he hadn't, so I made him some tea and told him to get whatever food he wanted to eat from our fridge. I don't know where the village is but he had walked, without shoes on and just those few clothes, to report for duty. The mornings are bitter cold, too. People are telling me I must not mollycoddle our workers, but I can't see them wanting and not do something about it. And our two boys seem to really appreciate anything I give them and work twice as hard for us even though, obviously, that's not the reason I try to help them. We are very fortunate to have these good boys and I'm very grateful – but soft!

I'll have to start writing to the rest of the family very soon. Tell them, won't you?

Love

Keith and Anne xx

WEDNESDAY, 5 October 1966

DEAR AUNT ALICE AND GRANDMA,

We arrived here safely, none the worse for the train journey we had to take from Cape Town to Malawi.

We had our own compartment but it was terribly small and we spent most of the time walking up and down the corridor for exercise. Fortunately, we were next door to a couple we met on the boat and we were able to have a bit of fun with them until they had to change trains in Salisbury. They were going to Zambia in northern Rhodesia.

It was just like a travel film, going through the different countries on the train. The Africans really do live in mud huts with thatched roofs. At every station we stopped at, children would crowd along the track, holding out both hands, begging. I was in tears at one station because I found it heartbreaking seeing the little ones, wearing rags so torn that you wouldn't use them to clean the floor, limping along the track, their huge eyes which seemed too big for their faces, looming up at you, pleading for anything you can give them. There is a great deal of leprosy in the poorer countries and so many people seem to be affected by it. Some of the children were being led by others, either because they were blind or because their deformed hands or feet were not much benefit whilst begging, The unfortunate thing was that we only had English money and traveller's cheques, so had we given them anything, they couldn't have spent it anyway.

The only wild game we saw while travelling was an ostrich and a few groups of baboons. But there are some beautiful birds in Africa; I'm looking out just now at some little birds, similar to canaries, and they are all colours, pale blues, greens and some with red breasts like the robin.

It's the dry season here at present and nearly all the vegetation is going brown through lack of water. The rains come just after Christmas, and we have been told there's a treat in store for us then because all the greenery comes to life and the trees blossom and the colours really glow. We have a beautiful garden, about one acre, and employ a garden-boy full-time to keep it in order. We have lovely trees and shrubs but they are dying off, even though they are watered just about every day. Our neighbours are more fortunate than us because they have fruit trees growing in their garden – apples, oranges, lemons, pawpaw – therefore never have to buy fruit. The person who lived in our house before us made a small vegetable plot and planted cabbage, peas and tomatoes, but the cabbage is now like broderie Anglaise it's so full of holes, and the tomatoes are so small they look like peas.

It's an education to visit the market on Tuesdays and Fridays. It's not a bit like Batley or Dewsbury! They don't have stalls to put the goods on. Instead, everything is laid out on the ground on paper – peas, potatoes, tomatoes, even fish. And the flies… phew. You buy everything by the heap too as the sellers don't possess scales, so you just walk around looking for the biggest heap of whatever you want.

Unfortunately, they don't have paper bags either. I bought 3d worth of tomatoes the other day (about fourteen small ones) and I had to carry them in my arms and pockets because I'd forgotten my shopping bag. Very awkward! Just about all the shopkeepers are Asian, and not African as I would have expected. It surprises me. We have been here a month now, and I haven't been into a shop yet to buy anything from an African or European shopkeeper. The market is in the open and surrounded by shops (non-European, of course), which sell anything from fabrics to bread. The Africans sit on the verandas with their Singer treadle sewing machines making clothes to measure, and the customers (Africans) sit in front on benches, the women breastfeeding their babies and not batting an eyelid; of course, nobody else bats an eyelid, either. It's even more amazing to see the babies feeding as the mother walks along the street doing her shopping. This is Africa and it is as natural as breathing.

I go to the cathedral on Sunday mornings – an eleven-mile drive each way – and except for about ten Europeans, the congregation is African. It's a gigantic place, though very plain inside and not as impressive as an English cathedral. Mass starts at nine o'clock and finishes at 10.15 a.m., and throughout the service, children wander in and out, presumably to go to the toilet. It's really bustling and reminds me of Briggate in Leeds! The little girls will carry their baby brother or sister on their backs, wrapped up in cloth, just like their mothers, and very often the girls are not more than eight or nine themselves. Also, there aren't many benches in church so the Africans mainly sit on the floor. I've been lucky so far, I've always managed to get a seat. Despite all this difficulty, the church is always full to capacity.

Do write back, won't you? I'd love to hear any news you have to tell.

Love to you both.

Keith and Anne xx

THE HOUSE ITSELF WAS INCREDIBLE. We had left a tiny, three-bed terrace house in England and replaced it with a huge house that had an enclosed veranda (khondi) surrounding most of it, the khondi being wide enough to accommodate a single bed with space each side. The house didn't have many individual rooms but each room was almost big enough to hold a dance. The floors were bare coloured stone and the walls were whitewashed concrete. There was plenty of furniture but it was all heavy, dark and old. However, because we paid to rent the house, we looked after it. The garden was well laid out with fruit trees that came to fruition in the spring and produced an abundance of fruit and flowers, some of which we had never seen before.

During those first few weeks, we were introduced to members of staff of all nationalities: American, Canadian, French and Irish but mostly British, and I felt that we 'gelled' expertly, even though I was well aware our antipodean American friends were less than enamoured with our colonialist past. It was at the house of Pops Papan, a real American Indian, that

I first tasted chilli. I thought it would burn a hole in my throat. In the 1960s, we still appeared to be relying on the know-how we learned during the deficits of WWII and seemed not to have caught up with the rest of the world so far as good food preparation was concerned. Our English cooking must, by all standards, have seemed bland and boring to our American friends, but we did our best!

TUESDAY, 11 October 1966

DEAR MAM AND DAD,

It was lovely to hear from you. The same day we received your letter (yesterday) we also had letters from Keith's mam and from Norman Wilson – the old so and so! He is on holiday in England for two months. We have been expecting him to call in to see us on his way back from Australia. As casual as anything, he says he changed his mind about Australia at the last minute and decided to visit his parents in England instead. He didn't tell anyone he was doing this, so can you imagine the surprise his parents would get when he just walked into the house? He flew from Vancouver to London (4,700 miles) in nine hours and says it took him another nine hours to get from London to Batley via Manchester (300 miles) because he had a four-hour wait at Manchester Airport. Amazing, isn't it? We reckon it would take us about the same time to get from here to London by plane, so we're not very far away from you really, are we?

I'm sorry to hear about Uncle John. I'll write to Auntie Mary and not to the hospital as you suggest.

Barbara sent us a lovely photograph of the babies. It made me feel very homesick. I've put it in a frame on the bookcase to keep reminding me.

Keith's mother says Denise (the friend who is expecting the baby) has had to go into hospital with blood pressure problems and being overweight, so everyone is very worried about her at home.

I forgot to tell you the last time I wrote but I went with Keith a couple of weeks ago to have a look around a school. It was riveting. I was introduced to the headmaster and, on visiting the classes with Keith as I walked in the rooms ahead of him, all the children stood up and said: 'Good morning, madam' and remained standing until told they could sit back down. I felt like royalty because I was then introduced to the teachers and told what the children were doing, and given a few minutes to either examine their books or needlework, or whatever they happened to be doing. Then, as we walked out, the children stood up again. The classrooms were really ancient and decrepit, although we were told it was a fairly good school. They were mud buildings with thatched roofs and just openings for windows and doors, and the woodwork class consisted of boys sitting outside, mainly under trees, chopping pieces of wood with blunt knives, but you'd be amazed at the things they were making. Then there was a class sitting outside under the veranda weaving raffia mats. It was a fascinating experience. I can't help but compare this school with a similar school in England. Oh, so different.

The garage at our house was originally constructed of bricks made from dried red mud and grass. It had long ago begun to fall down, and the college principal had kindly arranged with the local prison governor to send a work party to build us a new one. So, for the past three days, we have had prisoners in our garden from the local jail building a garage for our car. There was another batch of prisoners cutting the tall grass on the school compound with machetes (I think that's the spelling), which are long, lethal-looking knives. Altogether, I think there were about twenty prisoners walking around the compound, all carrying some kind of tool and being watched over by only two guards, who themselves were merely carrying small wooden truncheons. Yet, surprisingly, there was nothing frightening about it. There are very few escapees because, in jail, the men are assured of three meals a day and provided with a nice white uniform and sandals. We are told that most of them feel they have never been so well off. I could hear the prisoners laughing and joking with the guards, and I have to say, they didn't exactly kill themselves with work, either! However, while they were working on the garage, the prisoners kept coming to our back door asking for old newspapers, which we gladly gave them as, having read them, they were of no use to us. We thought this was strange and when we eventually asked one of the men why they wanted the papers, he simply answered: 'to smoke'. They were actually smoking rolled-up newspaper with nothing inside! Keith thought we ought to give them proper cigarettes when they had finished the garage, so the next time he was in Zomba he bought a few packs of their cheap local cigarettes called Tom Toms for 1d. a pack. When he gave them to the prisoners at the end of their work stint, you would think he had given them each a gold bar, they were so overwhelmed. It's touching to see how small acts of kindness are accepted with such gratitude by these lovely people.

John's wife came to see me last Friday and brought me four small eggs from their hens in the village. I was quite moved as they have so little to give. We shall have to return the compliment but we are waiting until we decide what they need most in their home.

I took out a provisional driving licence yesterday because I shall definitely have to learn to drive. I've got a job in the secretariat office in Zomba but they haven't told me yet when I start. They are a bit lackadaisical here, they don't seem to organise things at all. Anyway, I'm only giving them until Friday and, if they haven't let me know when I'm starting by then, I'll begin looking for another job somewhere else. It's terribly boring being at home all day, especially as all my work is done for me!

We sent the film of our journey here back to England for

processing (coals to Newcastle comes to mind) and it came back to Domasi last week. We are quite pleased with it, except that Keith had gone mad with the zooming effect. We are keeping it back for a while, though, to show to Derrick and Margaret at Christmas if they come (they said they would).

That's Keith's brother in Aden!

I had to break off writing just now to answer the door. I've just bought three lovely door mats for three shillings each. The Africans come around selling all sorts of things.

I'll say cheerio for now and we hope you are both very well.

Lots of love to you both. Write soon.

Keith and Anne

xx

I MENTION above that the garage was falling down but there is a funny story attached to that.

One day, I decided to bake a loaf of bread, although I had never baked bread before and the cooker didn't have a thermometer. Hence, I had no idea of the temperature and was only able to judge the heat by the length of time it had been switched on. You either got cool, hot or very hot. I think I was doomed from the start!

I followed the recipe for the bread, word for word, and remembered reading that it should rise to twice its size when blooming... but it didn't. What had I done wrong? Oh well, perhaps it would rise in the oven. I could only hope. When the oven felt hot enough, I put my newly made dough on the top shelf, closed the door and waited. After the time indicated in the recipe book, I opened the oven door to find myself looking at a well-baked brick. Pity I didn't know about Wimpey the builders at the time, as I could have gone into business with them.

I remember being so annoyed about the loaf of bread that I went outside and threw it at the dilapidated garage, thus starting the process of the demolition. The prison workers didn't thank me, though.

SUNDAY, 16 October 1966

DEAR MAM AND DAD,

We have just spent a hectic two hours driving to Lake Chilwa and back on a dirt road. The trip was terrible. If it's reasonably safe, then I drive. Like this morning, I drove there and back from the church but the dirt roads are dreadful. By the way, all Domasi is reached by dirt roads, and after the school lorry has driven along them a few times, particularly after it has rained, the road becomes corrugated. But irrespective of the bad roads, I have to admit my driving isn't wonderful. Keith and I keep having tiffs when I'm in charge of the car, but I can't seem to get into first and second gear without jerking the car forward. I'll have to persevere because Keith says he won't take me to church when the Domasi tennis court is ready. We clocked the journey this morning, and it's exactly thirteen miles from home to the church (a long walk, I think). Anyway, I shall have to learn very quickly because I am starting work tomorrow. I shall get £10. 4s. 0d. a week for working from 7.30 a.m. to 12 noon. Not bad, is it! (For comparison, in England my wages at the time of leaving my job in July 1966 were £11. 0s. 0d. for full-time work). But I shall have difficulty getting there because Keith has lectures some mornings at 6.30 a.m., so on those days I'll have to beg a lift from someone who happens to be going into Zomba (that's where I'll be working as there's only the college at Domasi and the Africans do the work necessary there for which they get about £200 per annum).

Auntie Mary wrote last week and told me about Uncle John having a really bad hypoglycaemic episode. I wrote back the same day but I forgot to tell her that she doesn't have to put an extra 3d stamp on the airmail letter. It goes for 6d from England to Malawi. It's only from Malawi to England that it's 9d. I hope Uncle John is going to be okay and that you are also keeping well, Dad.

We'll have to go into Blantyre to get a tape to send back, so it'll probably be Christmas before we get that organised. We have received the first half of the film of our journey here from England (it cost fourteen shillings postage) and we took it to one of our neighbours to run through as our projector and screen haven't arrived yet. We are very pleased with the film. It starts as we are leaving Leeds City Station, going on to Southampton, and then there are bits of the entertainment on the boat. Anyway, you'll see for yourselves when we send it over. When we bought the films in Leeds – sixteen in all – we were told we could get them processed in Africa, but I don't think there's an Ilford film shop in the whole continent of Africa, so we're having to send it back to England and they are spending as much returning it.

I was bitten by a mouse the other day; mind you, it was my own fault. Keith and the garden-boy were digging up the drainage system (big laugh!). It's just an open concrete trough around the house with 'fingers' running off in various directions to the outer edges of the garden. One part of the trough had been covered in with stones, and the 'tunnel' had become clogged up with dirt so the bath water wasn't running away properly; hence, they were digging it up. We were hoping to find a snake but were disappointed and only found this mouse (a big one, though). Anyway, Keith picked it up by the tail and because I thought it would be hurting, having all its weight hanging from its tail, I put my hand underneath it to let it stand on my palm (like an idiot) but it gave my little finger an almighty bite. I was a bit scared afterwards, though, because it might have had rabies. Wild dogs and cats often do have rabies so I suppose mice could have it, too. But I was assured by a biologist at college that I would be all right, which is a relief as I needn't start having the dozens of injections you must have if you are bitten by a rabid animal. The injections are said to be very unpleasant because they have to go straight into the stomach. What a thought!

John, our houseboy, brought his father and another brother to see us the other day. There are ten in the family, so we're going to have a busy time! We have taken a bit of film of John and Cassiano with their wives and children, which you'll see, eventually.

I think the last time I wrote I told you we didn't have any fruit trees. Well, I was very wrong because I have found at least six lemon trees and about four trees absolutely covered with mangoes. The lemons are only small and very green but after the rains we should have enough for all the station. It's a lovely, carefree life and we are beginning to really enjoy it, but we still miss you, both of us.

The bungalow is starting to look nice now, too. We are making another room divider, just to remind us of home!

I'll certainly write to Mrs Popplewell when I get her address, but I estimate she will be at least a thousand miles away from us, so I doubt if we'll ever get a chance to see her, Mam.

Cheerio for now. Give my love to everyone.

Love,

Keith and Anne xx

PS. Please tell Auntie Alice to write also.

WHAT I OMITTED to tell my parents in this letter was that we had badly damaged the car during this journey out to see Lake Chilwa. The dirt roads were unbelievably dreadful, with huge potholes spanning the width of the road in some places, and in other places rocks would materialise from the dust like Mount Vesuvius, standing proudly waiting for a car to pass to cut through its sump like paper. Thus, it was important to keep an eye on the road in front at all times. Unfortunately, there were distractions sometimes, and on this occasion it was a big one.

We had been travelling along the most appalling road for some time, hoping we were heading in the direction of home, when a beautiful African lady stepped out onto the road and started walking towards us, her ample breasts uncovered. Suddenly, the front of the car fell into a huge hole and bounced back and forth a number of times before finally coming to a standstill. Eventually, all was quiet and the lady passed by without a second glance at us. However, when we got out of the car to look at the damage, we found the front wheels were facing a different direction to the steering wheel! That turned out to be a costly look on my husband's part!

In the same letter, the reference to Uncle John was related to the diagnosis of Type 1 diabetes, which was going to curtail many of the pleasures in his life. He was a lovely, lovely man who would give you his last penny. In my early childhood, my greatest pleasure was always the infrequent visits to see Uncle John and Auntie Mary who lived in Bradford. I remember one occasion when my life fell apart because of the anticipation of one such visit. My brother, Michael, and I had learned, shortly after we had returned home after attending Mass that particular Sunday that we were going to visit these lovely people later that afternoon. I was beside myself with excitement. At the time, Uncle John worked as a greengrocer, selling fruit and vegetables from a horse and cart, the horse being stabled in a field near their home, and my uncle usually took me to see it and to feed it carrots.

That afternoon, I was to be allowed to wear my next to best dress, which was special in itself. I was ready first and was sitting on the settee like a coiled spring, waiting to dash out of the door. We four people lived in a one-up-one-down house so everyday living was done in the downstairs room. My father, who was busying himself getting washed and shaved at the corner sink, looked over at Michael and me and said, 'One of you – and I don't care whose turn it is, but I want one of you to bring up a bucket of coal so that I can stoke up the fire before we go out.' Like almost everyone else at that time we had a coal fire, which heated the room as well as the water in the small boiler beside the fireplace, and often the oven for cooking as well. Immediately, my brother looked at me and said, 'It's your turn because I brought up the last lot.' I remember feeling indignant as he was wrong and told him so: 'No you didn't, I brought up the last lot,' to which Michael replied, 'No you didn't.' And on and on it went until suddenly, my father stopped what he was doing and looking at us sternly, told us that he would give us two minutes to decide whose turn it was and that we were not going out until someone had brought up some coal as he certainly wasn't going to do our job for us, it being the only thing either of us was ever asked to do. And there it remained, Michael and I both being stubborn and digging our heels in. I really hated bringing up the coal, particularly if my brother was in the house too, as he could put the fear of God into me by whispering scary stories about bogeymen waiting to pounce on me as soon as I rounded the dark corner at the bottom of the steps. I would usually be so spooked that I would rush down and rush back, hardly putting any coal into the bucket, thus being made to go down once more to complete the task. We didn't have electricity in the house and whoever went down into the cellar had to take a candle in a candle holder, which was spooky in itself! But this time, neither of us would concede. We both stuck to our guns. It must have been hard for my father but at the time, he obviously felt the need to prove that in life everyone needed to obey someone. I can see him now. He finished shaving his face and slowly began washing the razor under the cold-water tap. Everything was quiet – too quiet. Michael and I looked at each other, knowing that we had blown our chance and that something unpleasant was looming.

Suddenly, my father turned around from the sink and in a quiet rage told us to go upstairs to bed, that our last chance had gone and that we wouldn't be going out that day. I panicked and immediately said that I would get the coal, but I could tell by the look on my father's face that it was already too late.

It was about 3 p.m. when we went upstairs and not only did we miss going to see Auntie Mary and Uncle John that day, but we also missed our evening meal as my father wouldn't let us go back downstairs. I was utterly heartbroken and cried for hours, being upset both with myself and with my brother. I was still convinced that it hadn't been my turn, which added to my distress. The unfairness of it all. It was to be a taste of future life.

That spring day was the day I made a promise to myself. I vowed that I would never, ever, ever look forward to anything in life with so much emotion again, that I would never again allow myself to have reason to feel as sad as I felt at that very moment and, in that way I reasoned, I would never have to suffer so much regret again. It just broke my heart.

SATURDAY, 22 October 1966

DEAR MAM AND DAD,

It was so nice to receive your letter yesterday. We received one from Barbara the same day, so we had lots of reading.

Well, the rains have finally started and they are very welcome, too. We were in Zomba this morning; I was shopping and Keith was playing tennis as usual. After shopping, I went up to the club to watch the end of their match and, although it was sunny, I thought I felt it spitting with rain. Luckily, we just reached home in time because at 11.30 (it's 2.30 now), the heavens opened and it hasn't stopped raining since, and this is what I call rain! For the first fifteen minutes the rain dried off as soon as it touched the ground, but you should see it now. The soil is like swamp land; however, it will do the trees some good because they were really dying.

We entertained our neighbours last night; having been to dinner to their house a week ago, we decided it was our turn to ask them back. I bought a 2 lb 7 oz. piece of ham and partly boiled and partly roasted it. We cut some nice thick slices off and garnished them with fresh pineapple (a very large one for 2s. 6d.), and banana which I grilled for a few minutes. With it, we had the usual salad and cold potatoes tossed in mayonnaise. To finish off we had fresh strawberries.

I didn't envy John having to wash up this morning (it was his day off yesterday). But today I'm afraid John is in Keith's bad books. I had bought pork chops to have for lunch today, and at 11.30 a.m., I gave John instructions about what we wanted. At about twelve o'clock, Keith said he could smell burning, but with the rain, everything smells of burning, even the paintwork! So, I told him he was probably imagining it. Anyway, you know Keith! Suddenly, he jumped up, went through to the back of the house and then I heard a shout. A few minutes later, Keith came back to tell me he was right – there was something burning and John had fallen asleep in the kitchen with the chops smouldering nicely under the grill. He told him off good and sharp, and now it's come out about John having fallen asleep before. Keith said the other day he came in from college and found John mopping up the kitchen floor, and he just said he had filled the sink up too much by accident. Anyway, the same day, Keith went into the kitchen and found John asleep with the tap running and the plug in the sink (there's no overflow for the water, either). So, it looks as though he falls asleep quite often. I don't know what will happen if Keith catches him asleep again.

I started work last week and like it very much. I'm working three full days instead of five mornings and I'm finding it fits in nicely. I have my own little office again, and at my lunch break I talk to the telephonist when I want company. His office is next door to mine. He is a blind African and speaks very good English. It amazes me how he works the switchboard because he has to feel his way along the switches to answer the incoming calls. He is a Presbyterian and brings his Bible to work each day, saying he likes to read it when he has nothing to do. I spent an hour or so the other day talking with him about his family. His father is the village chief in his home village in northern Malawi, and he became blind when he caught smallpox as a boy. He is married but they can't have any children, for some reason, maybe because of the smallpox. He was telling me that his family expect money from him because they have no education, therefore, they can't get jobs. Even his parents say he should support them – the opposite to English 'laws'! Bye for now... no more room.

Love,

Keith and Anne xx

AT THE INDUCTION weekend at Farnham Castle in 1966 organised by the British Council for Overseas Development, I remember we had been told what to expect regarding some health issues in Africa, including the blight of malaria and the importance of always boiling water for drinking. I had vaguely heard the word 'bilharzia' but had no idea what it was and intended keeping well away from it! What we didn't and couldn't have known at the time was that John, the houseboy, probably had bilharzia (or snail fever), sometimes called sleeping sickness, caused by the Tsetse fly which carries the infection. If left untreated, this disease can cause severe internal organ damage, sometimes leading to death and sadly, one of the symptoms is fatigue. Keith and I were not worldly enough to realise the consequences of someone who was always falling asleep while working, and no-one on the campus ever mentioned the implications of this when we occasionally related an incident that had happened with John. The only time we were ever involved in a medical incident with our workers was when Cassiano had a bad toothache one day and we took him into Zomba to the European dentist. Again, we were inexperienced and not much involved in the outcome, except I remember Cassiano asking us to stop the car so he could be sick at the roadside on the way back to Domasi. We were not without feelings; it was just that we were hanging on by our fingertips in the hope that, if there was a problem, someone would give us some advice. We eventually learned the hard way.

SUNDAY, 30 October 1966

DEAR MAM AND DAD,

We received your letter on Friday, together with Karen's drawing, and we think it's really lovely. We have put it up on the wall. We also received letters from Auntie Alice, Grandma, and Elaine – you know, the girl I worked with at the Hospital – and one from Keith's mother. So, we had a bumper reading day on Friday.

We haven't had any more rain since a week yesterday and it feels to be getting hotter every day. Keith played tennis on Friday with one of the doctors from the general hospital in Zomba – he's an American of an Indian father – and the temperature on the courts was 108°F. It's 85°F in the house at present, but there's a nice breeze coming in through the windows, so it's not too bad.

Last night, Keith and I went to the college dance and thoroughly enjoyed it, despite being the only Europeans out of about 300 people. The teachers don't normally go to these dances, but yesterday was Keith's duty day, which meant that he had to be on call for twenty-four hours – from eight o'clock one morning until eight o'clock the following morning – and the head of the Students' Union told him that they wanted to hold a dance but their record player had broken. They had been told that they could, however, borrow the college record player, but the other equipment to go with it was too expensive to trust to the students alone, so they wanted Keith to supervise this. We had nothing planned, so decided to do it for a laugh. Wow. Can those Africans dance! Mind you, we surprised them a little because they imagined we couldn't do these 'modern' dances. But they found we could twist and shake as good as the rest of them. They opened the dance by playing a special record which usually opens it, and the boy who announced this also said: 'Mr and Mrs Walker would open the dancing', which happened to be a jive, and every time we did anything different, they would clap and roar at us – just like Victor Sylvester's Ballroom Championship. Then a boy plucked up the courage to ask Keith if he could dance with me, then another… Anyway, I learned a new dance this way. Some of the boys were exceptionally smart while others were way out, just like in England, but judging by the applause, they liked The Beatles and Cliff Richard better than their own African music. They aren't a bit shy about dancing either, they really go wild. But you would have died laughing, like we did, when the dance first started because the girls (all twelve of them) were late, and our eyes nearly popped out of our heads when we saw the boys dancing with each other. And after the boys had circulated amongst the girls a few times, back they went to their boy partners for jiving, twisting, shaking and everything else. But you know, the boys walk along the road hand in hand all the time. Apparently, there's nothing wrong with that here!

Keith's brother Derrick has written asking for Conditions of Service and an address to which to write to for a post in Malawi (preferably Domasi) on the same scheme as ours. There are also a couple of posts becoming vacant during the New Year. It would be marvellous if he came here. We wouldn't be quite as lonely.

I've increased my working hours for the time being to twenty-seven and I shall get £11. 9s. 0d. a week wage, which isn't bad. Just think what I'd get if I worked the full thirty-seven hours! But there's not much chance of that. It's hot enough working during the hours I am working, but I'm bored stiff at home, especially as I have nothing to do.

At the moment, Keith is asleep on the couch and the boys have gone to get their lunches. It's fairly quiet outside because nearly everyone has a nap in the afternoons.

In your letter, you mentioned sending a parcel of clothes for the boys. Well, I think maybe it would cost more than the parcel was worth, although I know it would be greatly appreciated, but don't forget, they are very slim people – 5' to 5' 6" tall – not 'giants' like us.

I hope you are both okay and that you, Dad, didn't have to go back into hospital again. We'll be thinking about you both at Christmas and wishing we could be with you, but don't worry, because we shall be eventually.

Love to you both.

Keith and Anne

xx

MY REFERENCE to hoping my father didn't need to go into hospital again related to a problem he had with his eyes throughout most of my childhood, emanating from the army training he did on call-up at the beginning of World War II. While training in Scotland, he and other recruits had been put through a test to check the veracity of the use of mustard gas. At the time, there was a belief that Hitler would use mustard gas at some point, and the military in command presumably felt that the soldiers should be tested on its use. I remember my father telling me that he and his colleagues were told to run into a room that was exposed to the gas, both with and without a gas mask. Afterwards, he had had to spend time in hospital as his eyes had been badly affected. By the time I was seventeen, my father had lost the sight in one of his eyes and he often had difficulty coping with the pain.

SUNDAY, 6 November 1966

DEAR MAM AND DAD,

How are things with you both? Here, it's getting really hot and I'm finding it almost unbearable, but when I flip the coin and think of the cold and fog of England in November I feel quite thankful it is hot, although I've probably picked the wrong time to start work because the days get cooler a bit nearer Christmas. Maybe I should have waited a bit longer.

Still, I'm really enjoying life now. I don't know whether I told you or not, but I'm working two hours in the afternoons now as well as three days, and I go to the club for my lunch. Mr Donnelly, my boss (Scottish gentleman) drops me off outside the shops and after I've done what I have to do, I walk up the hill to the club. I started having a proper dinner, but it's a bit expensive each day, so now I just have sandwiches and we have something hot in the evening. Last night, Bonfire Night, they had a firework display at the club and afterwards a barbecue and dance, but we only stayed for the fireworks and for as long as it took to pick up our chicken, steak and chops that were being barbecued (which we took back to our neighbours, the Kimballs, where we had supper and played bridge afterwards). The reason we didn't stay long at the barbecue was because Keith had a touch of dysentery again and wasn't feeling very well, and I have a bit of tonsillitis (hope we didn't pass it on!).

We also had a smallpox vaccination again on Wednesday because there is an outbreak in Zomba at the army barracks (eleven miles away). We were at the army barracks a week ago as Keith has taken up rifle shooting, and there have been at least nine cases of smallpox confirmed there, so there's a real effort being made to make sure everyone is protected. But you would laugh if you saw the health 'clinics' set up for vaccinations... this country is such an education. Every half mile or so, by the side of the road, you will see a table and on it a bottle with a

Castle Lager label, as well as a little tray with needles. It seemed hilarious to stand under a tree and have an injection after being used to sitting in an antiseptic surgery back in England, though I must admit, it wasn't quite as scary. But we are probably feeling a bit under the weather after having the vaccination, besides everything else. Richard (our neighbour) says they wouldn't let him out of the market yesterday until he had had a vaccination. While he was busy looking on his right arm for the vaccination mark to prove he had been vaccinated already, they were sticking the needle in his left arm!

Richard and Jane are a very nice couple, very American. I don't know whether I mentioned this before, but they have adopted an African boy from Uganda and his name is Francisco. He is thirteen years old now – he was nine when they adopted him – but it seems strange to think they have a son of thirteen when they are only twenty-six years old themselves. Jane is a fabulous cook, too. Whenever you go to their house, she can always conjure up something different to eat. They come from California and it sounds marvellous (our next destination?).

We received your letter the other day, on Wednesday I believe, and it was lovely and long. I hadn't realised you had put our 'emigration' in the paper. You will send the cutting if you can find it, won't you? Jack's phone number is Leeds 6xx xxx, but Keith has written to him about the presents which we left at the house on the day we left for Malawi, so I think it's okay to say that he will send them along before Christmas (this one, I hope, not next). We don't have TV in Malawi unfortunately, and occasionally, when we've nothing to do, we would give anything to have one, but the longing soon goes when we remember the rubbish we used to watch.

I'll write to Mrs Popplewell too, but it's a pity I didn't know her address before we left England because we spent about six hours in Cape Town and could perhaps have called on her. But there's more chance of us going to Cape Town for a holiday than to Tanzania where I originally thought she was. So, you never know.

You mentioned you thought maybe we would have to pay extra on a letter, but we've never had to do this on any of your letters, so it must have been okay.

Bye for now and look after yourselves. Give my love to everyone.

Love,

Keith and Anne xx

SUNDAY 13 NOVEMBER 1966

DEAR MAM AND DAD,

I was pleased to receive two letters from you (or rather, we were both pleased). I just don't seem to have time to write many letters these days myself, even though I don't have anything to do in the house.

We have started decorating the sitting room this week and are doing it as near as possible to our house in Leeds, except that wallpaper is unheard of here, probably because the white ants and cockroaches would eat it all off. So it's all paint. We decided to do some decorating because we were sick of looking at whitewashed walls. We are also out hunting for a three-piece suite, as our chairs are real back-breakers – they told us in the literature that hard furniture was provided and they weren't kidding. We have just had some cushions made filled with kapok, but they have made very little difference. When I think of the furniture we left at the house I could spit blue pips. On Saturday, we also bought a table lamp, the cheapest we could find, with the exception of empty wine bottles with light fittings plugged into their necks, which we are also using. We could have brought the three-piece suite and standard lamp had we realised it was like this.

But there are pleasures in life! Yesterday, we bought a lovely Siamese kitten which we are calling Ching-Chao (his registered name.) The cat cost us five guineas (it's all paying out, isn't it!) He is extremely timid and hasn't eaten or drunk anything since we brought him home. We had to go to Blantyre to pick him up – fifty-four miles – so he has cost us a pretty penny, what with the petrol etc. The lady we got him from comes from the Dales and she has a sister living in Keighley – small world. She had a mammy Siamese, a daddy Siamese and three kittens, as well as two dogs, two parrots... oh, and I forgot, a litter of Alsatian pups. Her house would have put Mrs Band's into the shade; it was absolutely fabulous, and the furniture looked like the most expensive you could buy – not modern and not old-fashioned, just very, very good quality.

Oh, before I forget, you say you will send the Batley News and this will be very nice, and in exchange, I can send you either the Rhodesian paper which we get every week, or the local paper The Times, which doesn't really have any news in it, but I can send it along if you like.

On Wednesday evening, we had a horrible bat flying around the sitting room. I've no idea how it managed to get through the ceiling, but you can't ever get rid of them once they are there. We had to have a visit from the Bat Man as soon as we moved in, but he obviously didn't catch them all. This bat scared me silly because it kept swooping towards me and it eventually landed on the couch where I was crouched, screaming! The following morning the neighbours asked Keith what he had been doing to me the previous night! It eventually flew into the dining room and out through the open window, but it couldn't get away because we have mosquito netting on the outside of the windows. Keith killed it the next morning with his airgun, which I thought was cruel until I realised they are extremely dangerous because they carry rabies. I must admit, they are ugly little things too, and they have two rows of very sharp teeth so

I've no wish to be bitten again by anything – I told you about the mouse, I believe.

Our katundu arrived on Monday from England (see, I'm getting Africanised). It's taken a long time but it now means that we have a few extra luxuries, such as pans, cups and saucers, but the house doesn't look any better for it. Only two things were broken: a Pyrex dish and that green vase which you once gave me, Mam, and the goods were insured so we shall be claiming a couple of pounds for the damage. But you've no idea how nice it is to have a wireless to listen to, even though it does keep fading away. But we can get England, which is quite something. Keith is going to fit an aerial on the roof, so hopefully, we'll get better reception then.

We keep trying to imagine what it's like to be cold, I mean really cold. The temperature here dropped to 78°F on Thursday and we were frozen!

We'll be thinking about you.

Lots of love to you both.

K and A xx

MONDAY, 14 November 1966

DEAR AUNT MARY AND UNCLE JOHN,

It was brilliant to receive your letter today. I've been meaning to write to you for about a fortnight but I never got around to it. I'm just lazy, that's what it is.

It's grand to know that you are out of hospital, Uncle John, and that you are making good progress.

It's amazing what those gorgeous nurses can do. But you will have to take more care of yourself now, won't you!

We are settling down fine and know quite an assortment of people, both European and American. People here just seem to make a special effort to get to know you as there are only about

1,000 Europeans in Zomba, the town near Domasi, and whereas in England you could see the same person day after day and only pass the time of day with them, here, people come over to you and introduce themselves. I had a fabulous watermelon given to me the other day by an American lady I met during my visit to the club for lunch. It was so heavy I could hardly carry it, and the taste! Well, you can take my word for it, it was gorgeous.

On Sunday evening, we went to our neighbour's house, as did the rest of the college staff, as they were having a barbecue. I must say, Americans certainly know how to entertain. There were about twenty of us, all together. I'm lost when I have to cater for four people!

On Wednesday, the rain started again and stayed with us until Saturday lunchtime. It was lovely to be cool again – the temperature dropped to 78°. It's been in the nineties for weeks now. Needless to say, it's back up again.

On Saturday, we got a Siamese kitten. He's really timid. If you move at all he crouches down, and if you put him on the floor, he runs into a corner and sits with his little paws on the wall and looks so pitiful. And Siamese cats cry just like babies. He's woken us up both nights with his crying.

Our things arrived from England last Monday, so it's beginning to look like home again in our bungalow. We've even started decorating it like Pudsey Road with green and black, and we tried to get wood to make a room divider similar to the one we had in Leeds. In fact, we ordered it from one of the African villages but when we went to collect it, we were told the man who was cutting and planing it had gone back to his home in the mountains. So, I guess we've had it for that for the time being. The divider will have to be in special lightweight wood (called balsa wood, I believe), otherwise, the weight would bring the ceiling down on us – bats, owls, cockroaches and all!

Keith has asked me to leave the last page for him, so I'll say bye for now and look after yourselves. God bless.

Love,
Anne xx
Keith says:

DEAR MARY AND JOHN,

It's now Wednesday evening. I'm afraid it's taken me two days to write this letter. Glad to hear you are recovering, John. In no time at all, you'll be able to sup as much as you like. I hope so, anyway. We don't want you to be drinking lemonade at our homecoming party!

The kitten is slightly less timid now than when we got him; I think he'll grow into a nice cat.

I must say I do miss the telly here. Sometimes we get very bored, though not for long. At the end of this term, I won't have to give any more lectures. The students take exams and then we break up for Christmas. It certainly will seem strange eating our Christmas pud when the weather is hot. Mind you, it's been too hot for the last couple of weeks. I never thought it could ever get too hot for me, but 97° in the shade sure is HOT! It's just unbearable in the sun around dinnertime.

Don't forget to save up and pay us a visit. It's only £195 return by VC10.

Well, that's it for now. Enjoy the cold weather while it lasts.

Look after yourselves.

Keith

SUNDAY, 20 November 1966

DEAR MAM AND DAD,

Well, it's Sunday again, the only day I seem to have time to write these days. We had a surprise letter from Gerald (Keith's brother) the other day. His letter had been posted on 23 October but unfortunately, he hadn't put enough stamps on, so it had taken all that time by sea mail! We learned that Denise (our friend in Leeds) had a baby boy on 6 November. Keith's mother wrote last week, too.

My driving seems to have fallen by the wayside these days. It's partly my fault, really, because it's been too warm to bother these past few weeks, and also, we were stopped by the police a while back because we were displaying L plates when Keith was driving and, apparently, this isn't allowed, so we took them off but now think it's too much trouble putting them on and taking them off each day. I'll have to wait until it gets a bit cooler and then have a good run at it. However, I don't really have an excuse because it's a bit cooler now, thank goodness, and it's been raining since yesterday lunchtime, which is a welcome change from the boiling sun.

We had to take our kitten to the vet on Friday because he wasn't walking properly – he limped about whenever we put him on the floor and preferred to lay down all the time, so we thought there must be something wrong with him. The vet assured us that he was okay but that he needed feeding up. He said he had been taken from his mother too soon. We were given some vitamins for him and told to give him as much raw liver as he could eat. I'm amazed at the difference these last two days. He isn't the same cat. He goes absolutely wild, and I have the bites and scratches to prove it. The vet said he would make a magnificent cat if he lives long enough. What a statement to make!

I know it sounds early to start talking about where we are going from here, but our Canadian neighbours have all but talked us into going to Canada, so who knows? Anyway, we have already decided that after our two and a half or three years here, initially, we are going back to the UK so that at least Keith can take his Bachelor of Education degree, which will take nine months. And these American and Canadian contracts can only be for one year, so it would be nice to have a year in Canada to see that part of the world. Mrs Turrell, the American we stayed with when we first arrived here, goes back to the States next Friday. She is a marvel, really. Her husband was a professor at an American university and when he died, she decided she must go back to work, so applied to come to Africa for two years. She must be in her late fifties or early sixties. I don't know how she dares come all this way by herself. I'll let Keith finish this off now. Cheerio until next Sunday.

Love to you both and look after yourselves.

Anne xx (next bit for Keith)

HI! By popular request, I am now going to finish the letter. I've been reading your letters, it's just that there are so many people on my side that I left it to Anne to write to you. What's up with Reggie? You'll have to persuade him to put pen to paper.

We were glad to hear from Michael and Barbara, despite the insults!

I've finished lecturing for this term. The students take their exams and then go home for Christmas. Some of them have a hell of a way to go, 500 miles some of them. Some students, called T3s, finish this week and start teaching after Christmas. Their salary is £120 per annum or about £2. 7s. 0d. a week. Great stuff, eh? Mind you, that's more than some of 'em are worth (present company excepted, of course). I'll be sending some film home in the next four to six weeks, so soon after that Gerald should call you to arrange to show the films to you.

We've had a real letter-writing day today. We must have written books full of news (all the same, of course) to dozens of people. Tonight, we are going to the club at Zomba to see a film – Paul Newman in *The Moving Target*. I hope it's good 'cause we haven't seen a good film since we got here! Ta ra for now.

Keith

WEDNESDAY, 30 November 1966

DEAR MAM AND DAD,

I left writing until later this week on purpose because we are having a week's holiday next week and going to Rhodesia, so I don't think I shall have a chance to write a letter next week, only a postcard. It's amazing really to think that you can suddenly decide to have a holiday and not have to worry where the money is going to come from. I am having a week's unpaid leave from work and I need it, I can tell you, I'm shattered. It's not only the heat, it's also the work. I hardly ever stop now, from going in at 8.15 until I leave again at 3.30, except for my hour and a half lunch break. I really do like the work, though and it passes the time, not to mention the money which comes in very useful; however, I paid £11. 16s. 0d. tax last month. But like all government jobs here, it's understaffed and overloaded with work.

We are setting off for Rhodesia on Saturday morning at 5 a.m. in the hope that we can drive the 385 miles in the one day, but the trouble is, for over a 100 miles the road is only dirt, no tar at all, not even the single strip in the middle of the road, and we've already had a sample of a complete dirt road when we took a drive the other Sunday to Lake Chilwa, seventeen miles away. You have to drive at forty-five miles per hour, otherwise, you feel every bump, and if you drive faster, you're liable to end up in a field because the dust is so thick in places you skid along and can easily lose control if you aren't careful. We are planning to stay in Salisbury for one day, go to Gwelo to see some friends of Derrick and Margaret, and then drive up to Victoria Falls on the border of Rhodesia and Zambia. On the way back, we are going to pass through the Wankie game reserve. We shall cover a few thousand miles in the week but it will be worth it. Anyway, we shall keep you posted on our journey.

We are anticipating that Derrick, Margaret and the children

will be coming on 22 December, so they will be with us for Christmas, which will be lovely. They are flying from Aden to Nairobi and from Nairobi to Blantyre where we will pick them up. We had been expecting that Derrick would apply for one of the posts due to become vacant at the college in 1967, but in his last letter, he says he has accepted a posting with the RAF schools in Singapore. I know he will get much more money with the RAF, but we thought it would convince him to come when he visited us at Christmas, once he saw the set-up, but it's too late if he has already accepted Singapore. Ah, well.

We shall be thinking about everyone at Christmas. Thank you both for your Christmas card, it was really lovely. I haven't seen any Christmas cards to buy here yet. It's the same with birthday cards. I suppose they don't think it worth getting large stocks of cards in for the small European population (just over 900 at the last census, covering the whole of Zomba and the surrounding areas). They will probably have cards in Rhodesia though, so we'll see what we can do.

I was surprised to hear about Auntie Alice (and also Grand-ma), but it's the ideal situation if it works out. Hope they've got plenty of bicarb. I'll write to my grandma in Beech Towers – they can always post it on to her if she has 'resigned' – pessimistic, aren't I? But I can still remember the Sheffield episode!

We were thinking about you at 6.50 p.m. our time. We had just finished our meal (chicken and rice) and Keith looked at the clock and said, 'I wonder what they're doing at home now.' We are two hours in front of you – so I imagined my dad getting ready for work and you cleaning your machine at the mill. Are you still at the same place, Mam?

I'll let you have postcards of our travels next week. So, until then I'll say bye for now.

Lots of love to you both.

God bless.

Keith and Anne xx

ON 11TH DECEMBER BELOW, I write letters to both my Auntie Alice and to my grandmother which relate to the mention above that I make in response to a letter from my mother previously.

SUNDAY, 11 December 1966

DEAR MAM AND DAD,

It was nice to have your letter waiting for us on our arrival back in Malawi. You'll be receiving a postcard written from Rhodesia at about the same time you receive this letter. It had to be posted in Malawi because it was written the night before we left to come back and we set off very early in the morning; therefore, we couldn't get stamps as the post office was closed.

We thought we were going to have a fabulous time but were mistaken. It took us two days to get to Salisbury because we stayed overnight at a small hotel about 150 miles outside Salisbury. From there, we travelled to Gwelo – the town Derrick and Margaret used to live in – and stayed in Gwelo overnight.

We went to see the house D and M lived in and went next door to the neighbours to see if they could remember them from two years ago, but the neighbour had only lived there for eighteen months, so we were disappointed. Margaret had given us the address of an old lady to visit, but we were out of luck there too, because she had broken her arm and gone to live with her daughter.

We left the next day (Monday) for Wankie Game Reserve in Zambia (now named Wange National Park). Though our intention was to leave Gwelo that morning, nonetheless, we hung on until midday because it had said on the news that a decision was required by the British government by noon whether or not Mr

Ian Smith's government had agreed to conditions discussed between himself and Mr Harold Wilson, but when noon came and there was nothing, we thought it best to push on.

[Author's Note: In December 1966, Smith and Wilson met on board the British cruiser Tiger off Gibraltar and worked out a set of constitutional principles in line with the original British terms for a settlement. To begin with, Smith made several concessions. In exchange, Wilson agreed that majority rule should be postponed beyond the end of the century. But the talks broke down over the issue of how Rhodesia could return to legality. Wilson's demand that interim powers be handed over to the loyalist governor of Rhodesia, Sir Humphrey Gibbs, proved unacceptable to Smith, and the Tiger proposals were rejected.]

We arrived at the game reserve in the afternoon and had time to see a part of it before it became dark. I didn't like the place we stayed in at all; everyone had a rondavel – an African-style hut which was a small, round, one-room hut containing two single beds, a small table, two chairs, and a stand with enamel bowl, jug, bucket and 'potty' – no running water. It had a straw roof which was another thing I didn't care for, and there was a massive space under the door for all and sundry to crawl through. Mind you, you can't expect the Ritz for 10/- each (meals not included). To make matters worse, I came down with malaria the next day, even though we have taken antimalarial tablets since we came to Malawi. I hope I never have to spend a night like Tuesday night again as long as I live. I died a thousand deaths. To just lay my head on the pillow caused me the most atrocious pain in my head and the sweat was literally running down my body, dripping off my finger-ends. I have never felt so ill before in my life. I really did feel dreadful.

On Wednesday, Keith took me the seventeen miles to the nearest medical centre (and there, not even a doctor). A sister gave me an injection and lots of pills to take and then sent us back to the 'jungle', telling me to go to bed and stay there – horror of horrors! On Thursday, I felt well enough to travel, so to prevent having to spend another night in the 'torture chamber', we set off for Salisbury. Sadly, we didn't even get a glimpse of Victoria Falls, after travelling over 1,000 miles to get there – imagine!

As soon as we reached Salisbury, I began to feel a little bit better in myself. It was late because the car had broken down and we had to be towed to a garage – and was it raining! But my goodness, Salisbury is stunning, I've never seen anywhere like it before in my life. We hadn't booked a hotel previously, of course, so started looking for a hotel and came across a six-storey new hotel building. More for a joke than anything else, Keith went in to ask how much they charged for bed and breakfast while I stayed in the car, and he came back out saying he had booked us in. I thought he was still joking, but he wasn't and I was so relieved. Oh, how beautiful the hotel was. We had a wonderful room with private bath and toilet, all the furniture was modern and the room had fitted wardrobes and cupboards in teak. Our room was at the front, so we had a lovely view from the window. And all this for £4.10s. 0d for both of us. We decided we would like to stay an extra night at the hotel to give us chance to see the place better, but after having taken the car to have a proper repair job done so it wouldn't let us down halfway along the disgusting roads through Portuguese Mozambique, and finding it was going to cost more than £6, we realised we didn't have enough cash. When we explained the situation to the hotel manager, he very kindly told us not to worry as we could send the money on, and he even suggested we didn't have to pay for the first night and could just send the other two night's money on when we came back to Malawi. He didn't even ask for proof of identity; he merely told Keith he had an honest face (big laugh).

We arrived back safely, but the roads had become rapidly worse than when we were going. I don't even want to travel that journey again. For 350 miles, the roads were dirt but not smooth as you might expect. The rock had penetrated the soil and stood out like pieces of glass, then in places, it was like driving over a ploughed field – literally. We banged from one great stone to another, and this went on and on and on for mile after mile. When we eventually reached the tar, I wasn't surprised that the car let us down. We shall have to fly to Salisbury the next time. I've got more bits and pieces to tell you but I'll write again during the week.

Love to you both.

Keith and Anne xx

THAT JOURNEY to Rhodesia was both a trauma and a joy. It was only after we had returned to Domasi that we remembered how dangerous the travel through Portuguese Mozambique had been on our initial journey to Malawi. We didn't see a car from one hour to the next – and remember the train with the metal shutters? At any moment, we could have been captured and put to ransom. This isn't as silly as it sounds, as it occasionally happened.

But in those carefree days we would often set off on a long hot drive without even taking much to drink, usually only a couple of bottles of Coke. Oh, how stupid the young can be!

We loved Salisbury, we really loved it. Even now, in my seventies, I still feel the joy and delight of those few days. I can remember leaning out of our second-floor hotel window at the Jameson Hotel and looking down the street, left and right, and thinking how lucky those people below me were. Did they not know it? I suppose they did.

Oh, and we did send the money to the hotel as soon as we returned to Domasi.

9 December 1966

MONDAY, 12 December 1966

DEAR AUNT ALICE,

Well, this is a surprise, writing to a different address. It was nice to receive your letter(s) recently. Auntie Mary gave me your new address, but my mother told me of all the changes. I have just written to my grandma (that's why my writing is still so large – I fitted about five words to a page!)

How are you liking your new job? I honestly thought you'd never do it – leave Batley, I mean. I know it's difficult to do these things on your own, but once you take the first step, the scope is unlimited. Your next plunge will be to come over to see us. Keith's mother keeps saying if she wins the pools she will come, but that means never because who do you know who has won the pools? No-one!

We spent last week on holiday in Rhodesia. What a fabulous place. Everything is so new and clean. We stopped off in Gwelo (this is where Keith's brother used to live) on the way through to the game reserve. We went to look at his old house and it felt quite strange, as though we were prying on Derrick's private life. I can't really explain what we felt.

From there, we went to the game reserve and came across a herd of elephants even before we reached the reserve proper. They look even more terrifying as they amble across the road ahead of you, and the bull, being the bravest I suppose, is the one to let you know you are in their territory. He turns to face you, waves his ears and makes the most awful noise while throwing his trunk in the air. In the reserve, we saw more elephant and warthogs, deer, zebra, wildebeest, baboons and monkeys. The main camp was closed because the rains are due and the roads are dirt, so we didn't see all the animals there were to see. We were looking forward to seeing the lions but didn't see any.

The day after we arrived at the camp I fell ill with malaria, was in bed Tuesday and Wednesday, and because we couldn't see very much on the reserve and I felt fit enough by then to travel, we set off back to Salisbury on the Thursday. We found a fabulous new hotel, much better than any in Leeds and possibly London and, after the first enjoyable night, decided to stay an extra two nights to enable us to see a bit of Salisbury. Our room was amazing – everything was contemporary. The wardrobes were fitted and in teak, so too the various shelves, cupboards and dressing table. The beds were lovely and soft – there seem to be no double beds in Africa, not even at Domasi! We had our own telephone and wireless, beautiful wall lights, and private bathroom in lovely pastel shades. We even had fitted carpet everywhere. We enjoyed our stay so much that I personally didn't want to come back to Malawi, but needs must I'm afraid, and after the shocking roads we had to travel on coming through Portuguese Mozambique and Malawi, I was glad to get back and rest. We spent the majority of the journey going up and down over bumps – the car was shaken to pieces. It was just like riding over a ploughed field in places. Anyway, I'm back to work again now – worse luck (I don't mean that)! I'll say bye for now.

Write back, won't you? We'd love to hear about your new job.

Lots of love.

Keith and Anne xx

MONDAY, 12 December 1966

DEAR GRANDMA,

I was pleased to hear you had gone into Beech Towers for a rest. I bet you will have a lovely Christmas and you will be much better off than if you were in your own house away from everyone.

I hear the weather is very cold in England. At present, we are waiting for the rains to start properly, and until they do, the heat becomes almost unbearable.

We had a week's holiday last week and went to Rhodesia. We stayed in Salisbury (the capital) for two nights and also went to the game reserve where we stayed for three days. But we didn't get the chance to see too many animals because I became ill with malaria. I'm okay now, though.

We saw plenty of elephants, though some were too close for comfort as they just wander across the road in front of you as you are driving along in the car. If you get in their way, they turn and look at you, flapping their ears and bellowing. They are really terrifying animals. We saw lots of zebra, small deer and monkeys too so it was a worthwhile trip despite my sickness. However, our return journey was very tiring - 1,000 miles each way - and we were pleased to get back to Malawi, though, I must admit I much prefer Rhodesia to live in. It is a wonderful country.

We are expecting Keith's brother to visit us over Christmas. He came over from England in January this year to live in Aden and is intending coming down to spend a few days with us. We shall be having a very quiet Christmas and shall miss everyone at home, but we are fortunate to have nice neighbours, mainly American and Canadian.

I do hope you can read my writing, Grandma. Perhaps I should have printed it. If you have read any of my previous letters to my mam and dad, you will know that we have a lovely cat now. He gives me a terrible time particularly when I'm trying to write as he won't leave the pen alone. I'll say bye for now, Grandma, and hope you are keeping well.

Lots of love to you, look after yourself and have a nice Christmas. We'll be thinking of you.

Love,

Anne xxx

BEECH TOWERS WAS a government home for the elderly. By this time, my grandmother was in her eighties and finding it difficult to look after herself. She had already spent some time in a Catholic home for the elderly but had hated it preferring, of course, to be around her family. However, I can only assume that by going into Beech Towers, my grandmother had now exhausted the goodwill of her family. Unfortunately, she was a very difficult person to live with and couldn't stay with people for very long. I remember the short time she had spent living with our family when I was in my teens had been disastrous. But now, as I'm nearing my eighties, I feel utter sorrow for her. She didn't get on with people, yet was unable to live alone. I am very fortunate to have the love of my family and my life partner and know I won't spend my final years in turmoil as she did.

FRIDAY, 16 December 1966

DEAR MAM AND DAD,

Hope you are both well? I can hardly believe it's nearly Christmas – there is barely any sign of it in the shops here in Malawi. However, it was gorgeous in Salisbury, the streets were all illuminated and there was even a giant crib in the main square.

I hope you will excuse the writing but I trapped my thumb in the car door this evening and it's giving me jip.

I didn't get much chance to tell you about our trip to Rhodesia in my last letter, did I? We left Domasi on the Saturday morning at about six o'clock, and our first stop was at the Portuguese Mozambique Customs post. I'm sorry to say but I'm not keen on the Portuguese authorities as I find them surly people who don't give you time as you wait for clearance for Customs. They demand your passport etc., rather than ask for it, and do they say thank you! We had to pass through Portuguese Customs once again before leaving their territory – and what an awful territory. If I thought I had to go along that road to Rhodesia again, I'd jump in the river. However, they do have nice wine!

On the way back, while at a customs post, we met some friends of ours who live in Zomba and who were on their way to Rhodesia for a holiday. They have my deepest sympathy. This week it has rained at least twice every day, so I dread to think what the journey back will be like for them on the washed-out roads. We heard that someone travelling along the road from

Rhodesia on Wednesday arrived in Zomba with their car covered in mud from top to bottom.

On the Road

While waiting for the ferry to cross the Zambezi, we also met two young men who were travelling around the world. One was from Newcastle and the other was a New Zealander. They said they 'palled up' two and a half years ago, work until they have enough money to travel a little further, and when the money is finished, they get another job until they can go a little further. Then in Salisbury, we met a man – a former Londoner – who has lived in Rhodesia for nine years and said he taught in London with someone from Batley, a former St Michael's College pupil named Terry Finn. He asked if we could find out where he is now. He will be about thirty-five years old, I should think. I thought about a Mr Finn who teaches at St Mary's, but I don't know his Christian name. He may be older than thirty-five but I'm just going by the age of this Pat Morgan (an R.C. of course) who looks to be about that age.

I had to laugh when you were telling me about the girl Alice's employer is going around with. It most certainly isn't Jack's ex because her name was Jean, and in any case, she was married the Saturday after we left England.

We are expecting Derrick sometime next week (minus family and Margaret – fares too expensive), but he won't be staying more than a few days as he is flying on to Rhodesia to settle a few things.

I accidentally found out the other day that our offices here, where I'm working at the moment, are moving to Blantyre next March – fifty-three miles away. So, I suppose I shall have to start looking for another job.

If Britain makes the sanctions any harder for Rhodesia, Malawi is going to have a rough time. Things get more expensive every day here – admittedly it's only the British stuff, but I bought some sandals the other week – M&S ones which cost me 18/11d. in the Leeds M&S but here I paid 29/11s. for exactly the same thing.

Bye for now. I'll write again before Christmas.

Love to you both.

Keith and Anne xx

SUNDAY, 17 December 1966

DEAR MICHAEL AND BARBARA,

Thank you for your Christmas cards. I hope you don't mind sharing with my mother and dad, but there aren't many cards here at all. I was only able to get four altogether. One of the girls at the office said there was a queue outside the stationers during the week because they had just received their stock. I can hardly believe that it's Christmas next week. There are hardly any signs of it in the shops and nobody even talks about it. There's no doubt about it, snow really makes Christmas as when it's sunny, you feel as if you're in the middle of your summer holiday, not a Christmas one.

We were infested with flying ants last night; they have large fat bodies and four large wings, but they only fly for about twenty minutes then their wings drop off. I don't know whether or not I've already told you, but the Africans consider them a great delicacy as they are only available for about two months in the year when the rains are beginning. Apparently, they are great fried, like our fish and chips! It was funny yesterday because we could see our immediate neighbour's houseboy with his three or so children at the end of our garden, bending down every few seconds and putting something into a dish. Keith, being nosey, went to see what they were doing and found they were standing over a hole in the ground about two inches wide, waiting for the flying ants to come out – they were like ordinary flies with yellow bellies – and as soon as one popped its head out of the hole, the child would squash its head between the fingers and drop it in the dish. These ants came out every second or so, so you can imagine how many they had. The Africans said they tasted very good fried – how sickening!

Our African neighbours are really very astute. We have some trees in our garden that are full of mangoes, which is an African fruit about the size of an apple, but the texture is peculiar to us as it's very stringy and sweet and wet and a bit sickly. Needless to say, our neighbours like the fruit. Their children have started coming into our garden without asking and are just knocking this fruit off the trees with a stick. Keith was going to tell them off but thought better of it because (a) we don't like the fruit anyway and it would just rot, and (b) because you have to remember that to an African there are no boundaries. As far as they are concerned, the land is there and what is grown on it belongs to anybody (especially if it happens to be growing wild). So, we didn't stop them, but you can imagine our surprise when we saw our neighbour's children sitting at the side of the road the other day with rows of these mangoes, selling them! Good entrepreneurs eh? We are going to have to warn the kids about taking our pears, though, as we only have one pear tree and don't want the fruit 'nicked'. Our lemon trees are almost bearing fruit now too, but when Keith saw our neighbour's boy the other day, he mentioned that we would prefer that they didn't take any of this fruit, and the cheeky fellow just shrugged and said he didn't like lemons anyway. That's not to say he won't pinch them to sell, though.

I think we only get a Monday and Tuesday holiday from work, but Keith's brother is coming next weekend, although we don't know exactly how long he will be able to stay. Anyway, I might take a few extra days off.

It must be lovely having children at Christmas and watching their faces as they open their presents, but I bet it's going to cost you both a fortune. I was just asking Keith if we had to buy the houseboy and garden-boy Christmas presents, but he says no as they don't recognise Christmas. They are both Muslims and John said it was their big feast during the week and he had to fast from Wednesday until Saturday. They are still alive, I'm pleased to say. Here's hoping you have a very nice Christmas and give our love to the children.

Bye for now.

Love,

Keith and Anne xx

CASSIANO, our gardener, had been complaining about the large holes that were appearing all over the ground in the front garden and Keith decided to take a look himself. Armed with a spade and a bucket (not the seaside type), he started digging in an area furthest from the front door, and to his and my amazement, filled the bucket halfway up with scorpions! Knowing how dangerous these animals were, it was important to kill them swiftly, and the only way available was drowning. Our main fear, having 'woken the tiger', was that the scorpions would move their nest. But we needn't have worried too much about their welfare as, on looking around the back garden, we found plenty of their cousins already ensconced in their little homes.

Sometimes, they would search for new environs and we very occasionally found the odd one in the house. Much to John's disgust, he one day found one in his shoe where he had left it by the back door. Unfortunately, he found it the hard way, by touch. He got a very nasty sting on his foot which swelled almost immediately, but the scorpion got something much worse…

THURSDAY, 22 December 1966

DEAR MAM AND DAD,

By the time you receive this letter it will be after Christmas but I hope you both had a good one. I get Monday and Tuesday holiday the same as you will, I suppose. I've no idea what we shall do. It's so quiet here – there's a dance at the club on Christmas Eve, but we shan't be going. We miss the organised entertainment as much as anything and strangely, Keith misses TV much more than I do.

Well, you'll be sorry to hear that, unfortunately, we have had to sack John our houseboy. Keith gave him his cards and a week's extra pay with my blessing as he had become extremely unreliable. For the first few months he never set a foot wrong, he was wonderful. Then suddenly, the problems started. He would go missing for fifteen to twenty minutes every so often during the day and come back with his shirt covered in grass (Keith doesn't know this, by the way, as it happened before I started working and while Keith was at college). And I told you about the time he was asleep in the kitchen. All this on top of the fact that his work had begun to be shabby. He spent each afternoon every day ironing about four articles. Well, in all, Keith caught him asleep five times and there were many times when we would go in the back door and find John in the kitchen 'tickling' the sink, supposedly washing it, and his eyes looking like lead, obviously just awakened by the sound of the car engine. Anyway, I agreed with Keith that the next time he faulted in any way, he should sack him and on Tuesday, Keith parked his car at our neighbours so that John wouldn't hear him coming, and sure enough, he was asleep – this was at about ten o'clock in the morning and the dirty washing was on the floor, pots in the sink etc. I'm sorry to say I feel he had asked for it, as he probably had the least work to do and yet was getting the highest wage on the station. Our Canadian neighbour's boy has four children to prepare food for and wash afterwards, but he was getting much less than John. As Keith told him, he was a fool to himself. The odd thing about it was that John asked if he could work his notice, this after Keith had given him wages in lieu of notice. We've been told that this would have been the worst possible thing to do as he could have taken revenge on us, probably bringing cockroaches or scorpions into the house, or maybe something worse as he did prepare our food sometimes. I'm not pulling your leg – apparently, this is what can happen, though I'm sure John would not have done this to us as, despite the problem, we did have mutual respect. However, I prefer to manage on my own now with possibly a little help from Cassiano.

We received a letter from Auntie Alice, one from Auntie Winnie and one from Auntie Ethel during the week, so I'll have a lot of letters to catch up on over Christmas.

We posted the film of our journey here to Gerald last Monday, so I reckon you'll be able to see it in three or four weeks. In his last letter, Gerald said he hadn't forgotten about showing the film to my family.

We had a letter from Derrick during the week to say he couldn't come to see us after all as he couldn't afford to bring all the family and didn't like leaving them in Aden because of the situation there. We were really looking forward to seeing him too, although in my heart of hearts I didn't think he would make it!

I saw my first snake on Monday. It was in the office garden, partly hidden by grass and stones. It was very thin and not very long, but it was venomous. It had killed a frog more than twice as thick as itself and when I turned away, it was just starting to eat the frog's legs, ready to swallow the rest of him, which seemed impossible to me, but I didn't stop to see!

I would have loved to have had a camera at work today because the wives of the civil servants who live in the servant's quarters where I work must have been up all night catching flying ants. They had two double newspaper pages completely covered with them all fried and ready to eat, and every time a messenger passed on his way to the post office, he would bend down and take a handful. I could have been sick. Rebecca, the African girl I work with, says she can understand how I feel because when she was in England she used to feel ill when she saw people eating oysters, prawns and shrimps. I suppose she's right really – it's what one gets used to. You must admit, oysters do look horrible!

I'll say cheerio for now and wish you both a very happy New Year with lots of good health (and if you are still doing the pools, Dad, lots of wealth).

Look after yourselves, Mam and Dad.

Lots of love,

Keith and Anne xx

TUESDAY, 27 December 1966

DEAR MAM AND DAD,

Hope you both had an enjoyable Christmas. I'm sure you would have seen Auntie Mary and Uncle John at least one night so it wouldn't be so disappointing. I'm afraid we have been most miserable. For one thing, it didn't feel like Christmas with the sun boiling down on us and there is no place to go for an evening meal out or to the cinema, except to the club and there you see the same old faces every time. We were also very disappointed because Derrick couldn't come. The Kimballs came over on Christmas Eve for an hour to play bridge, but we stayed in most of Christmas Day.

At the prison, the prisoners were giving a dance display on Christmas Day, and after I'd been to church we went down to watch them. Because it was such a nice morning we walked the half mile or so. We were going to take lots of film because I'm sure nowhere in the world could you get prisoners and public mixing so freely. All the village turned out but Keith and I were the only Europeans there. It was funny to see all the prisoners streaming out of the prison onto the football field – about one guard to every fifty men – and they were puffing away at their cigarettes. We were standing near the entrance and every now and then we would get a 'Muli bwanji, sir' from someone, then Joseph, a prisoner who looks after the tennis court for us, left the party and came over to talk to us – just like that! Out came the dancers, making their 'war cries', and we thought we were in for a good time, but then the rain started, so we all had to run for shelter – prisoners and all. We stood under the thatched roof of a house for very nearly an hour before it stopped raining, and by this time it was almost twelve o'clock. As you now know, we have no houseboy as such, although Cassiano comes in each day to do the heavy work such as floors and washing, so I had to get the lunch ready.

We had just started walking back when it began raining again, and can it rain! Unfortunately, there was nowhere to shelter, so by the time we arrived back we were wet through – lovely Christmas Day.

I started writing this letter at about 9.30 a.m. this morning and it's now 8.30 p.m.

We have just arrived back from a trip to Mlanje Mountain, ninety-six miles away by car, and the amazing thing is that on a clear day you can see Mlanje from Domasi – it is two miles high. We decided to go on the spur of the moment and intended climbing at least part of it, but when we reached the foot we couldn't find the path and ended up in the middle of a cluster of African houses. Fortunately, someone came along in a car to ask if we were lost and it turned out to be the government agent for Mlanje district. We thought we could detect a bit of an accent as he was speaking and it turned out he was from Halifax. He said the path up the mountain was overgrown and that it wasn't advisable to try to climb at present, but invited us back to his house. Goodness, what a fabulous house and garden he had. There was an open-air swimming pool fed by the water coming from the mountain and a beautiful waterfall. His back garden was directly at the bottom of the mountain and had just about every fruit tree imaginable – orange, banana, mango, pawpaw, peach, lemon, avocado, and pear. He even grew his own pineapples, hundreds of them. We spent the afternoon with him and his wife and decided to round off the day by going into Blantyre to the cinema – sheer luxury. But unfortunately, we took the wrong turning on the way, not knowing the road from Mlanje to Blantyre, and instead of sitting in the pictures at 5.30 p.m., we were bumping along a dusty road in the opposite direction to Blantyre. We asked at an outpost police station and were directed back the way we came, so we travelled 238 miles in all today, and the funny thing is, we didn't seem to travel so far. When we arrived back, Cassiano, his wife and baby, and presumably another of his brothers, were sitting on the path outside our back door waiting for us. They don't go inside and wait unless you tell them they can. Anyway, today has made up for the disappointing beginning of the holiday.

I am sorry to hear about your job, Mam, but I'm sure you'll get another one – you'll have to go with Auntie Alice to 'sign on'. That'll be a first if you do!

Hope you are keeping well, Dad. We think about you all a lot.

We both wish you a very happy and better health New Year, and we hope you had a happy Christmas.

Lots of love to you both.

Keith and Anne xx

Gwelo, 1960s

FOUR

Letters From 1967

MONDAY, 9 January 1967

DEAR MAM AND DAD,

It was lovely to receive your letter this morning telling us how you had enjoyed the film.

I bet you are wondering why I haven't written for two weeks, but just lately we don't seem to be in the house for five minutes by ourselves – we're either being asked out to dinner or we're asking other people to dinner. We had a holiday from work on New Year's Day (the Monday) and went with a couple we have palled up with (who live in Zomba but come from London) to the Mlanje mountain again and Likibula Falls – a beautiful spot under the mountains to go swimming, but it was a bit off-putting because the Africans were doing their washing in the Falls. Yesterday, we went with the same couple – Chris and Wendy – to Lake Malawi. There are dozens of miniature beaches along the lake's shores and we chose one called Monkey Bay, so called, presumably, because of all the monkeys! It was really beautiful – the sand was clean and the sea blue. Actually, it's not sea, but fresh water, and a bit salty if you happen to take a gulp by mistake. There were only about twenty people there all day and we were comparing it with the beach at Blackpool or Scarborough for crowds. We went swimming if you'd like to call it that – Keith isn't much of a swimmer and I never really learned how to. At first, the sun was behind the clouds and it was warmer in the water, but in the afternoon the sun came out, and didn't we know it! I've had to take the day off work because my back and legs are burnt bright red, and Keith was supposed to be going to Blantyre for five days on a course, but he can't walk because his feet and ankles are badly swollen. The strange thing is, we didn't sunbathe and in fact, we were in the water most of the time, which only goes to prove how strong the sun is.

It's funny to think of you all shivering with cold while we are burning hot. All in all, though, we enjoyed the day and shall go again in a few weeks' time – it's only a good two-hour journey, on empty roads.

Today, we also had a letter from Michael and Barbara and one from Gerald telling us how much they enjoyed the film. And Mam, Gerald tells us that he has 'never been made more welcome anywhere in his life' – this is a direct quote from his letter.

We have sent another film for processing and are waiting for the return of the second film, so we should be able to let you see more of Africa very soon.

I wish you could see our cat now. I don't think he has grown a great deal but his face has filled out and his ears and paws are getting darker. We are going to have him doctored in another five or six weeks when he's six months old because he likes to go out now just as it is getting dusk, and the African family next door have a mangy old cat and, although I don't know its sex, you never know! Our cat's a funny little thing really; he will eat anything with the exception of Kite-kat, but he likes the insects the most: flying ants, cockroaches, spiders, moths etc.

He even 'plays' with the geckos (small lizard-type creatures which live in the house and are supposed to kill mosquitoes etc.). The gecko will drop its tail in the hope the cat will go for the wriggling tail left lying on the floor, but our little kitty isn't fooled so easily.

I've been offered the position of private secretary to the director of the International Development Association and I've accepted the offer, but I hope I shan't be working all that long.

My driving lessons have all but finished now because it's too hot. Never mind. I'll learn sometime. Bye for now.

Love,

Keith and Anne xx

ON THE WAY to Lake Malawi from Zomba, Keith once more managed to upset the animals and children! Our friend Chris had very kindly offered to drive us all to Monkey Bay in his car – a VW Beetle, there being no point taking two cars. As mentioned before, the roads were treacherous and, sitting in the back seat, Keith and I were being banged about like rag dolls. I had my eyes closed most of the time as I didn't want to see the mountainous rocks looming ahead which I knew we either needed to circumnavigate or carefully approach head on, and I wasn't at all sure Chris was aware of this living in town. But I needn't have worried... at some point during the drive, Keith must have decided he had been sitting on his hands for too long. He suddenly lunged from the back seat, through the gap between the front seats, and grabbed the steering wheel from Chris's clutch, loudly declaring that we were going to hit a rock. To say I was shocked was an understatement! But Chris, being the sweet man he was, merely accepted Keith's driving instruction and braked to an almost standstill, then once more took the wheel from Keith and carefully negotiated the lumps in the road. As we drove the remainder of the journey I once more kept my eyes closed, hoping someone would laugh and thus relieve the tension in the car though, once at the Bay, our main concern seemed to be where to park. I was dreading the return journey, but Chris had learned his lesson and we were carefully delivered back to Domasi in one piece (or should I say two pieces).

WEDNESDAY, 18 January 1967

DEAR MAM AND DAD,

It was great to receive your letter on Monday. I'm pleased everyone is well and hope the New Year will be a better one so far as health is concerned. We have just had the hardest thunderstorm we've seen since we came to Malawi, but the sky after it had finished was really beautiful. I've never seen so many different colours in the sky before.

We had our American neighbours over for a typical English tea last Saturday and they seemed to enjoy it. As a rule, everyone has guests to dinner that is they arrive at about seven o'clock in the evening and the meal is always a cooked one. Anyway, as it was our turn to invite them, we decided to do something typically English. We had salmon and tuna and the usual salad to go with it. It's amazing how Americanised the English people here have grown. We are having our English friends from Zomba for a meal on Friday so I suppose we should be as un-English as we possibly can. We eat quite a lot of rice instead of potatoes and it's surprising how nice it tastes with lovely gravy poured on – anyway, I'm slimming again – I've put on 11 lbs since we've been here. I now weigh 10 stone 3 lbs – isn't it disgusting! Keith is just as thin as ever, lucky thing, despite all the 'wrong' food he eats.

Our arrangement with our garden-boy is working out quite well. He spends a few hours in the garden in the morning and comes into the house to clean up and wash later in the day. But Africans never fail to amaze me. One came today to the office asking for money. On average, we get one a week and because we're European, they tell us we have plenty of money and practically demand something from you. Apparently, it's only been like this since Independence, as before they seemed to be well taken care of. The one who came today started spinning a yarn about coming into Zomba to see someone and now had no money to get back to his village and no money for food. When I told him I couldn't help him, he got quite nasty, telling me his government had provided me with a job and a house – I think he got the situation reversed, don't you? I wouldn't give him anything on principle because he would never be away from the office if I did.

There was another funny incident in church on Sunday. I was at the front of the church and could see everyone going to communion, so you can imagine my amazement when an African mother suddenly started feeding her baby just as she was going to kneel at the altar. She fed the baby while she received communion too, despite the fact it was a European priest. I looked away as he came up to her, but I can imagine that he was a red-faced priest when he saw her. But as Keith says, this isn't wrong to an African – you see them every single day doing the same thing and the male Africans don't even notice. It is probably my strict Catholic upbringing that has made me such a prude I suppose. I watched the faces of the Africans as the woman walked back down the aisle but Keith was correct, they didn't even look at her.

We're glad you enjoyed the film we sent and shall be sending a shorter film very soon when we receive it back from processing – this one has only been sent to Johannesburg but it's taking as long as it took to send to England, though I am led to understand it takes nearly a week to reach Rhodesia by post for some unknown reason.

I'll say goodbye for now. We keep thinking about you all and wondering what you are doing at certain times of the day, but I suppose you will be doing the same about us!

Lots of love to you both.
Keith and Anne xx

MONDAY, 23 January 1967

DEAR MAM AND DAD,

How are you? I hope your cold is better, Mam – I've forgotten what a cold feels like – touch wood, so far I've been free of them.

We took the kitten to be 'doctored' today. Poor thing. We only left him at the vets for half an hour and he has been as lively as ever since we collected him (that's another 10/6d on his value!)

I've got some interesting news for you. Keith and I have been asked to take part in a documentary film promoting Malawi for the Malawi government. We haven't seen a script yet but we have accepted. We will play the part of a young South African couple on honeymoon, arriving in Malawi from Cape Town, I believe, and we will be taken all around the country, including on an aeroplane journey. We don't have to say anything, which is a great relief, but I know it's going to be smashing. They don't tell us how long the film will last, but as a tourism film it will no doubt be sent to various African countries as well as to Europe, and maybe America. It's anticipated that it will be shot sometime March/April and, although we don't get paid, we get to see places in Malawi we would never be able to see by ourselves, all financed (including meals at various hotels to advertise them). I'll let you know more about it nearer the time and when we know exactly what will be happening.

We have had two more small films processed and are sending them on to Gerald this week sometime, so he will probably be showing them to you all around mid-February.

On another matter, Aunt Alice sent us the cutting you put in the paper when we left England, and when Keith saw it he nearly went grey! It says in the article he has a degree but you can't get degrees by going to training colleges – you must go to university. Anyway, he says to tell you that we will have to go back to England for at least nine months after this Malawi tour if only to get the Bachelor of Education degree that he's supposed to have! (Phew, he's changing colour back to his normal pink now). I suppose it's as good as any other kind of degree. We have decided to do two and a half years here (we shall get the same gratuity as having done three years), so we shall be home two years in April. But I'm pretty sure we won't stay in the UK for long, as we would like to see a bit more of the world; however, if Keith can go back to college to take his Bachelor of Education, which is a new thing only started this year, then it will be worth the stay as it should go towards getting him a better job with more money. We are looking into the Far East for two years and, by then, we should be millionaires! If it's any consolation, we are proposing buying a house in Leeds (for cash mostly, we hope) and letting it out while we are away, which should have paid for itself in two years, and then who knows? We may buy another with our gratuity from the Far East if we get there, then we'll be property tycoons in a big way! To let you into a tiny secret, we have been trying to get our spare money into Rhodesia in order to buy a house we saw there during our visit last December, but it's proving impossible to get anything into the country because of UDI sanctions. As it is, our money from the sale of the house in Leeds is lying useless in a bank in the UK.

Notwithstanding the fact that we are still homesick, coming to Malawi has proved to be the best move we could ever have made. We do think about you often, as well as Keith's side of the family, especially Jack and Margaret. Unfortunately, J and M don't go out very often these days because John and Denise, our mutual friends, are having to cut down their outings with the expense of just having had a baby. I wish Jack and Mags could come out here, it would be brilliant. Still, as Jack has said, in Africa, the Africans can count the tins of beans themselves, so there's would be no need for him.

He's such a fool!

I'd better close now. Bye until next time.

Lots of love,

Keith and Anne xx

MONDAY, 6 February 1967

DEAR MAM AND DAD,

Hope you are both well and managing to keep clear of the flu. Rebecca, the African girl at work, has been away ill with it, so too our friends in Zomba.

I've just had to break off writing this to take a look at the fridge which we keep in the dining room – it's crawling with white ants. They are little devils. They get in from outside by somehow eating their way through the concrete floors and they leave a trail of red soil wherever they go. We have red 'channels' running along the bottom of nearly every wall in the house and, just now, there was a trail running up the wall behind the fridge and the blighters were all over it, some even inside. They are tiny things and although they are called 'white ants', they are really brown. These houses are so old I think they are held up with this ant soil. But we heard the other day that if the houses on the campus were to be sold, they would fetch £12,000 each. Our friend in charge of housing came to see us today because Keith had complained about the condition of a few things, such as the new 'garage' – big laugh. It's just a lean-to on the outside kitchen with a thin, thatched roof and only two sides of bamboo. As soon as it rains, we get all the water running off the outside kitchen roof coming through the thatch onto the car. What a mess. Also, the toilet is in a terrible state. The pot is covered in hairline cracks, and the room itself if so small, I'm not kidding, you can sit on the toilet and rest your head on the toilet roll in front of you. Your knees practically touch the door. Anyway, we've been promised an extension to the toilet. As for the bats well, they drive us batty. Despite the fact that the Bat Man paid us a visit when we first moved in here, the bats still come in through big gaps where the roof of the house meets the tops of the walls outside. We don't notice the noise of their twittering so much now, but every once in a while they seem to have a party up there; they bang and scrape about. But we think the thud we get occasionally is from an owl. It's so loud it really makes us jump – we expect the ceiling to come falling down. Also, one of our unpaid guests must have a bell up there because when we're in the bedroom we often hear a ping-ping noise from above the ceiling.

Filming is due to start this week in Zomba. We don't know exactly what it's all about and it probably won't make a lot of sense doing it as it's being filmed in bits and pieces whenever possible. We've been told we shall eventually be flying to Johannesburg and staying overnight (all free, of course). And this on the VC10 (Michael will know what I mean), so it will be quite an experience.

When the film is complete, we've been told we can have a full-length copy of the film in 16mm (the original is 32mm) for about £16, so of course, we are definitely going to buy one. Keith sent another of our films to Gerald last week, much shorter than the first one, and he should have received it by now. So, he will be seeing you anytime with it.

Could you apologise to Barbara for me, Mam – I completely forgot about Janet's birthday until the day and, of course, it was much too late then. I tried to get an 'apology' card but you might as well be looking for gold down the toilet. It's stupid really. There is just one card shop in Zomba and they are only selling Valentine cards – mad!

It's just gone ten o'clock and it's about time we were going to bed. Keith's lectures start at 6.30 a.m., so we go to bed fairly early these days.

Bye for now. Look after yourselves.

Lots of love to you both.

Keith and Anne xx

MONDAY, 20 February 1967

DEAR MAM AND DAD,

It was nice to receive your letter today. Barbara and Auntie Mary sent letters last week.

It was quite a shock hearing about Monica's mother dying, she was still young. I'm so sorry for Monica and Paul. I was also surprised to see that Monica had married and had a family, though I don't know why I should be surprised as she was a year or so older than myself.

Grandma seems to be settling into the care home and enjoying herself. I've been meaning to write to Alice for weeks now – I owe her at least two letters. If I get a chance when I've finished this one, I'll drop her a line.

You comment about a Mrs Ashton telling you about the Zomba Mission. Well, the friend of hers she mentioned me to wrote a nice letter before

Christmas and also sent a Christmas card, but I'm sorry to say I didn't reply to the letter (though I did send a home-made card), mainly because I was under the impression from the letter that the Mission thought I was 'one of theirs' and they seemed dead keen that I should go and visit them. Actually, I fully intend to visit them sometime but not just yet. We go into Zomba every day because I work there, but I'm afraid I don't have time to visit anyone after work because, by the time Keith comes to collect me, it's four o'clock and he is usually in a hurry to get back to Domasi either to finish marking books, to set the following day's work, or to play tennis. So, unfortunately, I don't really know if I will be able to see these people before they leave for England. Anyway, I'll do my very best.

It's no good, we'll have to get a tape recorder organised, especially now you have trouble writing. It's surprising the number of things you can't buy in Zomba (the administrative capital of Malawi). Keith wanted some white paint the other week but couldn't get any, so I'm pretty sure we shall not be able to buy anything as 'complicated' as a tape. We shall have to try to go into Blantyre (the industrial capital of Malawi). I know this country has only recently become independent but it's a shame that things haven't progressed as much here as in, say, Zambia, although Zambia is much larger and has the copper industry. We were talking to someone 'in the know' the other day and Keith mentioned the comparatively low standard of work the students pass out at school. This person confirmed that the standard of education was low generally, pointing out that Africanisation has meant that responsible posts were often given to Africans who were not quite ready.

In spite of the smallness of everything, we are enjoying ourselves here. It's amazing what you can get used to. I can see insects now and hardly bat an eye.

We are having some renovations done in the house at present. I mentioned in an earlier letter that we had complained about the toilet being cracked and the room itself being small – it's so small you nearly have to get ready to use it before you go in, because when you go in and close the door, you nearly fall into the pot. Anyway, the workmen are knocking down one wall to make the room larger and we are having a low flush toilet fitted. When they built the house originally, they must have added the toilet as an afterthought because the rest of the rooms are like barns. We had a burst pipe over the weekend too, to add to the difficulties, and needed to turn the water off which meant we had to keep popping in and out with a bucket of water whenever we used the toilet. We thought we were going to have to use Cassiano's toilet – heaven help us! It's just a hole in the ground outside surrounded by a straw fence on three sides. When it starts to smell, the prisoners come and dig another hole and presumably cover in the old hole with the rubble. We have that pleasure still to come.

We are progressing into the twentieth century and shall soon be getting a washing machine from the government for rent at 11/- a month. We shall save in the long run because when the Africans wash the clothes by hand, they pummel and tug at the fabric and tear it to shreds. Three of Keith's shirts already have holes in them and his pyjamas are a write-off. I've tried patching them but now, even the patches have tears in them!

Bye for now and take care of yourselves, both of you.

Lots of love as always.

Keith and Anne xxxx

MONDAY, 20 February 1967

DEAR AUNTIE ALICE,

I'm very sorry I haven't replied to your two recent and very welcome letters; the days fly by and I hadn't realised this until the other day. I'm sorry. I hear you are settled in your new job now. It sounds nice. I had to laugh when my mother told me about Grandma trying to milk the cows. It's a pity she can't go back to Ireland to finish her days, but Uncle Tom isn't on the farm now, is he?

I still can't believe that I'm so far from Batley – this part of the world isn't really so different from yours. People still get up each morning and do exactly the same things as yourself during the day, except, unfortunately, we don't have a TV. Instead, we play cards with our American neighbours or visit some English friends in Zomba.

As you probably know if you are reading my letters to Mam

and Dad, we sacked our houseboy before Christmas and, since then, we have had the garden-boy working in the house every other day. I don't let him cook for me. However, because Keith doesn't have much time at lunchtime between lessons to prepare a meal for himself, he started to teach Cassiano to make sand-wiches. Now, he has either changed his eating predilections or Cassiano doesn't understand. So far, Cassiano has produced raw cabbage and cheese sandwiches, uncooked bacon and lettuce sandwiches, and coffee made with Bisto (yummy!). Fortunately, Keith has always just noticed in time. The difficulty is that Cassiano doesn't speak much English and, of course, we are rubbish at learning his language so, although he has asked me to teach him to cook, I said I wouldn't until he could comprehend what I was saying.

You've no idea how hard it is trying to make conversation with him because his favourite word is 'yes' and he also uses this word whenever he isn't sure what you mean, which is quite complicating. You think he has understood what you say and it's only by seeing the expression on his face you realise he hasn't a clue, yet he still says 'yes' when you ask if he understands. But the people here are very humble and lovely. On Sunday I spoke to an African woman outside the church who was picking coloured 'weeds' presumably thinking they were flowers. I just said to her that they were pretty and she nearly genuflected to me. She said she was picking them for church and, before she left, she said: 'Thank you very much, madam,' presumably meaning: 'Thank you for speaking to me'. When they greet each other, they say: 'Morni', which means hello, good day, good afternoon, or any other salutation and they always shake hands, but if they are greeting an older person they always curtsey, and the older the person, the lower they bow to them.

I suppose you will have heard about the film we are making. The other Sunday we had some 'still' shots taken in the clothes we are supposed to 'arrive' here in, and during Easter, we are going to the plateau and having a meal in the restaurant there –

this is to advertise the hotel and plateau. So far, we haven't heard from the shops that have been approached to loan us clothes for the film, but we are living in hope. It will be nice if they do loan us clothes because we feel sure they will tell us to keep them, as they can't very well be sold after we have worn them because of the perspiration (which I'll make sure I have!)

The weather is a bit cooler here today – it's now 80°, which is much fresher than usual. We've also had fine rain most of the day but I expect the sun is just waiting to come out. It's lovely to feel cool again. In fact, I'm now wearing a woollen dress.

Hope you and Grandma are both well and not suffering from the flu or anything. I'll write again very soon, and I'll have to get your new address from you.

Bye for now and lots of love.

Keith and Anne xxxx

WEDNESDAY, 1 March 1967

DEAR MAM AND DAD,

I am writing this one at work, or rather typing it because there is nothing to do at the moment. After the third of May, you will be writing to us at a different address because we are being transferred to Mzuzu in the Northern Region. It will be good to move as I feel that Keith is getting frustrated teaching the students at the college in Domasi because they don't seem too interested in learning – pretty much like the students in England, unfortunately! It is supposed to be a teacher training college, but half the students don't even have a GCE Ordinary level (hence, they are so slow they're holding back the ones who do), and it's nearly impossible to teach such a group of people when they are so far apart in learning. It's driving Keith to distraction! Anyway, we are being transferred to a secondary school, though we didn't particularly want to go so far up into

Malawi and would rather have liked to have gone south to Blan-tyre. But having said we wanted to move, we couldn't very well say we wanted to stay here just because we were being sent somewhere we didn't know much about. From all accounts, Mzuzu is a very nice place – just thirty miles from the best part of the lake, and there is a beautiful beach with palm trees and golden sand, just like you see on the films. The houses are new and much smaller, thank goodness, and the European people are friendlier by all accounts. In Zomba here, they are mostly snobs. Keith has been trying to get a game of tennis with some of the good players here ever since we arrived, but they make all the excuses under the sun. He says it's probably because he doesn't talk as if he has a hot potato in his mouth, but I say they are afraid of being beaten because he's become a very good player since we've been here. He can give our neighbour a good run for his money and Dick is said to be the fifth best player in the whole of Malawi. Anyway, there is a tennis tournament in Blantyre on Saturday and Keith has put his name down to play in singles and doubles matches (he is playing doubles with Dick as his partner, so it should be quite a match!). I am going to watch, although I'm afraid I can't work up any enthusiasm because I don't have too much interest in tennis, never having learned how to play. But it will be wonderful if he wins something.

About Mzuzu... it is about 500 miles from here and we shall have to go up in two stages, staying one night in the new capital, Lilongwe. The drive up won't be too nice, I'm afraid, as there is no tar on the roads, just dirt, all the way up (even in Mzuzu, I'm sorry to say), and the food is going to be quite expensive because it has to be transported there by plane. But apparently, there is a way around this, as I understand people group their require-ments of food together, buy wholesale and get it much cheaper by buying in bulk. We shall also have new furniture... what a relief ...but we are a bit annoyed because we spent quite a bit of money on paint to decorate the sitting room of this house and now it's going to be wasted on someone else. These offices here in Zomba that I'm working in now pack up and move to Blantyre on 16 March and, although I've got this replacement job here and was quite settled, I'm actually looking forward to moving because it will be like moving to another country all over again – it is as far away to Mzuzu from here as it is from here to Salisbury in Rhodesia. I've written to someone up there to ask about a job, but so far have not had a reply. It's a fairly new town, about sixteen years old, and a bit underdeveloped. We have heard varying reports about the European population – some say about two hundred, some say about seventy, and some say about twenty-five, but I think seventy is about correct. There is a social club, like here in Zomba, where they show films once a week, and there is one supermarket. The local meat is supposed to be very cheap from what we hear, about 1/6d a lb, and fresh vegetables and fruit are cheap. You can also get fresh fish straight from the lake. We shall probably nearly live on the beach at weekends, especially as we hear the weather is cooler because Mzuzu is much higher than down here. They don't get the heavy rain that we get here, but they get showers all the year round. It has been described to us as another Scotland with better weather so, as you can imagine, we are now looking forward to going. We shall let you know the address to write to before we go, but as it is not for another ten weeks, there is no panic at present.

We have received a letter from Derrick, Keith's brother in Aden, saying he 'might' be paying us a visit in April, but I doubt if he will, although it would be nice.

We are still making the film and are starting it properly during Easter. It will take a few months to complete, but there won't be any trouble getting time off work as Dr Kamuzu Banda has approved both the making of the film and Keith and I taking part in it, and his is the word that counts!

I just seem to have rambled on and on but not to have told you very much. I've been having trouble with this stupid typewriter – it's been at the repairers twice in the last couple of months because it is so stiff. It's like dragging a sack of potatoes along every time I want to shift the carriage to a fresh line. Also, the keys stick and sometimes it leaves no space between the words, but they haven't improved on it at the repairers. It's like Keith's watch. He lost the winder so took it in to be repaired to an African shop (the only repairer in Zomba, unfortunately), and since he has had it back, the thing has gained one hour out of every four – I don't know how they do it! During a broadcast to the nation in 1941, Winston Churchill said: 'Give us the tools and we'll finish the job', but here it has been changed to: 'Give us the job and we'll finish the tools'!

I hope your arthritis is better now, Dad, but it is a thing which never really clears up once you get it, I think.

We have started making arrangements about a tape deck to record messages, but Keith suggested that it would be better if you recorded first as we have four speeds and don't know which to record on for your tape recorder. Anyway, we'll leave it for a short time longer and see how we get on.

Bye for now and look after yourselves.

Lots of love to you both.

Keith and Anne xx

FRIDAY, 17 March 1967

DEAR MICHAEL AND BARBARA,

Thank you for your letter. It's nice to hear how the kiddies are getting along. I'm sure I'd hardly recognise Karen now, she must be quite a big girl. I can't remember whether my mam said Karen had started school at St Mary's or whether she said she would be starting soon. It would be lovely to see them again – we didn't see them half enough when we were in England.

I've only just realised that it's St Patrick's Day today – 17

March. Happy St Patrick's Day! Somehow, every day seems the same to us now. I'm working in the Parliament for the next four or five weeks until we go to Mzuzu. The education offices where I worked have moved to Blantyre, fifty odd miles away, and as we don't have a 'jet' yet, I've had to transfer to another branch of the government. I'm working with a lovely Irish girl from County Cork and we get along like a house on fire. We talk a lot about home, which I was not able to do at the other place because I worked with an African girl, although she was very nice, too. Margaret and I are typists for the Speaker, Mr Surtee, and the report I'm doing at present is a revised copy of Hansard (the record of the last parliamentary debate), which is forty-plus, close typed pages long. I'm finding it very interesting reading.

The other day I had a look around the room in parliament where the debates are held and it was like treading on sacred ground. The person who showed me around was talking in a whisper – I felt like genuflecting as we turned to come out!

At the moment, Keith is asleep (it's 8.20 p.m. but he starts teaching at 6.30 a.m. so I can't grumble at him). He made me laugh today when he told me about his escapade with the cat who, since he had his little operation, has wet more chair cushions than a baby would – we have three wet cushions drying out on the khondi at the moment. Apparently, the cat had come to sit next to him on the couch this afternoon (I use the term 'couch' very loosely – it's more like a park bench) and he thought nothing of it at the time. However, for the past few days, Keith has been troubled with red spots on his nether region (he'd kill me if he knew I was telling you this) and, as I said, the cat was asleep next to him. Suddenly, Keith said it started stinging like heck in the region of his spots and it got so bad that he jumped up to see what was biting him. It was then that he noticed that his trousers were damp; he felt the cushion near the cat, and that was soggy also. You can imagine how furious Keith was when he realised that the cat had wet himself while lying or sitting next to him, especially as he hadn't even asked to go out like he usually does (the cat that is!) But now we wonder how many times Keith has sat on wet cushions that the cat has christened, without noticing the damp, thus getting spots from the ammonia in the urine!

The cat is out at the moment, but I am a bit worried because there is a big owl living in either one of our trees or under our under-drawing. He sits on one of the outside rafters most nights, although one night he was standing by the side of the road as we were returning home after seeing a film. I'd hate to think what would happen if the owl thought our cat was the chance of a tasty dish as he's still not fully grown.

Food here seems to be getting plentiful again as before. Up to Christmas the prices of certain things seemed to rocket, for instance, tomatoes were 1/- for five. Now you can get seven or eight for 3d. which is a huge difference. We have just planted our own lettuce and maize but are not able to harvest anything yet, so we are having to buy our lettuce from the market at 3d. a 'bob.' We bought oranges today, large ones – two for 1d. Whole pineapples, very large and probably enough to fill two tins, cost 2/- each, and we are still getting strawberries, from the little man who comes around, for 2/- a colander-full. Eggs are still 2d. each. However, we pay quite a lot for imported food, and it will be worse when we get to Mzuzu because we shall be 500 miles further north. Most of our imported goods come via South Africa and Rhodesia, so of course, there will be extra transport charges. Everyone tells us we shall like Mzuzu better than Domasi, so we are prepared to pay the extra for that plea-sure. The bungalows are very modern, so that is another thing in its favour.

Keith's brother says he may visit us in April, though if it's like Christmas, I won't place much hope on it. But he's visiting England in July prior to going to Singapore with the RAF schools.

I'm still not very suntanned but we stay out of the sun as

much as possible. Anyway, before we come back to the UK, I'm going to sit in the sun until I bake if I have to.

Hope everyone is okay. Give my love to the children.

Bye for now.

Love,

Keith and Anne xxxx

SUNDAY, 19 March 1967

WELL, Mam and Dad, here's another tome for you. We received your letter during the week and we also received one from Gerald to say he had received our film but that they hadn't shown it to you yet – this is because Richard, their youngest child, has been in hospital. They have been worried about him and are visiting him every evening. But by the time you receive this letter, you may have already seen it – hope so.

We start our filming on Friday (we get Good Friday and Easter Monday holiday here). 'The Boutique' in Blantyre are providing us with clothes – Keith thinks maybe they will either give us the things afterwards or else let us buy them cheap. A chemist shop is also providing some things because they are being 'billed' in the titles at the beginning. We shall also be going to Salisbury in the film, so we can have a good buy-in when we get there. Our friends in Zomba – Chris and Wendy – are going to be 'extras' on a train journey, and Dick and Jane, our American neighbours, are also going to be extras, with Dick and Keith playing tennis.

Dick and Jane have adopted another African boy. He is the 'son' of one of the teachers who retired about three weeks ago. I say 'son' because to an African, all his relatives' children are his sons and daughters and, in fact, this particular boy, Nicholas, is his nephew but he has brought him up together with his own five or six children. Anyway, this gentleman, Mr Chimwaya, retired from the college and has gone back to his village.

Nicholas, who is thirteen years old, has been going to school in Zomba, but his 'father's' village is about forty miles away, so Dick and Jane said they would take him so that he could continue his schooling. Also, he would be a friend for Fransisco, their own adopted African son. Last week, we went with them to the village so that Nicholas could see his family again – what an experience. We travelled in Dick's Land Rover, which is a good thing because the road was just a path which went on for about four miles, dropping sharply on first one side, then another – we were shaken to bits by the time we arrived. The village was merely a small group of huts near each other in which lived all Nicholas' relations. It's amazing how close-knit they are and, of course, we all had to be introduced, which meant shaking hands with everyone and asking: 'Muli Bwanji?' (How are you?). Then we were shown around the houses. The buildings were so low you had to bend to go inside. The rooms were completely bare except for a bed in the bedroom and a table and chairs in the living room, and all the walls were whitewashed. Also, some of the rooms didn't even have windows. But everything looked very clean. The communal 'kitchen' was separate from the houses and merely a brick building with a large opening for a door. They make a fire on the floor with wood and put their pans etc., on top. The smoke comes out of the door opening – there is no chimney. There were a couple of children lying outside asleep on straw mats with just about everything imaginable flying about them – the flies, as you see so often, landing on their little faces, and if their eyes were open, the flies drank the liquid inside the eyes. I suppose they like the salt. But the mothers made no attempt to wave the flies away. There were hens and dogs and goats wandering all over the place as well. Actually, this was a good class house according to what Dick and Jane have told us, as they say the parents of their adopted son, Fransisco, are Ugandan, and live in a house much more poverty-stricken than that, and they, Dick and Jane, stayed overnight with Francisco's parents in Uganda, but I'm afraid I'm embarrassed to say I couldn't have done so.

We went to a film show at the club on Saturday. Oh, what a farce. The film broke down twice, then there was a power cut lasting half an hour. We arrived home at twenty minutes past midnight. Can you imagine everyone sitting in pitch darkness all that time? We have power cuts on average once a week. There was one at home last Thursday at 9.39 p.m., so we just lit candles and made our way to bed. Then there was another one the following morning but it didn't affect us very much as we were leaving for work. It's amazing how docile we are getting. We are beginning to take everything in our stride now no matter how annoyed we feel initially. It's surprising what six months out here can do to you – as the Principal had promised when we first arrived.

I've just got another little lump on my leg and I see a mosquito flying around. I'm going to have no blood left if I go on being 'got at'. They make tiny red lumps where they suck the blood but you don't feel them until they are finished, by which time it's too late! Not to worry.

Bye for now and love to you both.

Keith and Anne xx

MONDAY, 27 March 1967

DEAR MAM AND DAD,

Received your letter during the week. It seems to take much longer for the letters to reach Malawi from England – I suppose it's because the VC10 has had to be rerouted a couple of times because of the weather here. For the last three weeks or so it has been a couple of days late arriving at Blantyre.

We started filming on Good Friday – we went up the plateau in the morning and took a picnic with us (there were twelve of us altogether – the others were acting as 'extras'). We were tired by the time we arrived back home. On Saturday morning, we had shots taken at the botanical gardens here in Zomba and then we went to the cathedral. (I wanted to go to confession, so Mr King decided it would be a good idea to take shots of the cathedral as it's lovely from the inside as well as the outside). There is a grotto at the back of the church which was probably beautiful at one time, but unfortunately, it has been allowed to go rack and ruin over the years as there seems to be no-one in charge of its maintenance. There are nuns going about their business around the church but the convent related to the church is about three miles away, so one can't really expect them to do much running about. Also, they have their own little church to look after.

There has been a meeting of parliament this morning and the President has been here. Margaret and I popped out of the office to see him leaving, waving his fly swatter as usual. The Africans always give him a slow handclap, which I believe is a sign of displeasure in the West, but which I understand is the same as cheering and waving to us. I was surprised to see how old he really looked – from photographs he doesn't look particularly timeworn, although I believe he is around seventy-six. Mr Donnelly – my ex-boss in the education offices here – once told me that he had been given a real rousting by the president in front of everybody and, apparently, this is the way he acts for the benefit of the Africans because then they see how strong he is. I can see his psychology too as it really works, even with the Europeans. He seems to be the only African ruler with common sense, don't you think? His visit to South Africa has been publicised all over the Rhodesian papers, and they even gave him a very good 'write-up', which is unusual.

Well, Mam and Dad, have you both seen our second film we sent yet? I hope you have by now. The professional film we're taking part in won't be ready for another year or so, but we are going to get a copy of it. However, Mrs King (the wife of the producer of the tourism film) is taking her own shots and, if her film is good, we shall also have a copy of that which you will be able to see soon – in a few more months' time, we hope. Of course, we shall be taking shots ourselves of our trip to the lake and the game reserve, so very soon you should have a lot to see (hopefully).

You mention in your letter that you wonder if Keith has put any more weight on since we came here. Well, as you will have guessed, he hasn't. In fact, he has lost some weight, if that's possible. Now he weighs a mere 10 stone 9 lbs (or thereabouts). He was just over 11 stone when we arrived here. But he has lost this because he plays tennis nearly every day and in this heat… well, you can imagine. Now for me… I put on weight around Christmas and I weighed 10 stone 3 lbs. Now I'm back to 9 stone 8/9 lbs, which is still too much I think. I keep telling Keith that I shall have to take up tennis (not!). Jane Kimball, our lovely neighbour, is much taller than I am but she only weighs 8 stone 7 lbs, which makes her look like a lovely Twiggy (jealousy will get me nowhere). But she plays tennis too, which helps keep the weight off.

On Saturday, we saw *Beau Geste* at the club cinema – I should think this was the tenth remake of this film. Nevertheless, I enjoyed it because each time they remake it, the story is a bit different. The following day we saw another film at Mr King's. He borrows films which the bishop at the cathedral shows to the priests (there is a seminary here.) We have seen films before at Mr King's and they are very enjoyable – full length with news and cartoons. I suspect the priests abroad have a much better time than the priests at home; whoever heard of Father Gallon going to a film show? In fact, you would not recognise these men as priests as they wear the same clothes as Keith – flashy sports shirt and shorts! (No dog collar, though, as it is probably too warm for them, and Keith isn't too keen on the things, either!)

Did you do anything for Easter? I suppose the weather wasn't up to much as it was an early Easter this year. We were looking at a film we took on holiday last year when we went to Temple Newsam – remember? The one where we took film of you lying asleep on the grass. I don't suppose you ever saw that film. Your hair was a bit ginger, Mam. Is it still blond or have you done something else with it? I have happy memories of that time. I miss you both. What arrangements have you made for your big holiday this year? It's a pity you can't go somewhere like Worcester for a change. That reminds me. I haven't written to Uncle George and Auntie Gladys yet!

I'll close for now as I want to go to the 'chim' – the toilet. I'm writing this letter at work, as you will have guessed.

Bye for now. Give my love to the kiddies.

Hope you are both well.

Love,

Keith and Anne xxxx

THURSDAY, 31 March 1967

DEAR MAM AND DAD,

Well, here's another letter, the second this week. Aren't I good!

We are waiting to hear from Derrick to say whether or not he will be coming in April. He said there was a chance that he could get a free passage on a plane leaving Aden for either Malawi or South Africa. If he comes, he may only be able to stay a couple of days, but even that would be nice. In anticipation of his coming we have sent him a list of things we want, such as cine film and a dinner service – you pay a fortune here for plates and cups and things like that.

There was another meeting of Parliament today. We listen to the debates on loudspeakers in the office. I would never have believed that I could be interested in such things, but I really am. The President gave his opening speech yesterday and received tremendous applause afterwards. The parliament room is just above our offices and we were nearly deafened by the foot stamping. I have a copy of the official verbatim report – I've started collecting souvenirs already – and there was a motion today to the effect that, as the President's speech was so good, it should be published universally. It was mostly about the recent visit to South Africa of three members of the Malawi parliament. He suddenly criticised Zambia, Tanzania and Ghana (though he didn't mention them by name) for the way they criticised him when they heard he was sending a mission to South Africa **.

We bought our cat a little collar today. He is quite a big cat now and getting really dark about the ears and snout, and he has beautiful blue eyes (not crossed). We shall have to have him inoculated against rabies before we shall be allowed to bring him back home, otherwise he will have to go into quarantine for six months and I should hate that. He follows Keith around just like a dog and he even comes in the car when Keith collects me from work. Unfortunately, he is picking up a lot of tics now which I don't like as, if he gets tic fever, he could die from it. We are following the example of others here with animals and are either snipping the ticks off or burning their bottoms with a cigarette as their grip is so strong you can't get them off the cat's coat any other way. The dogs go to the dip periodically but cats can't be dipped as they would never lick themselves again because of the chemicals. Our cat even pesters Cassiano now though I'm not sure he's impressed; whenever Cassiano goes into the kitchen to do anything, the cat follows him making his standard demanding noise. Cassiano surprised us one day by asking what the purpose was of having a cat, pointing out that we had to feed him, keep him warm and dry, spend money having him inoculated, and many other things, yet he didn't do anything! We were gobsmacked initially, but when we thought about it, it probably doesn't make a lot of sense to him as the Africans only keep animals in order to feed themselves.

Last Saturday at the film show at Mr King's, I was hit in the face by a bat – the flying funny-faced variety! I suppose it came out because of the dark as all the lights had been turned off. It initially just skimmed my head and dropped down a few feet behind me, but I turned around to see where it was just as it was starting to fly again, and it hit me in the face with its wing which felt like my cheek was being stroked by a piece of velvet, it was so soft. The other women ran outside, but I was very brave (oh big deal). In fact, I felt so sorry for the bat as someone trapped it under a paper basket and probably killed it when we had left.

We are also getting quite a lot of mosquitoes just lately. We were congratulating ourselves at not having seen more than half a dozen for the past few months, but now they're coming with a vengeance. You should see the blood splashes on the walls where we've battered them – probably our blood too, I'm afraid. But, as it's much cooler in Mzuzu, hopefully, we won't see as many up there.

We had a letter from Jack during the week and he said their brother-in-law had bought a new Jaguar car which cost around £1,500. The family is also hoping to buy a house up Batley Field Hill if they can sell their present house. Isn't that amazing… whoever said the rag trade was finished! Keith is of the opinion that it isn't worth spending time going to school and college because you get more money working with your hands or even just 'bumming' around sometimes – all you need is the gift of the gab to go with it (no comments please!).

It's 6.35 p.m. in the UK at present. I wonder what you are doing at this precise second. Getting ready for Thursday night devotions at church possibly? As for myself, I'm going to have a bath – it's 7.35 p.m. here.

Bye for now and love to you both.

Keith and Anne xxx

DURING THE FIRST decade of Banda's presidency, Malawi's

relations with its black-ruled neighbours were sometimes stormy. At the opening session of the Malawi Congress Party convention in September 1968, President Banda made a claim to extensive territories outside the present boundaries of Malawi. The claim covered the whole of Lake Nyasa and parts of Tanzania, Mozambique, and Zambia.

The Tanzanian government asserted that President Banda could make territorial claims only because he had the support of South Africa, Rhodesia (which at that time had a white minority government), and Portugal (which then still ruled Mozambique). In fact, in 1967, Malawi had become the first black African country to establish diplomatic relations with white-ruled South Africa in August 1971; moreover, Banda became the first black African head of state to be officially received in South Africa, which supplied arms and development funds to Malawi.

The Banda government also faced some internal opposition. In October 1967, the Malawi government announced that a group of rebels, numbering about twenty-five, wearing police uniforms and posing as insurgents from Mozambique, had entered Malawi with the intention of killing President Banda and his ministers. Eventually, eight of the rebels were convicted of treason and sentenced to death; five others, including Ledson Chidenge, a member of the National Assembly, were sentenced to death for the murder of a former official of the MCP. (Taken from National Encyclopaedia – Malawi History)

THURSDAY, 5 April 1967

DEAR MAM AND DAD,

Hope you are both keeping well, as are we, though for how long remains to be seen! Last Monday, we went to our neighbours to play bridge and, during the course of the night, we killed forty-four mosquitoes between us; I've never seen so many in my life in one place. At the time my legs looked as if I had measles and, even now, three days later, they are still covered in red spots where the perishers bit me (or rather drank my blood). The snag was we ran out of Paludrine (the antimalarial tablets) on Sunday and the hospital here is waiting for the supply to come in. Unfortunately, our neighbours had the same problem otherwise we could have borrowed a supply from them. For myself, I shan't know whether I am smitten or not until next week but Keith was okay because he was wearing long pants at the time.

Our neighbours on our other side are returning to Canada in July and they have had the removal truck outside their house most of the evening. They have quite a large family so it will take some time to get everything ready to ship back home. I must say seeing all the commotion has made us a bit homesick. An older couple on site are going back to the UK on leave this month but, as they like it here, they are coming back. They have made arrangements to bring a dog back with them as their house has been broken into a couple of times over the years. This is a huge surprise to us as the husband is highly allergic to dogs, the same as Keith. We have discussed it with them on a number of occasions but they tell us they have found the solution. Eric will be given desensitisation injections for the whole month they are in the UK. It will be interesting to see how the injections work as Keith is occasionally having a slight problem with our cat.

The Papan's family (Canadians) are moving to West Africa in July, and the Principal and family are going back to the UK sometime this year. Once everyone has left, including ourselves, Dick and Jane are going to be by themselves in Domasi. We shall be leaving three weeks next Wednesday, 3 May. Our plan is to travel up to Mzuzu by car, taking the cat with us (heaven help us), and a lorry will be following with our belongings, as well as Cassiano. It will take us two days to get there and the lorry three days. Luckily, we get a mileage allowance plus an 'upheaval' allowance to cover buying curtains etc.

We had a letter from Auntie Mary today, and reading between the lines, she seemed a bit upset about you (not with you). She didn't tell us much, except that Grandma was back home from Beech Towers. I'm just looking at your last letter where you say you will have finished with her (Grandma that is) if she doesn't settle in the home. I wonder! I think Auntie Mary was worried about you both being off work so much, particularly your poor health Dad. I wish you could get away from Batley, then you wouldn't be the one to get the blunt end of the stick every time. I know that blood is thicker than water (you've told me so many a time when I've "aired my views") but you both have your own lives to live like everyone else; we don't get a second chance. When Keith and I decided to come out to Malawi, although we knew you would be very sad, nonetheless we couldn't take into account your feelings much as we would have liked to have done, knowing full well that you would be upset at not seeing us for a few years. Yet here we are and here you are, all living happily without each other. Well, Grandma will have to do the same. But she knows you are a 'pushover' and have always made excuses for her – I wish I was there now as I'd really tell you off! Now, I've said my piece and I'll shut up.

We had another letter from Derrick yesterday. They are busy packing as they go back to the UK in July and stay a couple of months before going to Singapore. From what Derrick says, it's getting too hot in Aden (bomb-wise I mean). When there's trouble they can't even go out to buy a loaf of bread. They seem to be holed up in their house all the time. Recently, a curfew lasted from Friday to Tuesday and they weren't able to leave the camp during that time. They had a narrow escape a few weeks ago when, just as they were coming out of the cinema, about fifteen yards from where they were, there was a flash, then an explosion and everyone threw themselves to the ground. Soldiers appeared from everywhere, running over everyone with rifles raised, chasing a terrorist. They got him, too. Derrick feels they were lucky they weren't injured and it was very close. Margaret (his wife) has been having nightmares ever since but apparently, a lot of the women are affected like this (men too, I should imagine), yet they have to learn to live with it. I don't think I could.

Keith didn't get very far in the tennis tournament unfortunately, but there is another one on Sunday and he has been asked to play on the 'A' team (he is very pleased about this as he doesn't get a chance to play good opponents very often and this is the only way to improve).

I'll let you know our new address as soon as I know it. Another reason I'm glad we're going north is because the Catholic Church is only a couple of miles away from the school in Mzuzu. I've had to miss a few times here – to get to the church is about the distance from your house to Leeds and back, fourteen miles, which is an awful long way to go. Still, I'm sure God will forgive me and I will make up for it.

Bye for now. Don't forget what I say about looking after yourselves.

Lots of love to you both.

Keith and Anne xxxx

Me and Keith

THE ENGLISH COUPLE returned from the UK with their dog – a Great Dane who had been trained up for them beforehand. However, things didn't quite work out as expected because Eric found the desensitisation injections didn't work and he was instantly highly sensitive to the dog. Accepting that the dog would have to stay outside they brought him back to Domasi – at least he would deter burglars. Unfortunately, although the Great Dane is a large dog, it is also very gentle, loving, sweet, affectionate, and friendly and not a guard-dog type at all, and it became clear very quickly that the dog would rather lick the burglar than bite him.

SUNDAY, 10 April 1967

DEAR MAM AND DAD,

No more airmail letters at present, so I thought I'd take the opportunity of sending you a snap taken by Mr King and printed by his son. It's a bit bright, but Keith says it's because the paper is too rough for the brightness of the snap. It was taken in Mr King's garden in front of the palm trees.

We met the headmaster of Mzuzu Secondary School last night. He had come down to Blantyre for a meeting but was staying in Zomba for a couple of days and it seems he called on us yesterday morning while we were out shopping in Blantyre. He has left his address in Zomba, so we called on him last night. He is in his middle thirties, I should say, and maybe his wife is a little younger. They have been married eight years, have four children, and are from Lancashire (that's it in a nutshell!). They have told us that there are three Catholics on the station so I shall be okay for church without Keith having to take me. I asked about the hospital and Mrs Goodwin said she had her last baby there and that the nuns were marvellous, that it was just like being with your own mother. Apparently, they are building a new hospital section with more modern equipment and this will be ready before the end of this year. She said that although she wasn't a Catholic, she couldn't speak too highly of the nuns in Mzuzu.

We asked about food and were told that local meat is only 1/5d a lb and although it's tough, it's not too bad at all. The plane brings the expensive meat in from Lilongwe every week – about 300 miles away – and naturally, it's dearer, but people buy that as a treat.

We joined the Co-op in Blantyre yesterday so that we can have food sent up each month. It's the first time I'd been to the Co-op although I'd heard a lot about it, and I was staggered at the difference in cost of food there compared with our supermarket in Zomba. Here I pay 1/1d for bun cases, and the exact same box cost me 6d at the Co-op. We spent £5. 13s. 0d at the Co-op and reckon we've saved 15/- by buying there. We'd probably have saved more had we realised there was a butchery department because we bought the best steak for 7/- lb in Kandodo supermarket in Blantyre, but would only have paid about 5/6d at the Co-op. It cost £5 to join, the same as back home, but you get that back when you leave – no dividend, I'm sorry to say.

Keith and Dick were in another tournament today with the players from Blantyre and Cholo (they were mostly Italians who came) and both of them lost their singles matches but won their doubles match. They have to play again next week with the winners of the other doubles match.

We passed an accident last night on our way into Zomba. There was a cyclist being carried to the side of the road as we passed and a car was half turned on the tar. But it's difficult to have much sympathy for cyclists. There are no street lights at all outside the towns, and when it's dark, it really is dark here. As I explained before, there's only one strip of tar down the middle of the road wide enough for one car, and when you meet a car, you have to move half off the tar and onto the dirt at the side. Well, cyclists have no authority to ride on the tar at all, although they do, but they should move off when they hear a car coming. You can imagine how dangerous it is at night with no street lamps along these roads, especially as ninety out of every 100 bikes don't have lights of any description and you just can't see them. The cyclists are committing suicide every time they go out on their bikes if they only knew it. The police must be 'slack-set-one-up' (slow) because they never, or very rarely, check up on these cycles, yet they are constantly stopping cars to check whether the windscreen wipers work, of all things! No doubt the accident last night was caused by the cyclist not having lights. I've also noticed that the people walking along the edge of the road (no pavements until you reach Blantyre) wear the darkest clothes imaginable and it's impossible to see them until you are on top of them. We have had some extremely near misses ourselves many a time. The odd thing is they seem to think it's funny if they just escape with their lives; they are grinning all over their faces while you are nearly panic-stricken. It's a shame but they never learn.

Keith has finished lessons here now. There are exams next week and then he has finished teaching at Domasi altogether. I cease working in Zomba a week next Friday, after which we have a week of filming and then off to Mzuzu.

I shall have to learn to make my own bread because we are told the market bread isn't very good up there. I shall also have to learn how to use a wood-burning stove as there are no electric cookers either because the electricity is too expensive. I suppose once it's stoked up, like the coal ovens, it'll be as good as an electric one. I prefer electric to gas now too, though that's not going to help me this time. Since we've been here, I haven't had many failures at cooking and I put it down to the electric oven. By the way, the next time you write, could you give me the ingredients you use for fish batter? The one in my cookery book isn't very good, at least the results aren't. Keith bought me a lovely cookery book for our first African Christmas, but I'm afraid some of the recipes are a bit ambitious just yet.

At the moment, Keith and the cat are having their siesta. We cover the bed with the bedspread and they lie on top – Keith with his head on one of the pillows and the cat with his head on the other. I wish you could see them – they're a picture.

It's nearly 4.30 p.m. (3.30 p.m. your time) so I'd better start getting the tea ready now as Keith and the cat will be expecting their meal to be ready.

Bye for now. Take care.

Love,

Keith and Anne xxxx

WEDNESDAY, 26 April 1967

DEAR MAM AND DAD,

You will notice by the postmark that this letter was posted in Zambia (I hope). We are actually flying to Zambia tomorrow morning as part of the film and shall be flying back the same day – only staying a couple of hours unfortunately but I intend posting the letter there. I'm very excited about the flight but I'm also very apprehensive, this being the very first time I have ever flown. Keith is also a bit uneasy, although he has been up before for a short while. We are flying in a Viscount, which I under-stand is a very nice plane, but I'm sure it isn't as fabulous as the VC10 in which we climbed in (and out again, unfortunately) on Monday afternoon. This is the first week of proper filming and we are having a brilliant time. On Monday, we went to Blantyre and were filmed in and around the shops and bank. At first, we were feeling a bit anxious but it's amazing how you get used to having people stare at you. The best, though, was at the airport on Monday afternoon, when we were filmed supposedly going through Immigration and climbing on board the VC10. It is the highlight of the week in Blantyre when the plane comes in on Monday mornings, so we loved having this opportunity to go on board, but it was funny how it happened. We waited in the lobby until the plane landed from Johannesburg en route to London, then hid behind the doors until the passengers had been through Customs and were on their way to Immigration. Then we had to move into the line without anyone knowing, but previous to this, the arc lights had been set up in the lobby. People who happened to be hanging around were inquisitive about the lights, and every few seconds a face would peer around the corner to see what it was all about. Of course, all they would see at this stage was Keith and me with our suitcases, standing under the full blast of lights waiting for the doors to open. The cameraman was hanging around so people were asking him what was happening. First of all, the rumour went round that it was royalty, then someone said they thought it was film stars because I looked like Julie Andrews (I don't think a day goes by without someone telling me that), so you can imagine the buzz in the lobby. Eventually, the doors did open and we dodged into the queue without too much notice being taken of us. The Immigration people knew what was happening, of course, so they pretended to look up our names on the passenger list and pretend-stamped our passports; all the time, this was being filmed but the lights were so dazzling that from our side it was difficult to see anyone filming and it went smoothly. By the time we got to the main entrance to go out onto the tarmac there was quite a crowd outside. It was just amazing. The chief officer escorted us to the plane, and we had to pretend to hand our tickets to the stewardess and climb aboard, which we did. The inside of the plane was fantastic, really. You had to wade through the carpet it was so thick, and the seats were like miniature couches. We felt very important, I can tell you. The captain waited at the head of the steps to have a word with us, and afterwards, we were taken to the control tower to watch the take-off and hear the countdown. That was breathtaking, too. I've seen plenty of aeroplanes taking off on film but it doesn't compare with the real thing. I had a lump in my throat as it began to rise and disappear into the sunset. And imagine, they were due to arrive in London the following morning – Malawi to London in ten hours – that includes two stops en route. The plane tomorrow is smaller, but nevertheless equally as nice inside, so you can imagine how excited we are feeling at the moment. We went on the railcar to Salima today – a special complete train just for us, and the man who was in charge of all this asked if he could take my photo. He must have thought we were really special people.

There is a very, very slight chance that we may get a journey to London in August. But I won't say any more about it so as not to get your hopes up, but if any more news does come, I'll let you know straightaway, then you can both come down with the Walkers. We would only be there for about fourteen hours but it would still be lovely. But quite honestly, I don't think there's much chance.

The next time I write it will be from Mzuzu; we go up next Wednesday. We shall be coming down here again July-time to do some more filming, so we can see our friends again then, I hope. There is still quite a lot of filming to be done, I'm pleased to say. Our trip on the lake takes place in three weeks, but I'll keep you informed as things happen.

Barbara wrote during the week and the kiddies seem to be getting along grand. I hope Karen remembers us when we get back. I also hope you are both well and everyone else, too.

Bye for now and lots of love to you both.

Keith and Anne xxxx

Mzuzu At Last

SUNDAY, 7 May 1967

DEAR MAM AND DAD,

We arrived here on 3 May, our arrival not without glitches. The journey to Mzuzu was very tiring and even our little kitty was tired when we arrived. The headmaster and his wife were brilliant and made us so welcome, getting their boy to prepare some lunch for us. Keith was keen to know more about the school and the staff and we spent a pleasant few hours talking, then Jeff took us down to the house that was to be our new home for the next two years.

Our first impression was good. The house is at the far end of a long span of dusty garden, though it's not so much a garden as a wide, grassed-over path with two channels worn into the grass from continual passage of car tyres. Nonetheless, on reaching the house, we were surprised to see how modern it was. There is a carport attached to the house at the side and walking around to the front, we could see that the frontage looked out over a garden which contained some trees and flowers. We observed that we couldn't see our neighbours on either side as there was so much ground to the house. On entering the house we noticed that the room was spacious and contained everything a modern home should contain but again, the settee and chairs were merely functional with no cushions, not even on the seats. It was while passing through the door from the sitting room to the kitchen that we saw the 'horrors' again – there were lots of hairy legs hanging down from the door jamb, their wings 'glued' to the paintwork. Every room was the same. The headmaster had been at great pains to assure us that everything at the house was clean and that the place had been fumigated and freshly painted to await our arrival. However, we feel he got the wording the wrong way around as it was apparent to us that the place had been painted first and then fumigated afterwards. The paintwork was still tacky so we think it was probably done the day we were there. There seemed no point in complaining as we have been told often enough that this is Africa, after all. So we set about scraping the bodies off the paintwork and sweeping up as we did so. We've been here for three weeks now and are somewhat getting used to it.

But to our great sorrow, our cat has gone missing. We kept him in the house initially, though he was always ready to run out of the door as soon as it was opened, so after a few days we took him out on a 'lead', would you believe? Some string tied to his collar. We did this just to get him used to the new garden and after a while he seemed completely at home, playing around as if he had been here all his life. Unfortunately, we took our eyes off the mark and became careless. We let him out on Tuesday and he didn't come back. At first, we weren't too worried as we have a lot of garden to explore, but when mealtime came and he still hadn't come to the window, we knew then he had disappeared. We have gone out every few hours since calling him but nothing. As you can imagine, we are devastated. We have asked our neighbours to ask their house-boys to keep their eyes open while they are out walking, but so far there has been no sighting at all. Unfortunately, we are now living practically in the African bush, so are assuming the worst; we have seen hyenas walking along the road ahead when we've been driving back from town and goodness knows what kind of snakes there are around. We haven't totally given up hope, but are having to accept that he is probably dead. He is still only a kitten so doesn't have too much sense. I'll let you know if there is any news.

Keith has been over to look at the school and his laboratory in particular, and says he is impressed. School will start up again in a few days and Keith said his laboratory assistant was already there washing things out ready for use. He is a young African who has had a couple of years of education and who is working hard to get some qualifications. He gets paid for his job as a lab tech, but not much. Keith says he gets a good feeling about the place. While he was at school he bumped into another member of staff, Tom Newell, a Rhodesian who happens to be our next-door neighbour, and he asked us both around for a coffee. His wife Eunice is lovely and, from what I could see of her displays, a very good artist. She makes pictures by hammering out an image onto copper giving a 3D effect, then she burnishes the copper to give even more effect. It's difficult to explain but the result is stunning.

The other evening the head invited us to his house to meet a few of the older members of staff over a few drinks. I say older members of staff because there are quite a few young people here – VSOs (Voluntary Service Overseas) – who I understand get only a small salary but get everything else paid for. They are mostly in their late teens or very early twenties. The staff seem friendly but, as is usual in a place like this, half of them are nearing the end of their contract and will probably not be returning. The deputy head is a lovely old buffer about to retire, but who is giving us lots of tips for a happy stay.

I'll close for now but will write again soon – with hopefully good news about our kitty, though I have almost accepted that he's gone for good, poor little thing.

Lots of love as always.

Keith and Anne xxx

MZUZU WAS MUCH SMALLER than Zomba, although it was larger than Domasi, which wasn't saying a lot as Domasi merely consisted of a few school houses, a school and a prison; but no shops. Mzuzu had a supermarket, which was wonderful, as Zomba only had small independent shops owned mainly by Indian traders. We could buy most of the things we needed to live comfortably in Mzuzu, although there wasn't very much choice. Occasionally, one could even purchase M&S clothes if you were lucky with your size as, inevitably, there would be only one of each garment.

Kandodo supermarket

The supermarket was called Kandodo, which literally meant 'walking stick' in Chinyanja, and was named after the man who opened the first supermarket in Malawi. He happened to be lame and carried a stick.

Next to Kandodo was the Standard Bank, and next to that was the Northern Divisional Police headquarters. Behind this small group of buildings was the local African market which was always a hive of activity. Across the road from Kandodo were the headquarters of the Ministry of Works and various other offices, as well as a golf and tennis club.

It was a very small town and, at first, we didn't like the intimacy of the place. The majority of Europeans were 'old hands' having lived in Mzuzu for a number of years and were often in their fifties or sixties, which meant there was a distinct hierarchy and woe betide any whippersnappers who overstepped the mark. Unfortunately, Keith made his presence felt from early on and was considered one of those whippersnappers who had to be put in his place, as can be seen in later letters home.

FRIDAY, 19 May 1967

DEAR MAM AND DAD,

Received your letter of 8 May yesterday. It has taken ages to get here compared to Domasi as, presumably, the post is held for an extra day or so in Blantyre to await the next plane to Mzuzu.

Firstly, I must tell you about the cat. Would you believe it? Last Saturday, as I was outside in the back garden walking around and wondering about our poor kitten, I thought I heard a meow in the distance. At first, I was sure I must be hearing things but I ran into the house to tell Keith what I thought I was hearing and we both dashed back outside, calling for all we were worth. Then, through the trees, we could hear undergrowth snapping as if being stirred and as we called, miracle of miracles, our kitty came walking out of the bush looking the worse for wear. You have no idea how happy it makes us to have him back. I had nightmares worrying he would be scared on his own and, the worst scenario, that he must surely have been eaten by a snake. It goes without saying that we are thrilled to bits to have him back, and I bet he'll stay near the house from now on (hopefully).

Now to the house: I must tell you about my source of cooking here – it's by wood stove, similar to the old-fashioned coal oven but nothing near as efficient. In fact, I'm already sick to death of it; the wood is always wet because it's always raining up here and the cooking surface on top is only large enough for two pans at a time. The regulo on the oven is broken, and the oven door has a gap of about half an inch top and bottom. I made some buns the other day – what a laugh, you could have mended your shoes with them. After about two hours of stoking the fire, I managed to get the temperature to 350° (or so the regulo indicated) but as soon as I opened the door, the temperature dropped to 300° and then gradually lower. The buns were baking for about an hour and the tops of them by this time were like rusks but the bottoms still nearly liquid! Ah well, this is Africa!

We decided we should get a cook-boy in view of the problem so we let the 'grapevine' know and had a steady stream of people asking for jobs, although 95% of them could only clean, not cook. We finally chose one who had worked for someone on the station before we arrived and told him to report today for a trial meal – Keith's idea as we are having the neighbours round for dinner and bridge this evening. But I'm afraid I already know that I don't want him – he won't listen to what I say at all.

I went to the African market this morning to get local meat (1/5d lb!) which needs pressure cooking before roasting or frying. Unfortunately, the local meat doesn't get a chance to 'hang' to mature so it's always tough, tough, tough. We have noticed that usually when you go to the market for meat, you are told that it is being 'inspected by the vet', meaning the vet is checking to make sure it can be slaughtered. Once checked, it is literally killed there, on the spot, outside the butchery, which is just a shed at the side of the open African market. There is no privacy for the animal, which is killed (probably has its throat cut) out in the street. Europeans are given the privilege of 'going inside the butchery', which isn't very nice but preferable to standing outside beside a small black hole in the wall looking in and not knowing what is happening. Once dead, the animal is carried into the butchery, hung up and literally hacked into pieces with an axe. There's no use asking for 'spare ribs' or 'fillet of steak'; in fact, you get whatever lands on the floor! Yes, Mam, I mean it! There is also the small problem of bags to put the meat in as, if you forget to take your own paper, the meat is wrapped in a piece of Portland Cement bag, sometimes with the grains of sand still sticking to it. I'll never complain about germs again. Mind you, we are never ill so it can't be too bad.

Anyway, back to the meal - I told this boy to pressure cook the meat for one hour, knowing how tough it was going to be, and to then put it in the oven for another hour to brown, but he completely ignored me and put it straight into the oven and then complained to me that 'oven no good'. I could have choked him. I put everything out that he was to use but he has now just asked me where the curry powder is. He'll get Keith's boot on his bum when he comes in. By the way, we've heard this man has just come out of prison because he started to buy a second wife before he had paid for his first one. I think it does me good to have a boy cook a meal occasionally, as then I appreciate my own cooking more.

MV Ilala

137

We are continuing on the film and had a lovely trip on the lake on a boat called Ilala over the weekend and have come back with lovely tans.

We left Nkhata Bay on Saturday evening to go up north to Karonga about twenty miles from Tanzania and arrived back at the bay on Tuesday afternoon. It would have cost us sixteen guineas each plus 23/- each for food but because it was for the film, we had everything paid for. It goes without saying that the cockroaches follow us around.

There are three classes of tickets for the Ilala: first class (us), second class - I believe they have somewhere to sleep - and third class — these people sleep in the open on the deck below. Of course, only first-class people get their meals provided. There were only two or three cabins on top and we were told that the ship had been in dock for a couple of months being renovated so would be comfortable. We did our ablutions before going into the dining room for the evening meal with the captain, who sat with us at the only table in the dining room. He was a grand man and we had a few laughs during the meal. Eventually, Keith and I had had enough for the night so, after saying good-night to the captain and the Kings, we toddled off to our room, switched on the light, and the room suddenly became alive, roaches darting in every direction from the bed, from the walls, from the floor. Ugh! I'm not saying we have now become nonchalant but we didn't go screaming and shouting as we would have done a few months ago. We merely gave the bedding a good inspection and went to sleep leaving the lights on and hoping for the best.

The following day on deck we met a lovely old man who was there with one of his wives. The man was a village elder and both he and his lovely wife spoke perfect English. We have taken some film so you will see them eventually. All in all, we enjoyed our couple of days, stopping off in a few of the bays up river before we eventually set off back to Nkhata Bay. We think we will be going to Johannesburg in September.

On to an even happier note. I have now started my new job at the police station and I'm sorry to say I like it very much! 'Sorry to say' because I know I won't be there for very long, although I haven't told anyone yet. The reason for this is that I'm pregnant. Wow, bet you thought it would never happen. I'll tell you more in my next letter. We have told Mr King about the baby and he said it would be okay as he could take head and shoulder shots if I looked too bad.

We are going to the Luangwa Valley Game Reserve in August, as well as having a trip to Durban by railcar at some point. I must say we are looking forward to seeing the Batley News when it comes, but don't forget, Mam, we want to come home sometime, so hope you haven't made a big spread about us.

Hopefully by now, you will have seen the film – if I had a penny for the number of times I've said that I'd be a million-airess! What a coincidence Michael seeing Gerald at the club. That is the kind of thing we miss most being up here; there isn't even a proper cinema.

Mrs King is going to Salisbury over the weekend and is bringing me baby patterns etc., but if you fancy knitting something we'd be grateful, as it'll take me ages 'cause I don't like knitting.

Give our love to everyone. Hope you and Dad are well.

Bye for now.

Love Keith and Anne xxx

BY THIS TIME, Keith and I had been married for almost four years and my parents were wondering if they were ever going to have a grandchild from their only daughter. Naturally, they were over the moon when I wrote to tell them that I was pregnant at last but, as I never kept my mother's letters, I don't remember exactly what she said about her thoughts. Sadly, because we were only able to communicate by letter, the time lapse between giving the good news and the bad news (below) meant that my family were hearing the sadness long after I had accepted it. By the time they responded to my miscarriage, I had already moved on. It may be that I am slow-witted or that I am just pragmatic, but the sadness lasted for just a short time and I was already consoling myself that I hadn't really had a chance to get used to being pregnant. Strangely, from memory, it affected my Aunt Alice (who was also my Godmother) more than anyone as, apparently, she was inconsolable for a time at my loss.

TUESDAY, 30 May 1967

DEAR MAM AND DAD,

I'm so sorry to have to pass on the bad news, but I've lost the baby. I had a miscarriage on Saturday evening and have been in hospital since Sunday morning, merely for observation. I hope to be able to go home tomorrow. I'm upset, but not so much at losing the baby, more so that I had only just written to tell you about it and by now, you will have happily passed on the good news. I'm so sorry, Mam and Dad. Still, you are not to worry as I know there will be another time. My hopes had been raised a few times during the last six or seven months, but after about six weeks, each time I found I wasn't pregnant after all. Anyway, next time I shall wait until I'm well and truly 'going'.

People were right, it is a lovely hospital here – everything comes up to my expectations. The staff are wonderful – the nuns, the Malawian nurses and the three Swiss nurses. They are all really kind and there's always one or another of them popping in to ask if I'm all right. It's a lovely room too; all Europeans get a private ward automatically, and the Africans' wards are better than any I've seen in England, probably because it's all new and modern. Everything is provided for Europeans: soap, towels, facecloths, own sink in the ward, even nightdresses which are much nicer than my own, and not a uniform night-dress as you would expect, with the hospital logo on. The first they loaned me was a brushed nylon one from Marks & Spencer, and the present one I'm wearing has harp designs on and lots of frills and buttons. The walls of the room are painted in lovely pastel shades and the pastel shade bedcover matches the curtains. All in all, it's like a nice hotel room and the only outward sign that it's a Catholic hospital is the crucifix on the wall over the bed.

The female doctor, who is Australian, has been ill herself the past day or so. She was telling me that she nearly passed out on Sunday evening during a Caesarean operation she was perform-ing. It was only by grim determination that she was able to carry on, knowing that there was no-one to stitch the mother up if she fainted. Before she did the operation on Sunday she came in to see me and said then that she felt awful, that she thought she had malaria. Anyway, today she felt better but looked nothing like as fit as I and she told me so. I could sympathise because if she had malaria, I know what she was going through.

I understand that by now you have seen the film; my good-ness, it has taken ages, hasn't it?

We also hear that Jack and Margaret have bought a house up Soothill, so there's no-one left in Leeds. That means nearly the whole of the Walker family is living in Soothill: Keith's mam, Gerald, Jack, Mavis. Luckily, the family is a very close-knit one and they all get on very well together, but if we ever come back to live in the UK, we think we shall still live in Leeds, if only so that people will be able to say they are 'going out' when they visit us!

We received a letter from Keith's mother the other day. Oh Mam, what on earth have you written in the paper? I wish she had sent a copy so that we could see for ourselves. Keith thinks perhaps you should have waited until we told you the full facts about the film before saying anything about it. I personally don't mind just so long as you have the facts right because, in the piece you had printed when we came out here, everything seemed to be mixed up. It looks like we might have to go straight from here to Canada, I think! Never mind, eh?

We had a lovely surprise last week when we received a parcel from Jane and Dick, our Domasi neighbours. I've told you how kind they were – how Jane baked cakes at Christmas for nearly everyone on campus and we've had far more meals with them than they have had with us. Jane knew how we liked Surprise Peas and that we couldn't get them in Mzuzu, so she sent on four packets – they cost 2/- a packet over here. Having been here now for a while we have met a number of Americans and they are all extremely nice.

Well, I must go to the 'chim' now (toilet in English, as I mentioned before!).

Bye for now.

Lots of love to you both.

Keith and Anne xxx

TUESDAY, 13 June 1967

DEAR MAM AND DAD,

How are things? Hope you are both okay. The weather should be nice and warm in UK at present.

Is it Whitsuntide yet? We don't recognise it as a holiday here and I can't even tell by the Epistle and Gospel at church as it's all in Chitumbuka. Talking about church – I notice that they have started a new way of getting the offertory collection. Is it the same back home?

The cook-boy of one of the other teachers here has just been to cut my hair. I dread to think what Keith will say when he sees me – he will no doubt raise the roof. I sat in the kitchen to have it cut and I never thought to have a mirror handy. When he had finished I was extremely keen to see how I looked, but my goodness, what a shock. I look just like a man with very short back and sides. The boy assured me that he cut women's hair all the time but I never thought to ask whether it was European or African women. Now I know! There's no hairdresser here in Mzuzu and I have been cutting my hair with my dressmaking pinking scissors for a while now as I have no hair scissors, so it often looked 'shaggy' and I told Keith that was the style hoping he would believe me. He wasn't happy but accepted it. One of these days he will refuse to go out with me! I've taken up driving lessons again, only this time I have one of the African police drivers sitting in with me. He charges 5/- an hour – they're getting almost as astute as we Europeans. I'm not doing too badly and am putting in for my driving test on 24 July, so be thinking about me, won't you?

We went to a party on Saturday and were a really mixed bunch. There were Europeans (English and French), Americans, Canadians, Israelis, Malawians and West Africans. We were the only marrieds there and felt in the way a bit, so we left at 11 p.m. The following morning on our way to church we picked up one of the partygoers having just left the party house – this was 9.15 a.m. What a shindig!

On Sunday afternoon, we went down to the bay expecting a quiet hour or two but, on arrival, found it looked like Blackpool on a good day – everybody and their grandmother was there from Mzuzu and the surrounding area. Occasionally we have a trip down on a weekday afternoon, after work, and the beach is often deserted, except for a few African ladies doing their washing. The bay is a mere twenty-six miles from Mzuzu, but it takes more than an hour to get there because the road is in such a bad condition.

I was so taken up with my hair earlier in this letter that I didn't finish what I was saying about the offertory collection at church. When it comes to that part of the Mass, instead of passing the plate around as we normally did, we now have to traipse down the aisle to the altar with our collection money and put it in plates being held by the altar boys! This is going back to the olden days when people would go up to the altar and lay their sheep or bread or whatever on the altar floor.

I felt a bit of a 'twit' clomping down the aisle and back and disturbing everybody as I got in and out of the pew.

(Keith has just come in, taken a look at my hair and told me I look a bugger and should wear a beret until it grows. Did I expect a compliment? Well, is the sea salty?)

He has a hectic time teaching. He started today at 7.30 a.m. and, apart from a couple of hours off at lunchtime and teatime, has been over at the school all day. It's now 9.45 p.m. The girl whose job Keith took over was single, consequently, she was glad to spend most of her time at school and started things like the Science Club in the afternoon school hours. Now, of course, Keith is expected to continue with this, which is a bit unfair. But there's no point in grumbling, especially as he is going to see about a transfer in a week's time. He has been dreading telling the head, but we have just heard that the head himself is leaving at Christmas, so now we don't feel too bad about it.

I'm back at work again and enjoying it. Everyone is so nice and the work is interesting and steady. I work six mornings, but the time passes very quickly; in fact, we seem to spend most of the morning drinking tea and coffee. We have a break at 8.30 a.m. and another at 10 a.m., then I finish at 12 noon. I work in a room with two African police colleagues. The younger is a police constable and the other is a police inspector. They are both lovely men and tell me all about their families. I was surprised to learn that the police inspector was only in his thirties as he walks so slowly and looks much older, but was even more surprised to learn that the retirement age was around forty, as the mortality age was approximately fifty on average.

We think Mzuzu, in general, is a bit of a disaster though. My watch strap has broken and I've tried everywhere to get another. As a last resort, I asked for some elastic, but I might as well have been asking for the impossible. Well, I was asking for the impossible as I didn't get any! But never mind, I can always take some out of my knickers.

We had another present from Jane from Domasi the other day. She knew how much we liked Andy Capp so she bought us the Andy Capp book and sent it on. She's really wonderful.

By the way, I've only just found out the order of the sisters at the hospital – they are the Medical Missionaries of Mary from Drogheda, Co. Louth. Remember, I used to get their magazines to sell when I was about thirteen?

Bye for now.

Lots of love.

Keith and Anne xx

SATURDAY, 17 June 1967

DEAR MAM AND DAD,

Received your letter yesterday. Oh dear, what an outburst! Well, I might as well get it off my chest, too. For a start, Keith's mother hasn't done anything to justify your remarks. It's a pity you don't wait and ask what has been said before making your comments. You can imagine how I felt after letting Keith read your letter first! If you read my letter through again, you will see that I merely say 'we received a letter from Keith's mam – what have you written in the paper? And not 'what on earth have you said?' … which is slightly different! I also said that I don't mind so long as you have the facts right, and as you are telling me that you gave the reporter my letters, this is okay. I'll quote you the bit Keith's mother says in her letter, shall I? She says: 'There has been quite a piece in the Batley News about you and Anne making a film to boost the tourist trade out in Malawi. It says Anne is Batley's Julie Andrews. We are hoping we shall see the film.'

Mam, if you had told me this in the first place, that you had shown the reporter my letters, I wouldn't have been worried, but I dreaded that perhaps you were letting your imagination run amok, though I didn't say so, did I?

In every letter we have received from people back home, we have been told they had read the article but no-one has said what the article contained or even had the gumption to send a copy. Even you yourself haven't sent a copy yet. What on earth do you suppose we should think? Even Derrick in Aden saw it. In fact, Keith's family think Keith and I sent the article to the News ourselves; they have said so in their letters. As for people knowing about the baby before you did. Well, Keith and I sat down on the same night and wrote letters to you and his mam and posted the letters on the same day. Also, it wasn't meant to be a secret! Oh Mam, I don't know. The Kelly family!

I hope you have cooled down now, but I'm only sorry it takes so long to post letters from here because by now you may well have said things to other people in the heat of the moment that will get back to Keith's mam. Don't forget, Keith's sister used to work with Mrs D at the hospital and, although she may seem nice to you, she wouldn't be human if she didn't pass on any messages she may hear. Anyway, I hope the misunderstanding has cleared up now. I know you mean well, Mam, but unless you explain things, being so far away, it's a bit frightening not knowing what's going on.

I'm really sorry, Mam, but your letter had just come at a bad time. I'm feeling really upset just now about the fact that we've been politely told today that we are no longer welcome at the club here in Mzuzu. This is because Keith wrote a complaint in the official club book. I think I have already told you about it. The thing is, unlike you, Keith doesn't say anything until he's sure, though I know this still gets him into trouble, not unlike yourself! I'm not upset so much for myself as I only went to the club for films, but there is nowhere else in Mzuzu for Keith to play tennis and, with nothing else to do here, he lives for this. Anyway, he says it has sealed the decision to ask for a transfer back south. In fact, I am beginning to hate everyone and everything here myself. There are less than one hundred Europeans here and it's like a tiny village, everyone knows everyone else's business. I love my job at the police station and everyone is very nice there – the Africans as well as Europeans, but I don't intend working for the next one and three-quarter years (not if I can help it).

The cockroaches are very few and far between now. We see a couple every other night or so but not the dozens we used to see every evening. However, I did take one to church last Sunday though goodness knows where it had been hiding. I was kneeling down for the Offertory, minding my own business when, shock of shocks, something jumped off me and landed on the seat of the bench I was leaning on. Sure enough, it was my old friend the roach. I wasn't about to clobber it, at least not with my hand, so I left it to scamper along the seat, silently praying that some large gentleman would sit down quickly and send it up to the insect heaven.

There aren't many mosquitoes either as it is perishing cold at the moment. We have a wood burning fire (when it lights) and lots of blankets on the bed. The roads are in a terrible state. The workmen had just put down lorry loads of new dirt to cover the potholes and corrugations when the rains started – three days of it. I couldn't control the car the first morning because it was like a skating rink, except that we were wheel-deep in mud instead of ice. The car is supposed to be white but it is red all over. In fact, the house inside is the same, with mud trails all over the place.

I was talking to someone today who brought their cat over from the UK and it cost £10. I dread to think what the fare for our cat will cost on top of the cost of food and accommodation when he is in quarantine for six months. Also, a stray has adopted us, so if we're not careful, we shall have to double that amount. We leave the window open for our cat when we're out and keep coming home to find our cat sitting outside meowing and the stray asleep on the couch after having eaten all the cat food. He had made himself at home in our kitty's basket the other day while our cat was outside again, crying to come in. He's such a dope! Bye for now.

Love to you both.

Anne xx

I FELT REALLY sad that my mother and I had had words as we were normally very kind to each other and didn't fall out ever. As I mention above, I think the problem was made worse by the fact that Keith and I had been banned from the only place to socialise in the whole of Mzuzu, but I did explain more fully to my mam and dad what had happened in the following letter.

THURSDAY, 29 June 1967

DEAR MAM AND DAD,

Thanks for your letter. It made good time this week – dated the twenty-fifth, received the twenty-ninth. Must have just been in time for the VC10 on Monday.

On Tuesday, there was great excitement when I went to school and saw a Batley Reporter in Keith's mail rack. But you can imagine my disappointment on looking through from cover to cover and not finding anything in it about us. It seems they have sent the wrong week's copy. The one received was dated 26 May. So, after all this time, we still don't know what the story is! Keith has also written to his mum telling her off for not sending a cutting. If you have a spare copy, could you send it to us to put our minds at rest?

I was gobsmacked to hear about cousins Patsy and Kathleen Kenny visiting you. It's uncanny that Patsy should lose her baby two weeks after I did – she would have been two and a half months at the same time I was. It's unbelievable! Do you know her address? I'd love to write to her. Actually, she is one-year younger than I am – she's nearly twenty-five years old. I went to London with my grandmother and Auntie Alice when I was about ten and I met Patsy then. When we were together people thought we were twins or sisters! Do we still look alike?

As I mentioned in my previous letter, we have been banned from the Mzuzu Club. The club is nothing more than a wooden hut but it is the heart of the area and the only entertainment for 350 miles. It consists of a golf course, six tennis courts, Saturday cinema, library, pub etc. Being banned means we cannot use any of these facilities. The trouble started very soon after we arrived. You know how Keith loves his tennis, and he soon found another player of similar ability to play against. They began making arrangements to play each other a couple of times a week, Keith usually booking the court as he had to come into town to collect me when he would pop into the club to sign the book to reserve a court. On a couple of occasions, while he and Ray were playing a singles match, someone would arrive on the courts, but instead of going onto one of the empty courts, they would open the door onto Keith's court and say something like: 'When you have finished this set!' then stand by watching in anticipation. The first time it happened Keith didn't understand what they meant and continued playing the game but, after being interrupted a couple more times, he asked what they wanted (you can imagine his tone!). At being told the newcomers would like to play doubles with them, Keith told them that thanks, but he and his partner preferred singles, and continued with their game. Ray is a very quiet American and didn't want any trouble, but Keith was adamant that they had paid for their game and so should continue.

This happened a couple more times with the same reply from Keith, but one day, when he arrived to sign the book and pay the court fee, he was told that the club secretary wanted to speak with him. So, off to the office Keith went, probably practicing his swing as he walked! The secretary was some old duffer who had been in Mzuzu for a long time and thought he owned the club and he was more than happy to put this young upstart in his place. He told Keith that, at the club, they were all gentlemen (even the women by the look of them!), that they played 'social tennis' rather than competitive tennis, and that the rule was if, while you were playing singles, another couple came onto the courts then, at the first opportunity, you were expected to stop your game and involve the other couple and play plonkety plonk (Keith's words) with them. Keith was furious and told the secretary what he could do; that he, Keith, had paid for the use of the court and was only interested in playing singles. Ray was waiting on the court when Keith got there after the 'meeting' and, after a short discussion, they commenced their game. There was a book in the bar at the club for members to write comments and after the game Keith decided to add his remarks about their system of booking tennis courts. Well, on the Saturday when we turned up to watch the film, we were ceremoniously asked to leave (me, as well!). Keith was absolutely furious and, before we departed, he left them in no doubt about what day of the week it was. But now, of course, he has no tennis and I have no films!

By now we felt we had had enough and a few days ago we went to tell the headmaster that we wanted a transfer back south. We showed him the letter I'd typed up explaining everything about our decision, which was addressed to the chief education officer in Blantyre, and the headmaster took it very well. He said, in fact, he knew that we weren't happy, that we hadn't wanted to come to Mzuzu in the first place (not sure where he got that from), and said we would almost certainly get back south but probably not until Christmas. It would have been nice to have been able to move in August but we can put up with this place for a further four months, I think. (The cat keeps sitting on the page as I'm trying to write and smudging the ink where it's still wet.)

I was surprised to hear that Miss L had transferred her affections. Mr B's wife was very nice – ten times as nice as Miss L. It's amazing what some men will do for a bit of a change. She's no oil painting, is she? She's progressing, though; firstly, finance officer, then administrative officer, now a surgeon. She must have something extra we don't know about because it's neither looks nor figure.

I heard on the Rhodesian news this afternoon that Jayne Mansfield had been killed in a crash, but nothing further. I wonder, did it happen in the UK or had she returned to the USA? What terrible news.

She has four or five children, too.

Alice seems to be doing okay for herself. I'd better start saving up for a wedding present I think, but tell her to wait until we get back in eighteen months or so. I must write to Aunt Mary tonight. She told me how the accident happened. Can't she claim from the corporation if it was their fault for leaving the road unsafe?

I also hope Michael is okay. He should have been in hospital by the time you receive this letter (we hope). He must be fed up. Oh, I had a letter from Babs last week, too. I'd better get cracking and get some replies made.

Bye for now.

Love to you both.

Keith and Anne xxxx

UNFORTUNATELY, I don't have the letters telling me what had happened to my aunt, nor do I now know what had been wrong with my brother, Michael, and my memory is dimming as the years go by. My brother and aunt are both long dead, so I can't even ask them. How sad. I am trying to make sure my daughter and grandchildren know whatever they need to know about me, as they know they have to ask now, before it's too late.

MONDAY, 3 July 1967

DEAR MAM AND DAD,

How are things? I'm glad to hear the weather is nice over there at present. It's terribly cold here in the mornings and I particularly feel the cold at work. I wear a thick skirt, jumper and cardigan (and sometimes gloves), yet I'm still cold. Don't know how I manage to type wearing gloves but manage I do! Fortunately, it does warm up nicely by lunchtime, though I'm usually too busy in the afternoons these days to sunbathe. We did go down to the beach yesterday after church and stayed until around four o'clock (having taken sandwiches for lunch), but the sun sets earlier each time we go down. Of course, this is the African winter so we cannot expect anything different.

We have written to the education people about a transfer (I believe I told you in my last letter) but the reply we received wasn't very optimistic, I'm afraid. They say they will consider us for a transfer but can't do anything until the New Year. I suppose they are hoping we shall have settled our minds to staying here by then. I don't mind it too much but Keith says he would rather pack in his contract than spend the next eighteen or nineteen months up here with nothing to do in our spare time. He said this to the headmaster who seemed shocked on hearing it, he not realising how strongly Keith detested Mzuzu. He told Keith he was quite friendly with the chief education officer (the person who has the say as to where one is sent) and that he would be seeing him in the 'near future' and would 'put him in the picture'. So, we have a small hope, I suppose.

I wonder if you can do something for me? I have tried many times to buy those scented sweets I used to get at the Batley bus station sweet shop, you know which ones I mean, Phul-nana cachous. They were 10d half an ounce, either orange or pink. I don't know whether or not it would be possible to get some and send them over. The only thing is I couldn't pay you for them at the moment as our postal orders are only valid in Malawi, Rhodesia and South Africa. Would they cost too much for you?

I don't think I told you but we had an earth tremor a few weeks ago. It was fairly late in the evening and there was a sudden noise like a very heavy lorry coming towards the house at full pelt, which surprised us as we are quite a way off the road. Then the house started to shake with the pictures on the wall vibrating. It only lasted about twenty seconds but it was really frightening. Strangely, neither of us said a word all the time this was going on, we just looked at each other. It was uncanny. As soon as it stopped, we realised what had happened, and we got our voices back. But it just shows how one's reactions are slowed even when you know what is happening and we would probably have still been sitting looking at each other when the roof came in on top of us had it been a bad tremor. They have had a couple of tremors in the south which were felt at Domasi in the last few years; in fact, there was quite a bad one only a couple of months before we arrived there. I remember the Clarks telling us how things had been shaken off tables and that the lights were swinging. It would be all the scarier in Domasi as the tremor happened while they were in bed. Can you imagine switching on the lights seeing what was happening and wondering if the ceiling was going to come down on top of you?

The southern part of the Rift Valley is only about fifteen miles from Domasi, so that possibly accounts for it there. I read that Lake Malawi is part of a distinct rift basin and is one of the largest, deepest, most ancient freshwater lakes in the world. It's Africa's third largest lake and the eighth largest in the world and fills a stretch of Africa's Great Rift Valley approximately 380 miles long and forty-four miles wide, reaching depths of more than 2,000 feet. Although estimates of its age vary from 40,000 to one or two million years, it's considered an 'ancient' lake in global terms. It has a comparatively small drainage basin, most of it in Malawi, and its outflow feeds the Shire River, a tributary of the Zambezi.

We have two days' holiday this week for Kamuzu Day (President's Day). This is good because it will give us chance to visit the beach again. At least we can be sure of a visit south in August to complete the film. I'm not sure what is planned yet.

We have just written to Mr King telling him when term finishes up here, but we are hoping a trip to Salisbury will be planned for August or failing that, a trip to Johannesburg.

The Kings went to Salisbury a couple of weeks ago to see the film so far (it is being processed there) and they said they were pleased with the result. If we do go to Salisbury, Keith has promised me some new clothes (it will be nice to have something bought for a change, especially as I am working more months than I anticipated, with the baby an' all).

It is Keith's duty day today, so when he gets back he will have a hurried tea and then needs to go out again. It's a long day – 7.30 a.m. to 8.30 p.m. with only one and three-quarter hours at lunchtime and one hour at teatime.

I shall have to either read a book or listen to the radio, which is hopeless up here. TV would be ideal in Mzuzu but it won't reach Malawi for about another ten years. Even South Africa doesn't have TV, which is very surprising, but I understand this is for political reasons!

Bye for now.

Love to you both.

Anne and Keith xxx

I guess it was a short detention!

THE DUTY DAY meant doing the normal teaching duties during the day but then spending the evening in the classroom overlooking detention. The main punishment was to 'fill in' every other square of a sheet of graph paper, both sides if it was a long detention. Several staff played bridge and, as was often the case, the single blokes would go over to the detention room and join up with the teacher on duty, making a fourth for bridge. This relieved the bachelors' boredom to some extent. It certainly passed the time and made the evening worthwhile for every member of staff, including the teacher on detention duty.

I also notice that I mention being pregnant again but I don't have the letter in which I told my parents the joyful news, nor an indication of their feelings, which I know would have been excited but anxious for me.

TUESDAY, 11 July 1967

DEAR MICHAEL AND BARBARA,

Sorry I haven't written for a long time.

Hope that by now you have been in hospital and had your operation, Michael, but knowing what the hospitals are like, well....

We have had a few days' holiday for the Republic celebrations here. Actually, Keith had three days off and I had two. The weather was a bit unkind in the mornings but it managed to clear up by lunchtime, and each afternoon there was something happening. One day there were dances by the students, each group dancing according to their traditional village dance. One group was in animal skins and carried spears and shields, and another had 'war paint' on. Keith filmed some of it, so we are hoping we shall have some record. Another day there was a football match between the staff and prefects. The result was a draw 2-2, but Keith scored one of the goals for staff, believe it or not! It was the funniest thing I ever saw. The ground was a mud bath because of all the rain. Keith and some of the others didn't have football boots; in fact, the pumps which Keith wore were so smooth it would have been silly to even play tennis in them. You can imagine what antics they got up to trying to remain on their feet. In the evening, there was a dance to records. There was also a 'big' match in Blantyre between Malawi and Oldham, would you believe, which we were able to follow on the wireless, but there seemed to be a slip-up as the referee blew 'time' ten minutes before he should have done! Enough said…

Recently at school, Keith witnessed a racial incident between Africans which surprised him. He isn't yet used to the 'name to the face' characteristic of the Africans, particularly as they have unusual names such as Kidney, Innocent, Chitedze, Kuku etc, which is a problem to remember, anyway. During the chemistry lesson, having shown the students an experiment, he asked one of the boys to explain it to the rest of the class, saying 'Mtumbuka, what happens when we mix…' but he was pointing to a boy called Mulomole. Immediately, Mulomole responded with indignation saying: 'But sir, I'm not Mtumbuka. He's much blacker than me!' The whole episode was a surprise, as you can imagine.

The older African in my office died on Sunday. It was an awful shock because he was fine on Saturday morning when I was with him at work, and I didn't know his health wasn't too good. He had a wife and five children. They held a post-mortem which I understand they always do on government employees, primarily because there is an awful lot of jealousy amongst the Africans and it's not unheard of for one to poison another just because he has a better job. But I understand this particular person was a heavy drinker and the beer he drank was the cheap local brew which I'm sure contained only 'muck', as the average African is so badly paid that he can't afford the real McCoy.

You'd be surprised what some of the locals actually eat and

drink. At the market the other day we bought 6 lbs of mutton (2/- lb, which we thought was very cheap) and we also bought 2 lb of steak for the cat (1/5d lb). This shows how spoilt he is! As we were getting our meat, an African came out of the 'butchery' carrying the feet and head of a cow. The feet up to the knee joint had been hacked off and still had the skin on. In fact, that's all there was, black hide and bone. I can't imagine what it must be like to be only able to afford the remnants of the dead animal or even what concoction could be made from it, but the man obviously thought he had bought a prize as, once outside, he began to carefully stuff everything into his battered attaché case! It just shows how spoilt we are in the UK. You can imagine the shock on our faces as we were watching all this.

In Africa, they don't waste a scrap of an animal which is brilliant. The Europeans buy the steaks etc., and the Africans buy the intestines, ribcage and all the other parts, such as stomach lining (tripe, I think) which always looks so dirty, prob-ably because they hang the animal up on a hook as soon as it's dead and cut it open so everything loose inside just falls onto the ground. Poor Africans – I'm sure they would prefer the 'better' cuts of meat if they could afford them. Ah well.

I had to use the saw to cut the mutton leg I bought as it wouldn't fit in the oven. I felt like a surgeon because the meat was still warm (hadn't been dead very long), and at first, I thought I would never manage to get through the bone but I eventually got the hang of it, though I'm still squeamish. I still haven't become used to the hens yet, either. The Africans come on their bikes from the nearby village carrying a cage on the back crammed with hens. The hens look so pitiful when they blink at you and it's horrible to see the boys feeling the hens to see how much meat they have on before they choose one and then slit its throat. You see them walking along the road carrying the live hen by its feet and the hen flapping its wings, trying to get away. On the surface, they seem very cruel people but they are in fact the softest people I have ever met in many ways, always courteous and very humble. However, when illness comes into it, they are most pathetic – in a nice way. The boys will come to ask for 'pill because of cough' when we would just shrug it off and I imagine our boy is the worst of all! If it's raining even slightly, he won't run the thirty or forty yards to his house; instead, he waits inside until the rain stops. You can just imagine what Keith says to him! His favourite question is to ask Cassiano if he thinks he's going to melt.

Hope you are having better weather than we are having. It's so cold at the moment that we have a log fire every day and I'm huddled up in bed with three blankets and a heavy eiderdown at night.

Hope everyone is well. Give my love to the kiddies.

Bye for now.

Love,

Keith and Anne xxx

AS A NOW MORE INTELLIGENT and grown-up woman in my seventies, I understand why the Africans felt illness so keenly: they ate the worst food with very few vitamins and couldn't afford proper medication. They must have suffered greatly as they lived in terrible conditions. Sadly, the Malawian Africans haven't progressed very far in the many years since I left the country, it officially being classed as the sixth poorest country in the world, with 70% of Malawians still living below the poverty line.

THURSDAY, 13 July 1967

DEAR MAM AND DAD,

Last week, we received a second copy of the Batley News,

the same as the first one, dated 27 May. We thought we were doomed never to see the article about us, but a couple of days ago, Keith's mam sent a copy, so at last we can say we know what it was about.

Actually, I'm sorry but I must have made a mistake in one of my letters (or else the girl took it to mean the wrong thing) because in the article, it says Keith will be studying to take his Bachelor of Education, when it should have been Bachelor of Science – the BE (Dip Ed) is the one he got from Becketts Park Teacher Training College. Not to worry, it doesn't matter, as I don't suppose anyone will know the difference, anyway.

Julie Andrews' double gets 'star' treatment in Africa

LESS than six months after leaving Batley for Africa a local couple have been asked to make a documentary film promoting Malawi, the country in which they live.

Anne and Keith Walker left England last August and in January they were asked to take part in a documentary film. By now many scenes have been completed and the finished film may be shown in European countries to "sell" Malawi.

ANNE WALKER

Newspaper clipping

It's just after 9 p.m. and we have been across to the school so that Keith can do an experiment (how keen is that!) and we were very surprised to see some of the senior students working away in the classrooms. It is all spare-time study, not compulsory. Keith even leaves the laboratory open during the lunch hour so that anyone who wants to can do some work, and to his amazement, quite a number of them take the opportunity. Where in England would this happen? Keith gave them a 'mock' chemistry GCE exam during the week and only one girl failed, but she was in tears when he gave them their marks. You should see how much work she put in today to make up for her marks. Keith recalled how, when he was at grammar school, anyone who had bad marks would just laugh it off.

Here the students' parents have to pay for their education so it's very important that they learn and they seem good at the sciences, but we laugh when we hear them speak English sometimes, though I don't know why we should laugh, as I hardly know a word of their language. The Malawian languages of Chichewea/Chinyanga are spoken in the south and Tumbuka is spoken in the north. In both languages, the 'l' and the 'r' can be interchangeable. Keith related this funny story from school the other day:

For their English lesson, the students had been asked to write about the visit of their president, Dr Kamuzu Banda, who was staying in the Northern Region at the time, and one girl wrote:

'We were all assembled in the school hall talking excitedly when suddenly the door opened on the stage and the President walked out. Everyone stood up and crapped loudly.'

Last week was Republic Week and there was 'a lot of goings on' at the school so far as entertainment was concerned. One evening, the students gave a cabaret and invited the staff. I suppose it was good but we didn't understand a great deal of it. There was nothing organised about it at all. Someone would come on and sing (no music), after which someone else would dance (again, no music). Then there would be a play (in

Tumbuka, their language), and then jokes in English (which no-one ever got). One afternoon, there was traditional African dancing and we took film of this so you should see it eventually.

Mzuzu School Sports Day, July 1967. Keith is the second spectator from the right. I see that the Deputy Head on the right needed his cigarette to supervise!

Saturday was Sports Day. I was roped in to help keep score and make out the winners' certificates, however, Keith had the hardest job of all – he was in charge of timekeeping (but of course, stopwatches are very heavy). He was a tad bit annoyed that I had been given a job to do because I was so busy I was still adding up points after the sports had finished! As you know, I was never good at maths. Unfortunately, I held everyone up as the person presenting prizes couldn't hand them out until I had filled in some of the names... what a life!

I go for my driving test a week on Monday (24 July). Keep your fingers crossed for me, won't you?

Derrick, Margaret and family should have arrived in England by now. They were leaving Aden on Tuesday evening and will be staying in Keith's mum's house in Soothill until they go to Singapore in September. Keith's mum is staying with Mavis.

We are looking forward to the school holidays in August

because then at least we shall be visiting civilisation, if only for a short time. Mr King is trying to arrange the rest of the film, so we shall have some kind of a holiday at least. If we don't get a transfer soon, the car will have fallen to pieces. There isn't one garage in Mzuzu so if you want anything doing you have to go 250 miles to Lilongwe. We have a puncture but can't get it mended here and are having to send to Blantyre – nearly 500 miles away – to get an inner tube for the tyre which will entail the cost of the tyre plus air delivery charge. You can buy petrol and oil up here but that's all! Keith is tearing his hair out, as you can imagine. However, sometimes even the petrol isn't safe, as when we first arrived we were told that there had been a leak from the petrol tank to the diesel tank and we were getting a mixture. With this, after a couple of miles, I should think the engine would fall out. Lovely Mzuzu!

Keith has decided that, after Christmas, if they still haven't promised a transfer, we shall be scouting for another job in another part of the world (he fancies Singapore now that Derrick is going). It will all come out okay in the end, it always does.

Bye for now.

Love to everyone.

Keith and Anne xxxx

THURSDAY, 27 July 1967

DEAR MAM AND DAD,

Thank you for your birthday card. Would you also thank Michael and Barbara for their cards? They were lovely.

It seems ages since I last wrote but there is only a plane out of Mzuzu on Tuesday and Friday, so if I happen to miss the Tuesday plane there doesn't seem any point writing until time for the next one. Unfortunately, we have no contact with any other part of Malawi by road or rail, only by air twice each week.

You sound like you have a very good job at the hospital, Mam. As you say, it's a pity you didn't work there years ago. I do remember Janie, the Maltese person. Such a lovely lady, she bought me some beautiful flowers on the day I left Batley Hospital.

Did Alice manage to get the address of Patsy for me? We had a good laugh at your remarks about Alice's 'intended'. Don't worry about her – she always lands on her feet. If she has to practically dress him and take him to the toilet, then I doubt there will be any funny business going on between them (if you see what I mean). Glad to hear Gran is getting on okay too. I have written only once and would write more often, only it's difficult knowing what to say to her. Also, I suppose she reads a couple of letters which I send to you.

I took my driving test last Monday but failed! It was a very unfair test in my opinion, as I was only out five minutes and it should have been half an hour. It was an African examiner and he failed all eight of us on the day - three Europeans and five Africans. The traffic officer at the police station said he had heard that the examiner had been told to fail everyone taking their test for the first time, but I don't know how true that is! I'm quite confident that I shall pass next time and may take my test in Zomba next month when we go down to finish filming.

School inspectors visited the school last week and Keith had a talk to one of them about our disliking Mzuzu. We were cheered up because the inspector said he was sure we wouldn't be made to stay here and said he would 'put a word in for us' which is good. However, we're not the only ones with problems. Some friends of ours at the army barracks in Mzuzu are on the verge of divorcing. And all because of this place. When they came out they had only been married a year, but because of the smallness of the town and not being able to see anyone or anything different, unfortunately, they have got on each other's nerves. Jenny was in tears the other day and said she was going back to the UK in October and leaving John. She said John didn't want a family (this would keep her occupied as she doesn't have a job) and that he spends every evening drinking himself silly, which I imagine is boredom on his part. They were supposed to be coming around this evening for an hour but Jenny phoned me at work to say John had been on the 'binge' on Tuesday night and had been sick ever since. Fortunately, Keith and I always seem to have something to do in the evenings; Keith spends nearly every evening marking books or setting exam papers, and I either read or knit, so we are managing to keep sane. To keep herself busy, Jenny offered to do some sewing for anyone who wanted and one of the African wives from the barracks went to see her with some very nice material and a cutting from a newspaper of a dress she liked. Like myself, Jenny always uses a pattern so I can appreciate her difficulty, but the laugh came when she started to take the lady's measurements because the African lady would insist on feeding her baby – about nine months old - just as Jenny was trying to measure her bust, and the next day the same thing happened as she was fitting the tacked pieces of the dress to the woman. I can just imagine the scene, especially as the African women wear very little underwear.

I have volunteered my services as a 'seamstress' for the wife of one of the policemen at work. His wife teaches at the primary school and she gets £15 a month. As a policeman, he gets £18 a month, which is a terrible amount for Africans.

Did you say there was a bit about Derrick in the local paper? It should be called the Shirley/Walker News! We receive a copy of the News regularly from the news office free of charge now, for which we are grateful.

Bye for now.

Love to you both.

Keith and Anne xxx

WEDNESDAY, 9 August 1967

DEAR MAM AND DAD,

Sorry it's been a while since I last wrote. I find I put it off until near the time the plane leaves, then suddenly I find I have missed it! Ah well, here goes. There's nothing definite yet about our moving south but the good news is that a science teacher in Dedza (the Central Region) has asked to come to Mzuzu in place of Keith, so now they are trying to place someone from the Southern Region into Dedza so that Keith can take their place in the south. It looks like ninety-nine point nine per cent certain that we shall move south in December, so it's something to look forward to, at least. They break up for three weeks on 25 August so I am having a week off work and we're going to Domasi to stay with the Kimballs. We had been hoping to finish filming, but Mr King has to come up to Mzuzu during the holidays to cover the Malawi Congress Party Meeting, as the President is coming also. Mr King, 'Chief Technical Officer' being one of his other hats, has to lay loudspeakers and make recordings of the speeches etc. We have asked him to stay with us but don't know yet if he will.

We went to an African wedding a week last Saturday. What an education. We arrived at the village after the church ceremony, in the afternoon. On arrival we were led to some 'seats' that had been placed strategically around a group of chairs and a table (which were for the bride and groom and best man). I sadly say 'seats' because we had given away a better chair to Cassiano. The family was impoverished and seemed to have nothing of any value, yet I have to admit it's a bit difficult trying to perch on a deck chair which doesn't have any tacks in the top to keep the cover on and the seat is torn. Nonetheless, it was a wonderful experience and not easily forgotten. The ceremony began by the bride and groom appearing amongst the crowd of villagers, all dancing and singing. The couple eventually took their seats and an alternative kind of dancing started, theoretically I think, to evoke the gods to bring happiness to the couple. Then came the giving of presents. Keith and I were the only non-Africans there and the only ones from school able to attend, but to get a better present for them about six of us had clubbed together and bought a small tea service of four cups, saucers, plates, teapot, milk jug and sugar basin, and these were beautifully wrapped and tied with a red ribbon. We had been very, very careful to rub out the price so as not to offend, so you can imagine our shock when we were asked publicly how much the present cost. When revealed, the price was written on a sheet of paper with our names beside it. We then had to stand up so that the villagers could see who had brought a present costing 75/- and there was great applause and cheering – we felt right twits! The other guests gave their presents and declared the prices and these too were added to the list. Then came the ceremony where money was given. I'm not sure exactly how it works but I think the parents go to one side and decide how much the son and daughter are worth; in this case, the boy was worth £2. 15s. 0d. and the girl £3. 5s. 0d. Don't forget, to an African, a penny is valuable. After this sum was declared, the relations had to give money – again, it was entered on the sheet of paper. It came in pennies and threepences.

Then the groom's father (who was wearing worn-out shoes, no shirt, and a dirty old overcoat) came up and gave a £5 note. It was so very touching and I felt like crying on seeing this as, quite honestly, the father must have almost gone without food for weeks to save up this amount. Poor, poor people.

Eventually, we said we must leave as it looked like an all-night 'do', but they insisted that we have refreshments first. So, we clambered into one of the huts and sat on a bench by a table. The room was bare apart from this furniture and the floor and walls were made of dry mud hardened in the sun. Two girls gave us a cup of 'tea' and offered bread and margarine. So as not to offend, I forced a piece down. They tried to get us to stay for rice and meat but we turned down the invitation very politely and said we had an appointment. On reflection, they must have been disappointed as somehow we had been made the 'honoured guests' and probably should have tried to stay a bit longer. We ignoramuses will learn some day.

Well, that was our first wedding but now we have received another invitation, this one during the time we shall be visiting at Domasi, so sadly, we shall have to refuse it. Still, it was a good experience. We will take our camera the next time we get an invitation.

I have my old prolapse back. I seem to be at the hospital every week now. Amazing, as I never once saw the doctor in eight months at Domasi. Well, maybe we shall get back again – we hope so.

Bye for now and lots of love to you both.

Wish Barbara a happy birthday on the twenty-third and Alice on the sixteenth for us.

Keith and Anne xxx

TUESDAY, 22 August 1967

DEAR MAM AND DAD,

We're out of air letters, so this will be a longer letter than usual. Received your letter today, together with the Batley News. I know there's very little news in it, no more than our paper here, but it's still something to read and occasionally I recognise a name, so it's very welcome.

You asked in your letter about John and Jenny, our friends at the army barracks. Well, they aren't with us anymore. There was such a kerfuffle a week last Sunday. I was in a tearing hurry, getting ready for church and I wasn't sure of the time; our neighbour collects me at 9.15 a.m. but I knew I was nearing the deadline and had to rush. There came a knock at the door and when I went to answer it, I saw it was John. It was unusual to see him so early but I asked him in. I could see there was something wrong. He hadn't washed or shaved or combed his hair and he was very pale. But I got a shock when he said Jenny had left him. It seems that the night before there had been a farewell party for a friend who had been in charge of the building of the barracks, a Rhodesian chap who was a few years younger than John, who is about thirty-six and Jenny is my age, twenty-six. It appears it had turned sour at some point because John said they were pushing drinks down him all night. Also, he had had a row with Jenny during the party because he had caught her in the kitchen with the Rhodesian chap. Anyway, to cut a long story sideways, Jenny said she was leaving him and going to Rhodesia with this man, that she wanted a divorce. I must say I have had my suspicions about this Rhodesian and Jenny before, as she was constantly talking about him but, as though she could read my mind, she had said there was nothing going on between them (and still says so, apparently). I woke Keith and made John some tea while Keith was getting ready. After a short discussion John said he had to go as he must tell the sergeant major what had happened, that he couldn't stay in Mzuzu and be the joke of the year. We told him to come back for dinner but he never came, and it wasn't until Monday afternoon after the plane had left, which Jenny and this chap were due to catch that we ventured over to see John at the barracks. Well you could have knocked me down with a feather when we saw Jenny outside their house talking to someone. Apparently, the sergeant major had decided he would resolve the matter his own way. He had more or less pulled Jenny out of the caravan where the Rhodesian chap had been living, and told her he was now in possession of her passport and therefore she couldn't leave the country at that point. He then took her down to John and told them both to move out by seven o'clock on Thursday morning and he wasn't having any Africans seeing such carryings on! He then gave Jenny a dressing down, telling her what he thought of her etc., and that they were being sent to the Zomba barracks but must be prepared to be sent back to the UK. John's promotion has gone by the board which is very sad as he had only a couple more years to do. I can't really say who was to blame; Jenny blames John saying he will never discuss anything. But I had to smile because on the Monday, the day after she left him, while we were there, he was calling her his 'pet'. It makes you think, doesn't it?

We are going down to Zomba on Saturday for nine days, so it will be a nice rest from this place. There is just one snag, though – we gave Cassiano a week's notice last Friday though I'm not sure Keith actually means it. He wouldn't do as he was told and, on this particular occasion, Keith was so mad he gave him notice. I can see that Cassiano has been very unhappy in Mzuzu anyway (not unlike ourselves). Here in the northern part of Malawi they speak a different language (Chitumbuka) but Cassiano comes from the Southern Region, so speaks Chinyanja. While in the south, Keith and I learned a few words in Chinyanja but mainly only greetings: Muli bwanji (How are you?) Ndili bwino, kaya inu? (I am well, and you?). Ndili bwino, zikomo (I am well also, thank you). However, like Cassiano, our 'knowledge' of the language doesn't help us here in the north, though we had great fun trying to get the accent right, but I doubt we'll be employed as interpreters in the future! I feel sad for Cassiano and wonder how many friends he has managed to make since being up here. His leaving means that we will need to take the cat with us to Zomba and, unfortunately, they have dogs at both places we are going to stay. Cassiano was sick in this instance so Keith has offered him another chance (to both our benefit, of course), but he was having difficulty under-standing whether Cassiano wanted to stay or not, so was going to try to get someone to translate tomorrow (our 'greetings' won't be of any use in this instance.)

I had a letter from one of the lads where I used to work in Leeds, and he said that my old boss had been retired off in May this year; that they were a million pounds down in profits and that the '51 Cooker', which is the one they were making when I was there, was now on the scrap heap. I wrote to my boss's wife once early on our arrival to Malawi, but she sent a very short reply, merely thanking me for my good wishes, so I took the hint and didn't write again. Maybe she was a bit upset about her husband's health, but I took it to mean she didn't really want to keep up the loose relationship we had formed while I had worked for her husband. Anyway, I may try again now I know the bad news. I don't know how old my boss was, but I guess only in his late fifties! (Author: he was more like in his seventies when I picture him now, which just shows how younger people are unable to relate to older people sometimes).

We have had terrible rains these past few days and on Monday we had to abandon the car not far from the house because we couldn't move for the mud. The Ministry of Works sent a tractor to pull it out. Meanwhile, they had to send a police Land Rover to pick me up and take me to work and then bring me back. Even with the Land Rover's four-wheel drive, it was extremely difficult to get up and down the hill. To make matters worse, that same day the water was turned off all over Mzuzu because the pump broke. Great! I'm such a slow writer – it's now Friday morning. Cassiano is going back to Domasi after all – he says he doesn't like Mzuzu. Can't blame him.

One of the young guys on the station (a VSO) is having trouble with his cook-boy. He has been sending him to the market to buy meat, say 5 lbs to 7 lbs at a time, but the cook boy has only been asking for 2 to 3 lbs and pocketing the remainder of the money. Naturally, a single boy of about nineteen doesn't know how much meat you would get for 7 lbs. It was one of the other teachers who spotted it. Richard, the VSO, said he had just bought loads of meat and could let this other teacher have some – she had had some unexpected guests – but when she looked inside Richard's fridge, there was only a small piece of meat there. So, Richard set a trap and caught his boy out. I think I should explain what a VSO is. It means Voluntary Service Overseas and our young man is working as a teacher. He doesn't have a contract, like us, but instead is meant to live and work alongside the locals helping them to help themselves. He is provided with accommodation and food etc., but only get paid a nominal amount each week. Our VSO lives on our station and a house similar to ours and occasionally will share the accommodation with a second VSO. Because they get bored these lads often take over the study period in the evenings thus giving the 'old marrieds' more family time. However, we old marrieds do look after them in turn, as they regularly get invited to eat with us in the evenings.

Derrick and Margaret are planning to go Singapore sometime in September. I don't know the date, so they were probably shipping some of their personal items off when Mr Pratt saw the railway pantechnicon outside. There was talk of them buying a house in the UK because, apparently, Margaret can get concession flights very cheaply and it would be nice to have a house to go to each time. But I don't know whether they got one or not.

My grandma sounds to be getting worse for wear these days. I don't think she will be around when we get back home, unfortunately. She gave me two half-crowns the last time we saw her before coming out here, but I must have lost one somewhere as I can only find one now and I'm so sorry about that.

Today is the last day of term for three weeks and there will be the usual dance this evening which we shall have to attend. The dances are usually very enjoyable except that they must have the records playing as loud as possible (my dad would love it!). Halfway through they serve cocoa in chipped tin mugs.

Hope everybody is well and that you enjoy the show at the Variety Club. Wish we could be with you.

Bye for now and lots of love to you both.

Keith and Anne xxxx

DURING THE NINE days we were with our friends in Zomba filming, we spent three of those days posing as the 'honeymoon couple' holidaying in Lilongwe, the capital of the Central Region of Malawi. We were advised that we would be travelling by road, which didn't fill us with joy as we had travelled that same journey when moving to Mzuzu, though we cheered up dramatically when we were told we were going to be chauffeur-driven all the way there and back. Our mood improved even more when we saw the chauffeur-driven limousine chosen specially for us for the occasion.

In Lilongwe, we were to stay overnight at the Lilongwe Hotel and return to Zomba the following morning. However, we didn't know at the start of the journey that we would be counting the fillings in our teeth on arrival to Lilongwe that day! It was the most hair-raising experience of my life to date as the driver seemed totally unaware there was a brake pedal on the car, insisting on driving at great speed, sometimes over huge, partly hidden slabs of broken stone embedded in the dirt which formed part of the highway, then dropping into craters formed when drivers drove at excessive speeds over the road! We were swaying from one side of the road to the other, hanging on for dear life.

On occasion we stopped en route, both to film specific scenes and to also allow the Land Rover carrying Mr King and the assistant photographer/lighting technician to catch up with us. It was always a relief to get out and stretch our aching limbs, but we rarely had a chance to catch our breath and off we would set for a further bone shaking ride.

We were subjected to over six hours of crashing and jolting over the most atrocious dirt roads, sometimes at speeds of thirty miles per hour and more on road surfaces that could change in the blink of an eye from deep red dust to mountainous boulders. We felt sorry for the occasional African man or woman walking along the road, unaware of the dust storm coming their way, as we would leave behind red clouds that would cover the poor people from head to toe, leaving them looking like walking anthills. Intermittently, the sump pan would fill with soil causing the car to brake sharply, and all the time we were praying it would outlast the knocks to the bottom of the car. The driver assured us he had passed his driving test and that he knew well how to drive, and I have to admit he did get us to Lilongwe in one piece. But, we wondered, were we going to be ready for the return journey?

We enjoyed our short break from Mzuzu, arriving back in early September just in time for the visit of President Hastings Kamuzu Banda (to give him his full name) who, that year, was holding the Malawi Congress Party Annual Convention at Marymount School, the Catholic secondary school in Mzuzu. His State Lodge was at the top of a hill called Kamuzu Avenue on the way to Mzuzu Secondary School where we were stationed, and this portion of the road had the only section of tarmacadam in Mzuzu, in fact, the only section of tarmacadam for 250 miles. It was because of the president's visit that both Mr King and Richard Kimball were staying with us. Mr King, being the government photographer, was taking the official photographs of the visit and Dick was involved in education work in the Northern region at this time.

As I sit typing now, I remember a funny incident that happened on that particular stretch of tarmacadam road at about that time. Working at the police HQ, I was witness to a number of confidential operations in the area and I heard that for a whole week there was going to be a radar speed check on all traffic driving down the road from the State House – this stretch of road was only about 500 yards long. Rightly or wrongly, I mentioned this to my husband as, at the time, he took me to and from work because I didn't have my own driving licence until much later. For the whole of the week the radar was in place, no-one from our school drove more than twenty-five miles an hour down that stretch of road with a speed limit of thirty miles per hour, and it's doubtful that the African on his bike would 'freewheel' any faster! I never did learn what the arrest rate was.

I don't know for certain how popular Dr Banda was, although the Africans seemed eager to see him on this visit, crowding around the entrance to his State Lodge hoping to get a glimpse of him through the gates and yelling at the top of their voices when he came into view (it was more like a wooo wooo noise rather than a yell – the sound being made by putting a finger into the mouth, tightly wrapping the lips around the finger, then making a wooo noise at the same time as rapidly rolling the finger round. It was quite effective)!

Dr Banda relied on the Malawi Young Pioneers (MYPs) to help maintain the peace and they were always at the forefront of any gathering in the country, keeping 'the people' under his thumb, putting fear into them. The MYPs were a paramilitary wing of the Malawi Congress Party and originally founded in the early 1960s to carry out voluntary work for Malawi's development, such as agriculture. They looked like European boy scouts in their green shirts and khaki shorts but the MCP movement was far from the innocent Boy Scout movement of UK, their role having developed into one of menaces and eventually becoming a terror group infiltrating every part of Malawian life.

We were first introduced to these people on our arrival into the country in 1966 as, often during the drive from Zomba to Domasi, these young men, wearing the trademark shirt and shorts, would stand at the side of the road and frantically try to flag our (European's) cars down, sometimes actually standing in the road. We had heard they had been told that when the country became independent they would have the power to stop anyone in a car and demand to be picked up and taken to the place of their choice. Needless to say, we Europeans merely evaded them if they were in danger of being hit and continued on our journey. I wonder how long it took them to learn what a two-finger V sign meant. But they had huge power over the Africans who, rightly, were scared of them. These men had the power to stop any public African transport and order the passengers off. (We had witnessed this ourselves during our stay and wondered what we would do if we were ever confronted by these thugs). They would inspect the length of the women's skirts and, if the back of the skirt didn't cover the crease behind the knee, they would brutally rip the hem down with a razor.

At the same time, another section of the MYP group would be demanding that passengers prove they were holding party membership cards, and any passenger not carrying a card would be unceremoniously thrown off the bus, baggage and all. So far as Europeans were concerned, we didn't take much notice of the MYP, although we were always aware that a problem could easily arise, their power being so great. We Europeans thought it strange that there was no rule about showing a woman's breasts in public – they did this all the time – and yet it was against the law to show ones knees. We often wondered how the African would react if a European woman had walked around in the same mode? However, Europeans were warned not to antagonise the Young Pioneers, so we usually obeyed the rules and didn't wear either minis or shorts around town. The Young Pioneers, a group disliked by both the police and army, had power more akin to presidential bodyguards with menaces, eventually becoming a terror group for the President infiltrating every part of Malawian life, creating spies out of university lecturers, cleaners, messengers, garden-boys, office personnel, barmaids etc.

WEDNESDAY, 13 September 1967

DEAR MAM AND DAD,

Sorry it's been a while since I last wrote but it's been hectic ever since we arrived back from our stay in Domasi last week.

Cassiano left us the week before so we had a very busy day Tuesday. I was working in the morning but Keith is still on school holiday. On Wednesday, Mr King came from Zomba to stay with us and left on Friday afternoon. On Saturday Dick came and will be with us until next Sunday. Can you imagine what it's like trying to wash sheets and towels by hand? Fortunately, I only had to wash a little because last Thursday a young African man came seeking work and he was a godsend. It's amazing how quickly the African drums beat when there is a job vacant on the school site! His name is Christopher and he has been to school to Standard IV so his English is very good; better than mine I should say. If I can teach him a little cooking it will be very good for me.

I thought I was going to be able to give you some good news very soon. I had thought I must be pregnant again so had been to the hospital the day before yesterday for a check-up. The sister/doctor had said she couldn't really tell whether I was expecting or not without a thorough examination and it was probably too early yet to do that. She suggested I go back to see her next month when she would be able to get a better idea. I'm now feeling so disappointed again (Keith also). We had stayed with the Kerby's in Zomba for a few days and they have a new baby. Keith was thrilled with it (though he didn't pick it up) and we were both convinced that this time it was it! Ah well. I'll have to stop wishing then something might come of it.

When we visited Domasi and Zomba we took time out to go to see the Education Department people about our transfer. We really impressed upon them how miserable we were and they promised to let us know before the twentieth whether we could hope for a move or not in December. So we are keeping our fingers crossed. To try to make our life better for the time we expect to be here, we applied for temporary membership of the club yesterday morning and took the completed form back in the evening, together with our £2 for one month's membership (sheer robbery), but when we asked people to propose and second us they refused, saying they had been told not to. We were shattered! We felt so ashamed. But Keith was upset and mad at the same time, as we had gone to see a film with Dick, our friend from Domasi, and had had to come away before it started. Talk about apartheid! We want to make a complaint and are trying to think of a suitable person to write to, people like the British High Commissioner, because we think it is disgusting that we should be discriminated against merely for speaking the truth. We'll have the last laugh, I'm sure.

Derrick and Margaret should be in Singapore by now. We had a letter from Keith's mam today. She said they got off safely but she was waiting for their address. She has had a card from Istanbul en route and in it, Derrick has told her she could expect us back home soon. He must have gathered by our letters how fed up we are. Anyway, we have decided to hang on until next August even if they don't move us. We would have to pay back our fares etc if we left in December – about £600 - and for the extra eight months, we should get over £1,000 in earned gratuity. However, if we are moved and like the place, we may stay until a year next August. It would be worth it moneywise.

Keith has been cleaning out drawers and has just given me the 'painting' made from material and buttons which Karen did, and reading what you put on the back, Mam, brought tears to my eyes. If she does any more, please send them, won't you?

Hope you and Dad are keeping well. We think about you a lot and still miss you both very much.

Bye for now and lots of love to both of you.

Remember us to Mike and Babs. It's my turn to write so I'd better get my skates on.

Keith and Anne xxx

Letter from Keith

MONDAY, 18 September 1967

DEAR ALL,

You may be wondering why I've finally managed to get around to writing. Anne is in hospital again after suffering another miscarriage. We purposely didn't say anything earlier as we thought that this might just happen again. She was about three months gone (as before). She started having pain early yesterday evening (Sunday) but refused to be taken up to the hospital. We eventually went to bed but the pains became worse, so we had to get up and drive to the hospital. By this time, Anne was in a lot of pain and I was worried. It took two injections of morphine to put her to sleep and she continued to be in a great deal of pain until the drugs finally took effect. I went back early this morning and the doctor (a sister) confirmed that she had, in fact, aborted. Anne had minor surgery this afternoon and appeared comfortable but exhausted when I saw her. The doctor says she will be quite okay in a couple of days when she's rested, so there's no need to worry. The next aeroplane down to Blantyre isn't until Wednesday, so I'll add the latest news tomorrow before I post this letter.

We have received good news – we are definitely going to be transferred at the end of this term. We don't know exactly where yet, but presumably it will be either Blantyre or Lilongwe. It's just as well we are going. Mzuzu doesn't hold happy memories at all.

It's now Tuesday afternoon. Anne is convalescing at home. I picked her up about an hour ago and she is fine now, only needs plenty of rest. No doubt she'll be writing soon.

Ta ra for now.

Keith

I HAD BEEN pregnant after all! Having gone to the hospital for a check-up on 11 September, for some reason the sister/doctor hadn't been able to determine if I was pregnant and had sent me home telling me to wait another four weeks or so. Sadly, within days, I was having a horrendous miscarriage, much worse than the first one, and remember being in so much pain I thought death might be preferable!

I had just told my family that I wasn't pregnant so now had to tell them that I had been but now I wasn't! What a mix-up.

Sadly, over the years, I hadn't kept any letters from my mother, so I have no idea now how she felt, but I feel she and my father must have been worried about me. However, I was back up on my feet and running before I had a chance to realise what I had lost. As can be seen from my next letter 'home', I only bothered to use two small paragraphs to explain things. In my mother's life, there was never any time for sentiment and fortunately, she instilled in me the same tough attitude which has helped get me through some adversity over the years since this time.

SUNDAY, 24 September 1967

DEAR MAM AND DAD,

Well, here we go again! I seem to be living at the Mzuzu hospital. The sisters are marvellous, though no panic, everything is taken in its stride. Actually, they said they could probably have saved the baby had I gone into hospital the day I started feeling unwell but, as I told them, everything seemed normal and I didn't realise I was having another miscarriage. But I certainly knew on the Sunday – I died a thousand deaths – well, this time it was probably two thousand (much worse than the malaria)! They say they will give me injections the next time I'm pregnant to make sure I don't lose the baby. It's funny to think that that is two different babies we'll never bring into the world, as complete and real as any baby that is born after nine months. They took this second one away from me but didn't put me to sleep for the D&C (scrape), instead giving me an injection in the arm – another thirty minutes of absolute hell. Now I know how to get secrets out of women! I didn't ask to see the foetus as I'm sure I would only be upset thinking about it. I'm fine now anyway, except for a spell of trouble on Wednesday when the pills they gave me were having the same effect as on the Sunday. I shall be going back to work tomorrow – thank goodness.

We are being transferred in December but as yet don't know where. We feel sure it will be either Blantyre or Lilongwe, which will be very nice either way.

Keith's mam went to Austria (Blackenberg) with Gerald, Barbara and family. She said she enjoyed herself very much, but I think she feels it was a lot of money to pay for a few days abroad as I gather it was quite expensive.

We were finally able to re-join the famous Mzuzu Club yesterday. It felt very strange going after all these months. For once they were showing a good film – Walt Disney's The Living Desert. It cost us a fortune to join (annual fee £13), plus 5/- each to see the film. But blow me, if they aren't showing the same film to the students here at school this evening. We always seem to get 'seen off'.

We have also had to spend a fortune on the car these past few months – maybe more than £100 since April. Keith says that it's a good job I'm working for the extra money, and I must say I'm glad also.

Some new people have arrived on the station. Actually, they have come back on their second tour and asked specifically for Mzuzu as they thought it was the nicest place on earth. I haven't met the mister yet, but the missus is a bit strange. She is about our age and has two small children, but within a few minutes of being introduced to her, she was telling me about what the sisters had said when her babies were born, and how she was worried because her little boy has only a small penis! She is thinking of asking for my job when I go at Christmas.

We are still very pleased with our new garden/houseboy. He polishes the floor every time he cleans up, which is just about every day, but I don't doubt that the enthusiasm will drop off after another few more weeks.

We hear that there was an accident at the army barracks yesterday. A corporal was in charge of an ammunitions exercise (all Africans) and he was throwing grenades. He shouted to everyone to duck while throwing one but forgot to duck himself – the result being that a piece of shrapnel hit him in the eye, which had to be removed, poor man. It's amazing how the story soon gets around. The barracks is a mile or so away yet we know almost immediately most of what's going on. The whole of Mzuzu is the same – everybody knows everyone else's business.

This new person here seems like a 'caller', so I'm pleased I'm working as I don't want to know all her private domestic occurrences, or anybody else's for that matter. I think the people here think Keith and I are strange!

Bye for now and lots of love.

Keith and Anne xxx

THURSDAY, 5 October 1967

DEAR MAM AND DAD,

Received both your letters yesterday. Seven days to get here – not bad going considering the plane only comes up three times a week.

Only about eight weeks to our moving, but we still don't

know to where. It's funny, but the place has taken on a different setting. Now I'm thinking: 'Well, it's not too bad really', but I'd be still hating the place had we not been told we were being moved!

I had another couple of days in the hospital last weekend. I started haemorrhaging badly while at work and they sent for Keith, who took me to hospital where they gave me another D&C, but under anaesthetic this time for a thorough job, and the sister/doctor says I have a fibroid on the wall of my uterus which might possibly be causing the miscarriages if the baby is sitting on top of it, although she added that she doesn't really think it is the cause. Anyway, she says to wait and see how I go on.

We had a leak the other day from the hot water cistern which is in the ceiling. Water came bouncing down into the room (good job it's not our furniture) and, since then, we have had a fair number of roaches in the various rooms. The wet must have disturbed them. It's also the season for flying roaches, too. It's lovely and hot here and it seems unusual to think of you all being cold back home.

Last night, we had a barbecue for the lads who have just arrived. There were nine of us altogether, and it seemed to go down quite well despite the lack of variety of food. We had made a contraption to cook hamburgers on while Dick was staying with us (being American, he loved it) so we were well prepared. We have electricity all day and night, but it's so expensive that we only use it for the iron, wireless, kettle, toaster, and lights. The electricity bill is £4. 16s. 0d a month. Just for these few things, that's why we are not provided with an electric oven – no-one could afford to use one. The cost of electricity is 1/6d for the first twenty units, thereafter 9d per unit. I think you will pay about 1/2d per unit.

Keith is busy building a tennis court at the school, which he started when we were originally banned from the club. At least no-one can say he didn't contribute towards the school. There used to be two courts, but they were left to go to ruin. He is having to organise all the work, so you can imagine what he will say if, when it's finished, the rest of the staff decide to occupy it each day. The headmaster is giving him money to buy fences, soil and equipment, but the labour is hard.

We spent the afternoon at the bay today; it was lovely and quiet. If you go down on a Sunday the rest of Mzuzu is usually there as well. We are acquiring quite a nice tan, too and I went mad recently and bought a bikini to help with the tan. Our new 'boy' Christopher is doing really well. He speaks very good English and we have just learned that he had four years schooling. Apparently, he had to leave school when his father died as the mother needed the school fees to buy food. The Africans have to pay for their education – it's not compulsory or free like in the UK. Therefore, only the people who can afford to send their children to school do so, which is an awful shame. I don't know what will happen when the Europeans leave Malawi. The unskilled labour far outnumbers the skilled.

Keith has posted off a film to Gerald. It will take about three weeks to reach him, so within the next six or seven weeks, you should be seeing it.

The Commonwealth Development Corporation (which is the largest government concern in Mzuzu) is closing down in six months. This company employs most of the seventy or so Europeans in Mzuzu. When they go, this place will be dead of Europeans. Thank goodness, we shall also be going.

Bye for now. Lots as always,
Keith and Anne xxxx

FRIDAY, 13 October 1967

DEAR MAM AND DAD,
Hope you aren't superstitious – Friday the thirteenth!

We are much the same here. I now have a new boss at work. He is a bit younger than my previous one but equally as nice. I have started working afternoons for something to do, but there is very little to do at any time. I shall be getting £765 per annum, which isn't to be sniffed at. My boss writes fiction books which he usually types himself, but says that the next time he writes another book, I can do the necessary typing at work.

My other boss has gone on leave to England for six months but when he comes back in April, he will be posted either to Lilongwe or Blantyre, so we may see him again if we are moved. I was sent over to the offices of the Malawian minister for the Northern Region this morning so that I could take dictation of a letter he wished to send to President Banda who, I believe, prefers speaking and writing in English. I took the dictation, typed it out, showed it to my boss to check, and took it back to the Minister's office. I must admit that I do have an unusual job!

We had a letter today from Mary and Barry, the couple we met at Farnham Castle in Surrey before we came out here. The British Council for Overseas Development had arranged for all the people going out to work in the various African countries to spend the weekend in Surrey where we were given information about the countries' laws and customs.

We gelled with Mary and Barry immediately. I believe they came from Birmingham. While we were being posted to Malawi, they were being posted to Zambia, but didn't go until last Christmas. We have kept in touch ever since we first met and we have each asked the other to stay during the various holidays. Anyway, they say they will very likely be able to come to visit with us in December or January, which will be lovely. They are living further into the bush than us – there are only about sixteen Europeans where they live – but they love it. My boss also likes Mzuzu very much. I am coming to the conclusion that Keith and I must be antisocial.

I don't suppose there has been any news in your papers or on TV about the 'rebels' who have come into Malawi from

Tanzania? These rebels are all ex-Ministers from Malawi who decided they didn't want Dr Banda as President in 1965 and who caused unrest in the villages by telling people he was no good to rule. In the end, Banda's supporters chased them out. But since 1965 the rebels have been recruiting other rebels from Malawi and training them in Algeria to fight. Well, one of these rebel ex-Ministers came into Malawi through Portuguese Mozambique last week and brought with him forty others. They intended to make their way from Portuguese territory through to Zomba to kill the president, but they never got within ten miles of Blantyre because the villagers captured them and gave them over to the police, but the leader has been killed in the skirmish. It shows how irresponsible they are when some of them are captured with their own booby-trap. I couldn't mention this before because it was hush-hush, but now everyone here knows. Some people at the office seem to think it is a huge joke because they knew the Southern Region of Malawi was very loyal to President Banda. We heard months ago at work that the rebels were going to attempt to get through, but everyone thought they would come in through Tanzania or Zambia, just above where we are. Anyway, everything is quiet – in fact, there has been no panic at all.

The wife of the African in my office gave birth to a boy during the week. The father is thrilled to bits. I gave him some booties that had been given to me a couple of months ago and he thought they were lovely.

I have sent off to a place in England for a cut-out suit and blouse, but they won't despatch to Africa, so I have given your address. When the package comes, will you take off all the labels or at least any that mention the price (70/-) and put a label on with my name and address, writing on the package 'USED CLOTHING'. This way, it will get through without my having to pay customs duty. If you have to put a value on the package, say 19/6d but not more than £1, as anything above that amount is not duty-free.

Hope you don't mind! Ta.

Bye for now.

Love to you both.

Keith and Anne xx

TUESDAY, 7 November 1967

DEAR MAM AND DAD,

Received your letter the other day. Barbara has also written and sent a drawing from Karen. I have stuck it on the wall and it looks lovely.

We have re-joined the Mzuzu Club at long last. My new boss took the bull by the horns, saw the chairman, and squared it up with him. Keith is now happily in a tennis tournament being held during the next few weeks. We went through with our application to the Club again because there seems to be a bit of doubt about our moving now after all the promises that never come to fruition. But we've been told that there has been a complete re-shuffling in the Ministry of Education in Blantyre, and we have heard unofficially that we cannot be placed anywhere else at the moment. Still, it won't be too bad now that we have joined the club, although we still feel a bit peculiar seeing people there who know the reason we were banned in the first place.

Last Saturday we went to the Bonfire Dance at the school and really enjoyed ourselves. All the young students went, and we were joined by some more young couples from one of the outlying schools whom we had not met before but whom we seemed to get on with very well. We have also become friendly with a young American Catholic couple, Ray and Robin Perone, at the Catholic Secondary School here. They have a little girl aged fourteen months and are expecting another baby in April. They seem very much like Dick and Jane, our friends at

Domasi. Ray had a really good job in America, at Cape Kennedy I believe, and gave it up to come out here for three years. He gets very little salary, and one can see by their standard of living that they have a struggle, but they are such nice people. We play bridge with them about once a week, which passes away an evening nicely.

The rains have started now, but we have some good hot days. My boss gave me the afternoon off yesterday as Keith has every Monday and Thursday free, and we went down to the bay. It was wonderful, so quiet and peaceful. The only other people there were the Major from the army barracks with two African officers who were sailing a yacht.

I have set myself up as a hairdresser for the headmaster's wife. A few weeks ago, I sent off to William Penn in England for another of those haircutting combs with a blade inside. If you remember, I gave the old one to you as I didn't think I would ever need it again. Silly me. It was okay while we were living in Zomba because there was a hairdresser there, but not up here. I will soon be taking bookings as the only alternative is the African barber, and you remember what happened to me!

Keith has to go to Blantyre for ten days in December to mark Junior Certificate papers, but I can't go with him as all the teachers stay together in the dormitories at the European secondary school there. He will also have to go down again in January for a science conference, but we don't mind too much as each time he goes he gets travelling expenses. Mary and Barry, the couple we met at Farnham Castle in England and who are in Zambia, are proposing to come to see us just after Christmas. Then, maybe next Christmas, we shall be visiting them.

We have started sending our garden/houseboy to our next door neighbour every lunchtime to learn from their cook-boy how to cook, and he seems to be doing fairly well. I would still prefer to do the work myself, but I must admit it is better not to have to do so, especially with the silly stove we have.

We are now frequently receiving the Batley News. I was

surprised to read the other week that a couple from Batley were coming to Malawi. I believe they are those Jehovah's Witnesses who occasionally visited the houses in Copley Street, you know, the brunette couple. They are intending going to Blantyre to promote their religion but I am pretty certain they will not be allowed to enter the country as President Banda has outlawed that particular religion. Anyone found with literature, preaching, or selling for the religion can be sent to prison. There has been a great deal of trouble here about Jehovah's Witnesses as I understand the church leaders have been telling the local people not to buy party cards – every Malawian is supposed to pay 2/6d to the government to buy a card which is for the Malawi Congress Party – the people in power. There have been beatings of Jehovah's Witnesses by the Young Pioneers, but because the Young Pioneers have made the excuse that the Witnesses started it, they have been given a free hand and nothing has been done to prevent it. I hope they don't try to get into the country as there is no point in antagonising the government.

Anyway, bye for now.

Love to you both.

Keith and Anne xxx

SATURDAY, 25 November 1967

DEAR MAM AND DAD,

Thanks for your letter received the other day. Also, thanks for your Christmas cards. Batley is really getting itself on the map, isn't it, especially with the printed cards with the name of the town in them? I have to admit, Batley is much bigger than the capital of Malawi, even though we consider it a small place compared with Leeds. I have sent off a few Christmas cards myself, but am awaiting some special ones from Nairobi to send to you and Keith's mam. Hope the cards come soon or it will be too late to send them on this Christmas.

As I mentioned in a previous letter, Keith will be going to Blantyre two weeks from today to mark examination papers. He will be gone for about a week, travelling by car, but I will still be able to get to work as someone will be picking me up each morning. And in the evenings no doubt I shall not be left by myself for very long.

Keith is playing tennis regularly now. He has a competition game scheduled for this afternoon with one of the Special Branch officers at the police headquarters, but it is starting to rain so the match may have to be postponed until later in the week.

There was a bad accident a week last Sunday when a police lorry taking people from the station house and from the secondary school to Nkhata Bay to play a football match together was involved in a collision. There were thirty-six people altogether travelling along in an open lorry, when the driver lost control hitting a bank on his left and turning the lorry over. At the very last minute, he jumped out but was crushed under the lorry, dying shortly afterwards. Lots of young police were injured. The lad I work with had cut elbows from where he was thrown out onto the dirt road and many of the boys had cuts to their faces. It was fortunate that more were not killed. It's now believed that the lorry had defective brakes before it set off and, if this is the case, then the driver sergeant will be in very serious trouble.

We had a letter from Gerald yesterday saying he has received our new film and that he will show it to you all before Christmas. We have another one to send but it will have to wait a while longer until we have another one to add as it's too short to send as it is.

Keith's mam seems to be missing his father - she sounded quite melancholy when she wrote last. No matter what he was like, as she says, he was always there and was someone to talk to.

It is the second anniversary of his death this week and she will be putting a piece in the Memorial column of the Batley News from us all. Goodness, doesn't time fly? I can hardly believe that he died so long ago.

The other day I went for lunch to the house of one of the Africans I work with. It was brilliant. His wife cooked rice, Nsima (ground white maize flour, which is the staple African food), cabbage cooked in tomatoes, eggs (also cooked in tomatoes) and other bits and bats. I really enjoyed it, although I felt a bit strange taking their precious food. These Africans are such nice people and we get on well with them. The wife has now gone back to the village in the Central Region for two weeks to recover from the loss of her baby, which I didn't know about until it was mentioned at the lunch. We are returning the kindness and asking Lloyd to come one lunchtime to our house as he is by himself. He is taking Junior Certificate of Education exams next week at the secondary school (although he is twenty-three years of age); I should think this is equal to the 16+ in England. But if he passes it will mean a great deal for his future promotions in the police.

Our friends in Zomba, the Kirby's, are paying a visit to England; in fact, Chris will be there now. He was going to go by himself, coming back, and then Wendy was going over to the UK and taking their new baby to show her mother and father. In a way, we think they were a bit foolish to do this as they are going to spend all their gratuity when they will need the money they earn to buy a house when their tour is finished. They have been in Malawi just a couple of months longer than us. We consider we are nearing the time when we should start booking our passage back home and they will be leaving for good a few months before we do. Still, it's their money. I'm really looking forward to receiving the parcel from you. Once stitched together the suit should look very nice, don't you think? The package may not get here now until after Christmas, but it will still be warm here and will be really useful. I sent to UK recently for some dress material and this came a couple of weeks ago. But I didn't save on this really, as the postage cost me 5/6d on a piece of material costing 14/6d and I can probably get material nearly as cheap at the local African shop here.

Hope you are keeping well, both of you. We shall be thinking of you at Christmas, trying to imagine what you will be doing while we shall be sitting in the sun (we hope). It was very hot at Domasi last Christmas, although thankfully it is much cooler up here most of the time.

Give our love to everyone and to yourselves. Bye for now. Love, Keith and Anne xxxx

DECEMBER 1967

DEAR MAM AND DAD,

Just a short note as the plane will be leaving Mzuzu in an hour or so.

Sorry I have been so long in sending your card and this is not the one I expected sending. Someone at work was intending going to Nairobi and promised to buy me some beauties from there which had animals on, but at the last minute, they weren't able to go; hence, my order fell through!

Hope you are keeping well and looking forward to Christmas and the holiday. It is a bit Christmassy here at the moment as the weather is cold.

We are having the President visit Mzuzu for a day or two. He is opening the new army barracks. But goodness, there is an awful lot of fuss just for the short time he is up here – money is being spent unnecessarily. However, I must admit, he is an amazing fellow for his age. He left Mzimba about a hundred miles from Mzuzu early yesterday morning and did a tour of all the villages, speaking to the people at every village, arriving here in Mzuzu at 3.30 p.m. yesterday afternoon. He is an old man and I don't know where he gets his stamina from.

Yesterday, as Keith was going to play tennis at the club, he got caught up in the throng of people and had to stand and listen to President Banda's speech which, to a European, is very repetitive and terribly boring, but he knows that if he doesn't do this, the Africans will probably forget what he has said two minutes later (much like myself, I'm afraid).

Keith goes down to Blantyre on Saturday, and I have made out a long list of things for him to bring back. Hopefully, if he can get what I ask for, we should have a good stock of food for Christmas.

After being re-admitted to the Club recently, Keith played in the tennis competition I mentioned in an earlier letter and he won the Singles first prize, which was a Dunlop Maxply tennis racquet valued at about £10, plus a small silver cup for him to keep.

Although I'm not thrilled with tennis at the best of times, nevertheless, the match was really exciting and I clapped and clapped whenever Keith won a point. But it was remarkable to note that, at the end of the match when Keith had won his final point, I was almost the only person clapping. If the people at the Club could have booed, they would have done so! Such bigoted idiots. He was playing the singles match with Ray Perone, the American teacher from the Catholic school who himself is a good player, and the match was well worth watching. But I felt sad for Keith as he didn't get the acclaim he deserved.

I was intending to buy him a racquet for a birthday and Christmas present combined, but now I shan't have to bother (thank goodness). However, I shall have to think of something else! I am learning to play tennis, too. My boss's wife is trying to teach four of us. It's a laugh, if nothing else!

The couple who were at the barracks here still haven't made up; Jenny wrote to me the other week to say she was going back to England. She will probably be there now. But from what she says, John is not going with her. Unfortunately, it's just one of those things, I suppose.

Thank you for your Christmas cards. They are really lovely. Auntie Mary has sent a calendar of Yorkshire which reminds us of home and what we are missing very much. I must write and thank her. We have also received a lovely card from Auntie Alice. I'd better say bye for now. Love to you both.

Anne and Keith xx

AS I MENTION ABOVE, my boss's wife did start trying to teach a few of us to play tennis but it didn't last very long. One day our little group was short of a third for doubles as one of the other learners hadn't turned up and, as Keith was waiting for his partner to arrive at the club tennis court, he was asked if he would like to make up the doubles for a short time, which he did very reluctantly! He was partnering me and my boss's wife was partnering another 'newy', but the match was very, very slow, and I could see that Keith was getting extremely bored. The other side continually sent their ball towards me, and inevitably I missed it. 15-0, then 30–0; it was getting silly, and in his frustration, Keith intercepted a ball coming towards me, hitting it hard and catching my boss's wife squarely in the boobs. She yelped, then stopped the game, saying she thought he had deliberately aimed at her and had had enough. I never went to tennis practice again – ho ho ho. 'Another fine mess you got me into, Keith…'

THURSDAY, 14 December 1967

DEAR MAM AND DAD,

Was glad to receive your card last Friday.

As already mentioned, Keith has gone to Blantyre with a couple of the other teachers and although I thought I should have lots of time on my hands in which to catch up on my correspondence, somehow I don't seem to have a minute to myself.

There is now only one male on the station – all the others are in Blantyre either marking the Junior Certificate of Education papers (like Keith), visiting the government hospital (like our neighbour Raymond Larouche) or merely shopping for Christmas. So, as you can imagine, the women are sticking together.

Each day after work I call at the school to pick up any mail for us, as well as that of the Larouche's, which I take back to Bernadette. I believe I told you before, Bernadette is a beautiful Malawian lady and Raymond is French Canadian. He once studied for the priesthood but I don't know the reason he left the seminary. They are such a lovely couple and have a little girl aged ten months who is a beautiful pale coffee colour. Her hair is one mass of curls but not as close as the African hair, and she has very dark blue eyes. She is also the chubbiest little thing you've ever seen. She seems to be a slightly late developer though and has only recently cut a third tooth but has been extremely ill with it. However, she does seem now to be losing a little of her weight, probably because of her teething sickness.

The new Standard Bank here in Mzuzu is being officially opened on Saturday, but because Keith won't be back before then I declined the official invitation to the cocktail party. Anyway, Tony, the young Rhodesian from the bank, has told me I must go as he has put my name on the list of guests. One of the police here (the second-in-command) is also going and, as his wife is in Blantyre, I shall be accompanied by him to the cocktail party. There is a dance at the club in the evening too and I would love to go as they are having a cabaret. One of the guys from the Special Branch division is taking part – this man is about 6' 3" tall and thirty years old, and is quite a goon at the best of times so I can well imagine what he will look like in the cabaret. The headmaster's wife has asked me to go with them to this function but I feel I'll be imposing on them if I do. I wish Keith was back! Did I tell you about the headmaster's wife's parents having come out from England? The head and his wife are both from Lancashire and Sheila's parents are potentially visiting for three months. It's lovely to hear a familiar accent. They live in Morecambe and Sheila's father is something in education there! They are such nice, ordinary people.

But they had only been here two weeks when the father had to fly back to the UK in a hurry as his own father, aged eighty-seven, was seriously ill and had only days to live. He arrived before the old man died and now Sheila's father has come back.

Jane, a Canadian, also has her parents visiting, but Jane's contract has finished so they all three plan to take the long way back to Canada. What a lovely holiday.

You say you might put some more odds and ends in the parcel you are sending which will be lovely, but be careful because it will weigh quite a lot. If you mark the parcel 'used clothing', then I know I won't have Customs Duty to pay, but the parcel rate is fairly high and you may have to pay more for postage than the things are worth, so don't send very much, Mam.

Hope Michael and Barbara are settled in their new house. I'm glad they are near you. I bet Karen is glad too, as it's not too far for her to visit by herself now. Love to you all.

Bye for now.

Keith and Anne xxx

Keith and the boys from the school. This Junior Certificate of
Education marking is serious business!

FIVE

Letters from 1968

WEDNESDAY, 1 February 1968

DEAR MICHAEL AND BARBARA,

Well, at last, I've managed to sit down to write you another letter, I hope you are settled in your new house now and that the family are enjoying it. The children will be nice and near my Mam and Dad (and you will, of course, but not too near!).

Did you all have a nice Christmas? My mam told me about all the presents the kiddies got. I imagine that Karen is quite a little girl now – she still seemed a baby to me when we left – and Janet sounds a lovable little devil! Hope your mam and dad are keeping well, Barbara, and also your sister.

Not a great deal has been happening here just lately, except that term started today with two girls less than last year because they had managed to get themselves pregnant, though I don't know how as they are watched like hawks from getting up in the morning to being locked into their dormitories at night. But, of course, they go to the toilet without supervision. It's amazing what you can do in five minutes, isn't it! The headmaster we have now is really on the ball, though, and we understand it used to be far worse before he came.

We went to the club last week to see *Son of the Werewolf,* a great film... I don't think! I've never seen anything so corny in all my life, and to think we paid 5/- each to see it. We went to a good dance on New Year's Eve though with food provided. It was dancing to records and back home I would class it as a parochial hop. I probably wouldn't have wanted to walk two strides to go, but it's amazing how these two-penny-ha'penny hops are made into big affairs. There was a fancy-dress competition too, and my boss at work went as a South Sea Teddy Boy or something! He looked whacky. But one of the bachelors went dressed as someone from the Arabian Nights, a Nubian knight or some such, in a costume I actually made for him, and he won first prize, so I was quite chuffed. But neither Keith nor I would get dressed up. We weren't very popular, I know, but I'm not going to make a fool of myself in front of all Mzuzu. My boss writes a column in the Malawi News – 'News from the North' – but no-one is supposed to know he writes it, although everyone seems to know. However, as he always manages to mention his 'own' name in each article people think he's too big for his boots. But I get on fine with him, especially as he did the write-up on the tennis tournament which Keith entered and won. He is writing a fiction book, a murder story, and he's having me type it up for the publisher, but I get so engrossed in it that I'm making typing errors. I'll have to read it through when I've finished in order to get the complete story.

I had a row at work the other week with the second-in-command, a European. I was getting a bit sick of him slapping my bottom every time I went past him and of his sarcastic remarks, so I waited my time and then gave it to him. I didn't start speaking to him again until this week – it was lovely, as he hasn't been giving me any letters to type either. But Keith is biding his time to get one back at him, probably through his wife unfortunately.

This is the trouble living in such a small community. People tend to criticise each other more and get on each other's nerves. But on the whole, it's not too bad. In fact, there are people I shall probably miss when we leave here in thirteen months' time, believe it or not.

Bye for now. Give our love to the children, and hope you both have a very happy New Year with the best of everything.

Love to you both.

Keith and Anne xxx

THURSDAY, 22 February 1968

DEAR MAM AND DAD,

My goodness, you are nearly as bad as I am for not writing! Maybe there'll be a letter from you tomorrow. We had a letter from Barbara on Wednesday and they seem to be very happy with the house.

Malawi Prison

In my last letter, I told you about the prisoner officer, Mr

Smith, being prosecuted for shoplifting a 2/11d bar of chocolate from the shop in Mzuzu. Well, last week, he had to appear in court, before an African magistrate of course, as there is only one European magistrate in the country and he is based in Blantyre at the High Court. When everyone heard the sentence doled out to Mr Smith they were shattered. He was sentenced to three months with hard labour, and that to be spent in his own prison. He came to the police station on the Tuesday after he had been sentenced looking ashen and my boss was frantically phoning the magistrate, trying to get him out on bail pending an appeal, but the magistrate would have none of it. So, on Tuesday night, Mr Smith was in his own prison with his own prisoners. On Wednesday, there were urgent signals passing backwards and forwards between Mzuzu, Zomba and Blantyre, but by the time the High Court judge had been found and approved Mr Smith's release on bail, the magistrate in Mzuzu had left to attend court sessions elsewhere in the Region and couldn't be found. So Mr Smith spent Wednesday night in prison too. Goodness knows what he ate because the prisoners cook their own Nsima. This is cooked to the consistency of very thick porridge and can be so thick as to be cut with a knife and rolled into balls to be eaten like bread. It's tasteless, I'm afraid; I've tried it. But no doubt Mr Smith would have been too upset to eat. Anyway, he was finally freed on the Thursday. Meanwhile, his wife was staying with the headmaster and his wife. Last Monday, Mr Smith went down to Zomba to see the prison commissioner to hear his appeal and he hasn't come back yet. It's all terribly embarrassing! People are a bit wary about going into Kandodo store now. If this is what happens when stealing a 2/11d bar of chocolate, then woe betide the person who steals anything of value! In the paper, during the week, there was a case of an African who was sentenced to eighteen months IHL (Imprisonment with Hard Labour, I think) for stealing 1d. He didn't actually steal it but he broke into a house and was caught holding a 1d box of matches. At work at the moment is the case of the accountant at the Kandodo (same shop Mr Smith shoplifted from) who has fiddled £894. 18s. 1d. (I reckon he'll get life plus, judging by eighteen months = 1d. etc).

As from 1 March, I'm going back to mornings only. It's a bit too hectic just lately and I'm shattered when I get home. Anyway, I don't benefit all that much moneywise as I'm stung for tax. The thing is, I get sick time off with pay while working full-time, although I haven't been sick since I started full-time, drat it!

Keith is out playing bridge again and I've been busy sewing. This piece of material makes it over £5 that I've spent during the past two or three weeks. Keith is creating, as you will imagine, especially as he is telling everyone he's been waiting for the last four and a half years to get a pair of socks darned.

Also, he's been complaining about having no buttons on his tennis shorts for the last three weeks. They're all the same, men, aren't they? I keep trying to tell him I'm saving him money by making my own clothes but he says I'm not as he'll soon have to buy another wardrobe to put all my things in!

It's bucketing down outside and the cat is out in it somewhere. He'll be sheltering no doubt as he hates water of any description unless it's a very slow drip from the tap, then he'll drink it – just like your cat. Hope he comes back soon though, as it's getting on for 10 p.m. – bedtime.

Bye again for now.

Lots of love to you both.

Keith and Anne xxxxx

THURSDAY, 7 March 1968

DEAR MAM AND DAD,

Glad to receive another letter from you the other day. Also, one each from Alice and Barbara, which were very welcome.

Keith is out playing bridge once more, so I am able to catch up on my correspondence.

We went out to bridge and supper last night, so all in all, we seem to be pretty occupied. Keith has a fairly regular arrangement these days to play bridge at the house of the French teacher John-Pierre Gabille, together with two French-Canadian priests from the order of White Fathers (Pères Blancs in French). The White Fathers society was founded in 1868 by the first archbishop of Algiers.

They all get on very well, probably because the priests here aren't like the ones back home. I didn't know until later that John-Pierre was a Catholic as he never goes to Mass, but the priests still visit him every Friday evening for supper, and Keith goes up afterwards to make up a foursome for cards. The Fathers never ever mention religion and Keith says they swear as badly as anyone if they are dealt bad cards. I made up a fourth once as one of the priests couldn't come and the Father had to promise to spare my blushes! Even Keith is amazed at their normality, though he managed to show me up at the time as he told the priest who was playing cards with us that he took too long saying Mass on Sundays. Keith told him he normally comes to collect me at 10.30 a.m. but very often it's 10.45 before he 'lets us out' of church. He said we usually went down to the bay on a Sunday after Mass, and it meant that we had a late start when Mass ran over... I could have choked him! We are reciprocating the bridge at our home a week tomorrow with supper etc., so we shall see how we get on with the priests, but I'm afraid there's no hope for Keith, despite all this!

There's going to be a marriage at the end of the year between Sue, the VSO who has been here since September, and Ken who came in December. It's a strange thing really as they have only known each other five weeks. Sue is twenty-four and Ken is between thirty and forty. The marriage announcement has happened quite suddenly, and even now not many people on the station know. Bernadette, my neighbour, didn't know until I told her today but it made her feel a bit better when I did as she had seen them kissing and cuddling outside Sue's house on Monday and was shocked, as apparently Africans don't do that sort of thing in public, but Raymond, Bernadette's husband, had tried to explain to her that it doesn't mean anything to Europeans.

I find that the Africans have some very nice customs; whenever I visit Bernadette, she always walks me back to the end of our garden, probably because in their tradition it's rude to say goodbye at your door (which I'm afraid I'm guilty of doing whenever she visits me). She's an extremely nice neighbour and I shall certainly miss her when they leave in August on transfer to Dedza in the Central Region.

I do hope you will eventually be able to see our cat but I don't know exactly what we shall be doing with him. We are thinking of asking Liz and Richard Burton to loan us their boat on the Thames, though don't know where we shall get the £1,000 a week from for six months!

Wishing you a very happy Mother's Day on 26 March. Bye for now.

Love, Keith and Anne xxx

MONDAY, 27 March 1968 (Pay Day – Yippee)

DEAR MAM AND DAD,

Thanks for your letter received on Monday. We are glad you liked the film but it's taken ages to get it shown to you. Keith wouldn't believe me when I pointed out to him that we had posted it to Gerald last December. Still, they have been pretty busy one way and another and the youngest child has been in hospital, too. We sent another film to Johannesburg for processing and received it back on Monday also, but when we set the projector up we found that sadly it wasn't working, and this being Mzuzu there isn't a great deal of chance that we can get it repaired.

We were tickled pink by your comments about Jacqueline and Janet − fancy them remembering us. It will be nice to show the films again when we get back to the UK, then we can explain where we were when so and so was taken. In fact, I did look fat on one of the shots taken on the boat on the lake. It was taken when I was about two and a half months pregnant with the baby I lost and, like yourself Mam, I seemed to have put on weight around the middle. But it soon disappeared. This biro is dreadful and I'm afraid my writing isn't much better.

Somehow, somewhere, I've lost my spectacles. I took them to work but didn't wear them very often, then in January I decided I should bring them back home but I can't remember actually doing so. Anyway, they are missing and it will cost a small fortune to get some more here, but we seem to do an awful lot of reading now so I need them.

Hope you can send my cut-out suit along soon as my present clothes are getting threadbare. I sold my green suit to someone at work recently which was good, as I only paid 30/-d for it originally. If the parcel is expensive, I can send a money order to you but don't forget to put 'Used Clothing' on the outside and 'No Monetary Value'. If you post it now, it should get here in time for the cold weather from May to August.

I knitted a cardigan last year but it's too large for me. I can fit plenty of jumpers underneath (it's very cold up here, sometimes), but it really does look too big so I'll send it to you August-time for your winter and, when that's finished, we shall be on our way home.

We have decided upon two alternatives, i.e. if Keith can get into university in September 1969, then we shall be spending a year in the UK before gallivanting off again, but if he isn't able to get into university, then we may try for another contract job in Swaziland − more or less between South Africa and Rhodesia. It's a newly independent country and next door to South Africa, so things should be cheaper.

Hope you liked your Mother's Day flowers. I don't know what they would be like, but my boss's wife gave me the address and really recommended the firm.

Keith is out playing bridge again with the White Fathers. It seems to be the only free time I get to write a letter when he's out, because after tea (dinner here) we usually start talking and then reading, and before I know where I am, the night is over and it's bedtime – about ten o'clock every night, regular as clockwork. I make it sound like I'm rushed off my feet, don't I? Anybody would think I had ten kids and a house to look after.

The job in the pub sounds fine, but do you think maybe there would be too much responsibility? At least now you know your work is finished when you leave the hospital until you go back the next day, but not so if you have the worry of how much food to order and whether it's cooked properly. And the pay isn't so fabulous, is it?

Hope you and Dad are keeping well.

Lots of love to you both.

Keith and Anne xxxx

THURSDAY, 11 April 1968

DEAR MAM AND DAD,

Here we are again. This time next year we should be on our way back home. Keith has written off for particulars of plenty of jobs – one in Germany – though we don't expect any replies for another four or five weeks. In any case, it's a bit too soon to apply formally for anything yet.

We had a letter from our friends at Domasi: Dick and Jane. They go back to Boston in June at the end of their contract. It will be strange at Domasi now as it's been 'Africanised', apart from Dick and Jane and the Clarks. Even the principal is an African. Dick and Jane have sent Fransisco, their adopted Ugandan son, back to America already as he found life at Domasi very slow. He really loves America and fortunately was never involved in any colour trouble at his school there, but I don't know how he will find it now that Martin Luther King is gone.

It is raining (again) and the flying ants are out in force. The cat is having a lovely time eating them. They are peculiar things as they come out of the ground as soon as it starts to rain and take flight, but their wings drop off nearly as soon as they set off. We stood and watched them the other day as they came out of their little holes in the ground, and almost immediately out came the big ants with lethal-looking pincers in front of their heads. They attacked the smaller ants and dragged them off back to the holes, presumably to eat. The houseboy's little girl is enjoying herself collecting the flying ants too, also to eat. They are supposed to be very tasty fried – I'll take their word for it.

It looks like I may have to appear in court as a prosecution witness against a prisoner. I left my spectacles at work because I didn't need them at home, then one day I decided to take them home but couldn't remember having done so, although I couldn't find them at work. About the same time, my boss was missing about ten packets of cigarettes from his desk drawer. He had bought them to give to the prisoners who clean the offices and tend the gardens at the police station. Then one morning, I arrived at work to find my office being used as an interrogation room and three of the prisoners who do the cleaning work being questioned. Most offices use the prisoners from the local prison to do the 'dirty work' as part of their rehabilitation. Eventually, one of the prisoners admitted having taken Mr Marlow's ciga-rettes and Inspector Mumba, who works with me, took him back to the prison to report what had happened, but my boss didn't want to prosecute (we have a soft commissioner of police in Mzuzu). I casually mentioned my missing spectacles and

Mumba said he would keep his eyes open. This was about six weeks ago.

Anyway, apparently today the office messenger, who also knew about my specs, met this particular prisoner who had ironically just been released from prison. The messenger searched him and found my spectacles in his pocket. He must have hidden them on his way back to the prison one day after completing his work at the police HQ which would have been very easy as they walk about in groups without anyone in charge of them. Then today, after his release from prison, he collected his ill-gotten gains. Had it not been a cold day and this chappie hadn't gone to warm himself on a brazier near the local shop, I would never have seen my glasses again, as the ex-prisoner would have gone back to his village and that would be that. The ex-prisoner immediately ran away and although my boss sent some policemen out to look for him, he hadn't been traced by lunchtime when I left. But they will find him I'm sure. I wouldn't normally prosecute but I have been told it will help the messenger if I do, as he is only a trainee policeman. In fact, he was the one who discovered the prisoner had taken the cigarettes out of my boss's drawer. It will probably help him if it's made public that he discovered the thefts. I feel a bit mean about it but they were fairly expensive spectacles.

Hope everyone is well. It's my turn to write to Barbara and Alice, so I'll have to get a move on. Give our love to everyone.

Bye for now and lots of love to you both especially.

Keith and Anne xxxx

TUESDAY, 7 May 1968

DEAR MAM AND DAD,

Sorry it's been a long time since I last wrote, but by now you will have received my postcard from Johannesburg. Bet you were surprised, as were we, at being told that some filming was to be done in such a hurry (as usual with Mr King). We received a short, scribbled note on the Thursday saying tickets had been booked on the Monday's plane to fly to Blantyre. From there, we were staying with our friends that night, flying out to Jo'burg on the Tuesday morning very early – in fact, we had to be up at 4.30 a.m. However, Mr and Mrs King seem to be very much like you, Mam, if you know what I mean, as they are always the last minute. They blame each other. Mrs King says the only time Mr King has ever been on time was at the wedding, and the only other time will be at his funeral!

As arranged, we stayed the Monday night with the Kirby's, and the King's said they would be around to collect us at 5.15 a.m. to give us time to get to the airport without too much rush. But when they hadn't come for us by 5.30 a.m. we thought we had better set off to meet them, carrying our heavy suitcases. We had arrived at their house before we actually saw them, and there they were, darting about falling over each other. We eventually left their house at 5.45 a.m. – VERY LATE! Consequently, Mr King was driving at a terrific speed trying to catch up time; we had about fifty miles to go to reach the airport. Suddenly, there was a 'pop' and then thuds at intervals coming from the car, but he kept going until it became worse, then he had to stop. Can you imagine our thoughts when we saw that the tread had peeled off the tyre and it was smouldering? We spent about five minutes changing the wheel, arriving at the airport to see the plane engines in full swing and the commandant of the airport looking furious. We all four had free tickets and the commandant knew that we were making this film and therefore knew that we would definitely be catching the plane. We climbed aboard the plane and it immediately took off. There is a rule at airports that passengers must be there thirty minutes before take-off. Talk about feeling embarrassed.

We spent two days and one night in Johannesburg and two days and two nights in Salisbury having a wonderful time. But we were quite disappointed with Jo'burg and still think Salisbury is by far the nicest city we have ever seen. We didn't have much filming to do – only scenes at the various travel agents and airport. Now the film is complete, so we are anxiously awaiting the results. Mr King says he should be able to let us have a copy – 8mm – by September this year, so we shall be bringing it back with us in April next year! (Author's note: We never saw the film, being told that it had been put on hold.)

We stayed at Domasi on the return journey to Mzuzu. Sadly, this is the last time we shall ever see Dick and Jane as they are returning to the US next month. We had a very enjoyable two days with them but were really shocked to see Domasi now. It is completely Africanised with the exception of Dick and Jane and the Clarks. All the gardens are overgrown, including our own old one which we always thought was beautiful. We must have taken dozens of shots of it on the various films we have but we hardly recognised the place. The house next door where the Canadians had lived was empty and appeared derelict. The whole place seemed like a ghost town. Keith and I say we are glad not to be there now, especially as Dick and Jane are leaving. The Clarks were upper class and old school seeming much older (and wiser) than us, even though they were only in their thirties. Strangely, we weren't too upset at being back in Mzuzu this time.

Have you got a job yet, Mam? Maybe you would like us to help you out a little? If you need any financial assistance, let us know, won't you?

Hope you are both well and taking life easy (easier said than done, you will say!). I seem to owe lots of letters at the moment; I had better get a move on and do something about it. We still correspond with a couple we met coming out on the boat (the Smiths) who were visiting their daughter and grandchildren in South Africa; the husband is a retired detective inspector of police. He said the weather wasn't too good in the south, so that means you will be even colder. We are having nice days here, but it is getting colder in the evenings now the winter is drawing nearer. We shall be at our worst when you are in the middle of your usual heatwave in June/July! Grandmother still keeps plodding along, doesn't she? They can't believe me here when I say she is still living at eighty-seven or so and had continued to work well into her 70's. The Africans retire at forty-five and consider themselves very old at fifty-five. They look old too, but I imagine it's because of the hard life an African lives and not eating the best of food.

Bye for now.

Lots of love to you both and look after yourselves, won't you?

Keith and Anne xxx

PS. Thought I was at the bottom of the page. There is still no news about a baby, but you never know. If I do get pregnant now, it will be too young to bring back by sea, so we are half hoping and half not hoping. Actually, I wouldn't mind flying back – about a ten-hour journey, amazing – eleven days plus by the sea!

XX

FRIDAY, 24 May 1968

DEAR MAM AND DAD,

Received your letter on Wednesday. I am glad you have found a job, although it doesn't sound very good. It would have been better to have stayed on at the hospital, although I don't know how you worked nights. I am sure you will soon find something that suits you more and the warm weather is coming on with the lighter nights, so travelling won't be too bad. Keith's mam is still at the Welfare Centre but she only works for a few hours and, of course, she gets a small widow's pension from Keith's dad, so I don't suppose she is too badly off. We had a letter from her on Wednesday saying that Margaret (Derrick's wife in Singapore) had come home on a concessional flight with the RAF. She had been instructed by Derrick to look for a large house in Batley, so it looks as though they are planning to stay there when they go back. But on Wednesday we also had a letter from Derrick himself telling us that Margaret was trying to get a concessional flight to the UK (his letter took two weeks to reach us). In the letter, he was asking us what we were planning to do and he said he wasn't sure about their plans. He also spoke once or twice about a house in South Africa. I'm confused now. I would be surprised if he is considering Batley – he could hardly wait to get away. But he said Margaret's health had been bad ever since they went to Singapore and he also didn't like the school he was teaching at. He is like Keith (i.e. has a mind of his own), and apparently the headmaster is a bit of a stick-in-the-mud who won't modernise the ways of teaching. It would seem that Derrick is always having rows with him about this. Margaret also had a teaching job but in another school, and she left because she didn't get on with the rest of the staff there either. Derrick never mentions what the town (or city) is like and he doesn't seem to go anywhere. He just sounds generally fed up and, of course, he misses the rest of the family. I don't kid myself that eventually we shall feel the same and shall want to settle in Batley – heaven forbid! – or Leeds of course, but at the moment we still have the travel bug.

If Keith does go back to university – it will take about nine months – who knows, maybe we shall have settled back into the routine again by then and shall not want to move off anymore.

On Sunday, I was talking to Sister Pauline, the doctor at the hospital, and she was asking me how the baby was coming along. I told her there was nothing at the moment but that I hadn't given up hope. She said I could go into hospital again and have an operation which might help, but as I pointed out to her, if I did that, the baby would probably be due just about the time we were ready to travel home and I'd like to avoid that if possible. On the other hand, I'm sure I would be pleased and we would probably postpone our journey home for a couple of weeks or months. But I think I'll let things take their course. She did agree with me and said it would perhaps be better to wait until we got back to the UK as the hospitals there are much better equipped.

Jack's mother-in-law is quite ill at the moment. Before we came out here she had been in hospital for a few months suffering from a nervous breakdown and depression, then thankfully she got better. But since we came out here she has been in hospital again three or four times for the same thing. Poor woman. Now she has had a brain operation but we understand she is beginning to feel a bit better. Margaret is naturally very worried.

We go to the club on a fairly regular basis these days as it is the linchpin to everything in Mzuzu. On Fridays nights, we now have Candlelight Suppers; one of the wives from our station is a good organiser and, together with her own excellent house-cook, has taken on the mantle of providing these special meals. This is a welcome break from the usual ham, egg and chips of the daily menu. The Suppers are so popular and for a couple of hours each week we can imagine we are back in the sophisticated world once more. In order to get a table, people usually have to book at least a week in advance and we were fortunate to get a reservation for Friday night of last week. To make it more special, I decided to knock together another dress, preferring to make my own so that there was no chance of me turning up with the same dress as another woman. Knowing that Kandodo only stocked a few styles of dress – usually from M&S – there's always a chance of seeing yourself coming without a mirror!

On the previous Monday while at work, knowing the Dakota had arrived from Blantyre, I popped down to Kandodo to see what goodies had been delivered. I saw some rolls of lovely new cotton material which I thought would be suitable for my new dress and consequently bought the amount I would need. I spent the next few days making what I imagined was a lovely garment and on the Friday night, getting dressed up, I thought I looked the bee's knees, knowing that I wouldn't look like any other woman that evening. We duly arrived at the club, had a pre-drink at the bar and when our name was called, headed for the back room which has now been converted to a small restaurant.

Can you imagine my horror when, on walking into the room, my eyes were met by the sight of the curtains, curtain ties, table covers, chair back covers, seat covers, serviettes and staff aprons, all new and all made from the same material as my 'special' dress? I looked ridiculous. If I had fallen onto the table no one would have found me! I could have cried. But all I could do was laugh with everyone else and get on with my meal. However, the first opportunity I have I shall be selling the dress on! Though I did achieve my goal inasmuch as I didn't look like any other woman that evening!

Only ten more months and we shall be on our way home. In any case, we shall be in the UK by this time next year. Did you say you had sent a hair cutter? If you have, it will be very useful, but if not, don't worry as I am managing very well. I have a regular order on the station now to cut other people's hair as well as my own. Someone in town was asking one of the people on the station where she had her hair cut, and who did it, so I may be getting another customer. Pity I don't charge. I attempted to cut Keith's hair once but he wouldn't let me touch it again after that once.

Bye for now. Hope everyone is keeping fit.

Lots of love to you both.

Keith and Anne xxx

PS. I have written to those boarding kennels at Birstall about quarantine for the cat and given your address, so they may write to you about it for you to pass on to me.

THURSDAY, 13 June 1968

DEAR MAM AND DAD,

I had started to write to you yesterday but got broken off. How are things back home? We are still interested in the Batley News and look in our box every week to see if it has arrived. I am always keen to see what's new from home and was surprised to see our old neighbour Margaret's wedding pictures shown this week. I know the man in the photograph with her isn't her father as I remember him as being a tall thin person, but the man with her certainly looked old enough to be her father, if not older. If I remember rightly, she is a bit younger than me. It's quite unusual for someone of her age to marry someone so much older than herself but I hope they will both be very happy!

Keith was supposed to be writing to you. You'll have to tell him off again in your next letter!

Did you ever receive the postcard from Johannesburg which we sent when we were down there in April? Also, did you receive the cheque? As you didn't mention it in your last letter we were wondering if it had perhaps been stolen as I think anyone could have cashed it.

I'm still looking forward to receiving the parcel you sent. It's been about six weeks now so it should be due any time. Hope it's intact and nothing has been stolen. Are you still working, Mam? I always said I would prefer not to work when we came out here but I'd be lost without a job to go to. In fact, when I leave here there are two people in Mzuzu wanting to take it over, so they must be feeling the same way. There is absolutely nothing to do at the station except neighbour and that's not in my line.

On Wednesday afternoon, I'm starting to help out in the domestic science room at the school because Louise, the teacher in charge, is always very busy. I can at least help the students to thread the sewing needles and shuttles. It will be something to keep me occupied in the afternoons for a couple of hours, anyway.

There were seven of us for dinner on Saturday and I made a nice dessert of cake, ice cream and meringue, and it was very well praised. I'm getting used to the wood stove now that we are nearing our end.

Bye for now and love to you both.

Keith and Anne xxxx

THURSDAY, 20 June 1968

DEAR MAM AND DAD,

Received your letter today. Just think, in just over nine months we shall be on our way home to see you all.

I have just spent a couple of days in hospital again, this time for the fissure, which is about one and a half inches long, has fibrous tissue growing over it and doesn't heal. The doctor didn't seem to know what was causing my pain until she put me to sleep on Monday morning. I had a lovely day on Monday; firstly, I had a visit to the dentist who has a practice in the hospital, then I had to get straight into bed and get ready to be wheeled down to the theatre. My appointment with the dentist was for 8 a.m. but the doctor wanted me 'got ready' quickly as she had to go to the airport to meet some visitors (it's the Bishop of Mzuzu's twenty-fifth year of ordination and Sister Pauline, the doctor, must have been the only person who could drive a car to pick up the people who had come to help celebrate). Anyway, Sister Concepta took me into the dentist and I heard her say to him: 'Can you see Mrs Walker first as she is the next on the slab' – charming, isn't it! Unfortunately, the doctor tore the fissure a bit more when she was 'grabbling', and for a few hours after I came out of the anaesthetic I was in agony. She says the only solution is to have the operation my dad had done when he was in the army. She said she was tempted to do it while I was 'under' but I had specifically said I didn't want that doing so she was afraid to take it on her own shoulders. She asked me what my reaction would have been had she gone ahead, and I said I would probably have been glad, but then I started having pain and I thanked God she hadn't done it as it would by then have been ten times as bad. Dad, can you remember what the aftermath was like? It would probably be better to have it done here than in the UK as here you certainly get the 'treatment'. If you want the nurse, you have a brass bell to tinkle – I think mine had Napoleon on the handle. It's just like a hotel room with your own sink and mirror, wardrobe, carpet, easy chair, lovely curtains to match the bedspread and the food isn't bad either. I felt sorry for Keith because I had left the fridge nearly empty as I thought maybe I would be in and out the same day and so could do shopping the following day.

Anyway, I had a nice rest if nothing else. I went back to work today and had to suffer some humiliating cracks. But I was surprised on the Monday after I had just come round when the nurse came into my room and said I had a visitor. I said to send her in, thinking it was probably Bernadette, my neighbour. But I could see the little African nurse looking a bit strangely at me and I got the surprise of my life when my boss came into the room, dressed in his full uniform. The nurse probably thought I had done something wrong and the police were coming to question me! Well, now you have the episode of 'when I had my operation' – well, not quite!

I received a letter and birthday card on Monday from Alice, which was very nice, though I'm not all that anxious to remember my birthdays these days – twenty-seven next, isn't it terrible? It looks like I shall have to start writing to adoption societies because there are still only two of us (I'm only kidding, Mam). Maybe Michael and Barbara could lend us one of theirs?

We went to a party at the head's house last night and if you could have seen us dancing you would have thought we were sixteen years of age (in the head, maybe). Jeff, the head, goes mad and usually has to change his shirt as he gets so damp, but he's great fun to have at a party. The deputy head was there, too (an African), but we're a bit afraid of him at the moment. There's no saying what changes he will make when he takes over as head.

We also think he is sending for the girls to go to his house (hope no-one in this place can read this – I'll get deported). But Julie, the school matron, is keeping her head down. She's a half African/half Portuguese lady. I saw her dodging the deputy head at Jeff's and thought it very funny.

Hope you are keeping fit. Give our love to everyone (what shocking writing).

Bye for now and lots of love to you both.

Keith and Anne xxxx

TUESDAY, 2 July 1968

DEAR MAM AND DAD,

Thank you for your letters (three) received this last week. We also receive the News regularly. When you said Tommy Bloomfield had died recently, I didn't really know who you meant until I received the recent copy of the paper. What an awful thing to happen to someone so young! It didn't say what he died of, either. Our houseboy's wife is still sick. Did I tell you? He thinks someone at the village is bewitching her and that she is going to die. She's only twenty at that. We've told him it's senseless to believe people can wish others dead, but the Africans are so superstitious they really believe it can happen and, because their belief is so strong, it does happen. In effect, they seem to wish it on themselves. The Sisters at the hospital cannot find anything wrong with Christopher's wife so have been treating her for malaria but now Christopher has sent her to the government hospital twenty-odd miles away, and he says they confirm that there's nothing wrong with her. Like a fool, Keith is running her backwards and forwards (grudgingly, of course). We've suggested Christopher send his wife back to the village to her parents in the hope they can help her. Hope he accepts our advice as there's nothing to be done! He came the other day and wanted to know the difference between a flying-insect, flying-aeroplane, and flying bacon – you remember I told you they interchange L and R. Keith nearly collapsed! There's a Howlers Book in the staff room at school with some really funny comments made by the students unknowingly. I'll copy some out before we leave. We are still waiting to hear about this university degree for Keith. The time is flying and we still don't know what's happening. I'm just listening to the tape recorder. Herman and the Hermits are singing 'I'm into something good'. Do you remember, Mam, you used to like that recording? I can remember when you would sing and dance along with them! My writing is really bad just now, but my arm is killing me 'cause on Sunday I was playing darts with Keith at the club – don't ask. I ought to type the letters because, surprisingly, I don't make quite as many mistakes that way.

There was a barbecue at the club on Saturday and a dance afterwards, but it's so perishing these days that we didn't bother with the BBQ instead eating at home and only going to the dance.

Keith is still stirring it up here I'm afraid. He has now had a barney with my boss, again over tennis at the club. Keith said he was quite civil, but apparently, my boss lost his temper and Keith says he was shaking with rage. In fact, he couldn't speak he was so mad. Oh, Keith is a bugger when he feels he's in the right. Most people are wary of my boss because he's the Number One man in Mzuzu, holding the most important position in the region. He is also high up in the Freemasons in the Northern Region, being the Grand Worshipful Master, and whatever he says goes. So, you can imagine how Keith loves to antagonise him. But I will admit, he's the best boss I've ever had and I like him very much, both as a person and as a boss. When I was in hospital last, as I mentioned in my letter, he came up to see me and was most concerned. He even held my hand. Of course, it creased Keith up when I told him. I thought my boss might criticise Keith to me on Monday after the row they had, but instead, he went out of his way to be nice to me. Keith says he bets my boss thinks that he (Keith) leads me a dog's life, so he's going out of his way to make up for it! But I don't care what he does so long as he gives me a good reference when we leave here…

Our neighbours are being transferred in two weeks' time and being replaced by an African. By this time next year, Mzuzu Secondary School will be mostly staffed by Africans, although there are only two at present, but many contract staff leave at Christmas and Easter like ourselves and will no doubt be replaced by Africans. Jeff, the Head, leaves the term after ourselves.

Keith has just come back from tennis at the club and tells me he has been speaking to a committee member who says there is going to be a meeting on Monday to discuss the problem raised by Keith about having to stop playing singles when doubles people arrive, and it looks as though Keith might win after all this time.

Bye for now and love to you both.

Keith and Anne xxxx

MONDAY, 8 July 1968

DEAR MAM AND DAD,

Here's another letter but I don't know when it will leave Mzuzu as it is a national holiday until Wednesday. I say 'national' but Keith still has to teach. I have had five days holiday including Sunday, but the weather has been poor so we haven't been anywhere. The holiday is to celebrate Republic Day – five years' independence. On Saturday evening, there was a dance at school and all the staff went. Unfortunately, there was a shortage of girls for the students to dance with, and the Head had asked the sister in charge of the Catholic girls' school here if the girls could come over to the dance, but the sister had said no. So, as usual, half the boys danced with each other. But the highlight of the night was when one of the First Formers came over to Keith and me as we were sitting, and asked Keith if he would care to dance. He doesn't often blush, but he did this time. His shell just crumbled away (I wish you could hear me laughing!) But he soon regained some composure, enough to tell the boy to go away! We didn't stay long at the dance after that!

Last night, we went to a surprise birthday party for the wife of Ray, the American teacher we know at the Catholic school. It was a surprise in more ways than one. There were only seven 'civilians' and the rest were White Fathers and Brothers, about a dozen in all. We had an extremely pleasant evening telling jokes, Father de Repartini telling the best. He said it was a bit dirty but nevertheless, told it all the same. It was: Two Americans were travelling to Scotland from London (it's a bit long-winded so I'll cut it short) and missed the boundary sign between England and Scotland, but suddenly, the first American said to the other 'Oh look, we have passed the boundary, we must be in Scotland. See, there's the toilet paper hanging out to dry!' Pretty tame by our standards. Apart from one, the clergy were either American or French-Canadian with the exception of one, who was Scottish, and Father de Repartini is his best friend, believe it or not.

One of the other priests brought along an accordion, so we had a lovely evening listening to all the 'top' tunes. We are really out of touch with the top twenty songs now I'm afraid. De Repartini had given the sermon at Mass yesterday morning, so he said he had already seen me that day, but he took me by surprise when he said he had seen me smiling at his sermon. I was smiling but didn't think I had made it so obvious. He had been giving the Africans a 'dressing down' about taking care of other people's property and not stealing, but he had made some funny comments in between. Well I thought they were funny anyway.

Robin Perrone, the girl whose party it was, is expecting another baby. The second baby was only born in March – there are a couple of months between them. The first baby is about eighteen months old. The strange thing is she seems to thrive on it. She taught this time up to about three weeks before the baby was born, then when he was about three weeks old, she went back to work. The hospital is still under construction so it's not easy being admitted onto a building site.

Our next-door neighbours are being transferred on Friday to Blantyre. I shall miss them a lot, especially Bernadette, as she is the only one I ever really befriended. Their replacement is also an African but he doesn't sound very stable. He has been convicted three times of killing three people, on different occasions of course, while driving his car. One of the people he killed was the only Malawian in the country ever trained to be a pilot. It's quite sad really when you think about it. All the money the country must have spent training him, then along comes this man and knocks him down. The teacher has been demoted on each occasion as he was a Headmaster originally, then a Deputy Headmaster, now he's just a plain old teacher. Glad he's not teaching me to drive!

It's the highlight of the week this evening. It's the film show at the club. Isn't it pathetic? It's like watching home movies. I suppose we should be grateful really though, as we could be in a much worse place (I think).

Christopher, our boy, has just spent a few days at his village seeing his wife. When we asked him how she was, he said: 'She is a bit all right'. The trouble is, it's difficult to tell from that whether she's dying or whether she's better.

Bye for now. Look after yourselves. Lots of love.

Anne xxxx

THURSDAY, 11 July 1968

DEAR MAM AND DAD,

I've just received a fabulous birthday present – your parcel arrived today. It was like Christmas, unravelling all the paper, and I've not had so many pairs of stocking and pants since we left the UK. I buy a pair of nylons each week for 6/11d and they last exactly that long – one week. Not many people here wear nylons but I wear them for work, even if they are laddered! The parcel arrived intact and I didn't have anything to pay, but it certainly cost you a lot to send, didn't it? The hair cutter will come in very useful, but I won't let anyone on the station know about it or else I'll find myself inundated with haircuts. It works smashing on my own hair. Keith has at last started letting me cut his hair now and I've just been using scissors so maybe the razor will be good for his hair, too. The Frenchman has also asked me for a haircut. He says he doesn't have it cut very often because he usually feels ill afterwards. What an excuse! I've told him he must come for a cut before he starts tripping over it, which is anytime now.

We had an enormous mail day on Wednesday. A letter from yourself, one from Barbara, one from Keith's mam. In her opening paragraph, she said: 'Margaret has gone back to Singapore now and I do miss her so much. She was such good company.' I think she was just being kind and I suspect she's glad to have her own house back now. We also had a letter from our friend in Zomba and the Batley News.

On the beach

We enjoyed Barbara's letter and photos. The young one sounds a devil. I was surprised to see how Karen had changed in the short time we have been away. She's quite a big girl now. The 'babies' are lovely too and Janet still looks very much like Michael. But my dad doesn't change at all judging by the photo.

We nearly died laughing to see everyone on the beach (including Dad and Michael) dressed in dark suits and dress shirts. And did my dad have his tie on? It's very rare that anyone here wears long trousers, even for teaching, and at the bay everyone wears trunks. I guess I've forgotten what cold summers there are sometimes in England. But the 'African summer' you are having makes up for it.

I still occasionally take my hot-water bottle to bed it's so cold here and we have another six weeks of coldness before it starts getting warmer. Can you imagine trying to predict the English weather like this?

We are trying to decide how to travel back home – by sea or by air. It's only just nine months now (or eight depending on term finishing). I still haven't heard from those kennels in Birstall about the cat. We were discussing the other night how to smuggle him into the country. The trouble is he makes such a damn noise. If we flew back we could put him to sleep, but our faces would give us away going through Customs. Then we thought about going back on an Italian ship and arranging to meet Jack and Margaret in the south of France, having a short holiday, and coming back with them. The Customs wouldn't be as stringent from France to England. But it's still a risk!

Thanks again, Mam, for the lovely things you sent, including the Phulnana cachous, and I'm glad nothing was missing (my breath smells so sweet now).

Bye for now. Lots of love to you and all.

Keith and Anne xxxxxx

THURSDAY, 18 July 1968

DEAR MAM AND DAD,

I've just finished making the suit and blouse you sent. It looks quite nice, too. Poor Keith – he has no room in his wardrobe because of my clothes overload. The dress you sent is a little bit big so I'm going to take it in at the sides, and with the surplus material, I can make a belt. They are selling dresses just like that one at the African bazaar near the market and they cost 69/11d. Hope it didn't cost as much as that!

I had a smashing birthday on Saturday. They had a little party for me after the sports competition in the afternoon and gave me a lovely cake which had been decorated by the wife of one of the staff members. She used to teach cake icing at Salisbury University so you can imagine how nice the cake looked. Louise, the Domestic Science teacher, is going to start giving lessons at the school and will charge £1 a lesson for eight lessons. Keith thinks it's a waste of time but, nevertheless, I'm going to join the class. Then on Saturday evening, we were invited out to dinner. I also had two 'callers' earlier in the afternoon – the Frenchman and another young lad. They walked into the house just as I was standing at the door bargaining for oranges, and I noticed as they walked by there were flower petals on the floor where they had passed. They then hid their hands behind their backs – yes, you've guessed it – flowers and chocolates! I was staggered as I've never done anything out of the way for them. Keith was just as surprised – he said he had no idea they were coming round.

It's funny, but just now one of these lads came round to see Keith and started banging on the glass door – it's 9.30 p.m. I've just had a bath and naturally I am in my nightie ready for bed, but without my dressing gown. I was caught between rooms and had to make a dash for the far side of the house. The curtain wasn't quite pulled, so heaven knows what he saw! And I'm sure his impression of the quiet wife of Keith has now diminished. Of course, Keith has no sympathy for me as he had bought me a housecoat for Christmas, but it's too much trouble to put it on. I'll learn! I walk around in all stages of dress with the curtains open and never think, simply because no-one lives directly either side of us, although, of course, it's possible people could be prowling around the garden. This reminds me of you, getting washed in the kitchen sink, Mam, and your panic when someone comes into the house.

We have someone coming to stay with us next Tuesday for a week. We don't know who he is except that Mr King (the person who made the film) mentioned us before he left for the UK. This man regularly comes to Mzuzu on business and would normally stay at the Rest House, but the accommodation is tatty and you have to provide your own food, so we have been asked if we will allow him to stay with us. We can claim for keeping him – I believe it's about £2 per day, so we should come off about even. I will have to buy a pair of sheets as my present ones are in tatters. It will be nice to see a new face for a change. However, I hope he doesn't drink much beer as it's 2/2d for a half pint bottle, so the £2 upkeep claim wouldn't cover booze. It's also awkward using the toilet when someone stays as you can only flush it once every twenty minutes or so. We usually have a bucket under the bathroom sink to help with the flush, but if this chap is a bit lah-de-dah, he'll wonder what he's letting himself in for. The cat won't be very pleased either as he sleeps on the spare bed every night. Our kitty has only stayed out about half a dozen times since we got him (except for the time he was lost) but he will have to sleep in the sitting room when the visitor arrives. I have to admit, the house is a bit small for three grown-ups, and it's going to be difficult making conversation with someone we don't know, with no TV to help or distract us. It'll be great - one week of sitting around the fire trying to think of something to talk about with a total stranger! Should be fun. Of course, he may not be as bad as we imagine. I hope not. Then, of course, there's always the club to go to if we get totally stuck.

It's now ten o'clock and we were supposed to be having an early night. Ah well, maybe we'll get one tomorrow night. Ten o'clock is fairly late here as many people got to bed as early as 8.30 p.m., and some even sooner than that. It's only at the weekends that we stay up until eleven o'clock and I'm usually falling asleep by that time. Bye for now and lots of love.

Keith and Anne xxxx

MONDAY, 29 July 1968

DEAR MAM AND DAD,

Today, I passed my driving test! As you can guess, I'm very pleased with myself.

My driving license

I also received Keith's birthday present to me – a lovely pearl ring – something I've been hankering after for a long time. All in all, it's been a day worth remembering.

Our visitor leaves the day after tomorrow too, so that's something to look forward to. He's a really nice chap, but it's just a nuisance having someone around all the time. There's one thing certain, we shall try to rent a flat in Batley when we get back so that we won't have to palm our bones onto people because no matter how well you get on together, it's a strain after a while. This house is too

My pearl ring

small for three adults and the plumbing is from the Ark. I told you in my last letter about the plumbing and the fact that we have to leave a bucket underneath the sink to fill with water to flush the pan. When the chap came I thought he was a bit 'uppish' and was dreading him going to the lavatory but, after seeing him eat his peas from his knife, I settled down a bit! He's about fifty years old and has three grown-up daughters. He bored us a bit telling us how good the girls were, how they had been to the best private schools and how his wife was such a good secretary that she was getting £150 a month in Zomba. In fact, the first night I doubted whether he and Keith would hit it off, but I needn't have worried. The only real worry is what to provide for meals. It wouldn't be too bad had he just been a friend staying for a week, but as the government is paying us to look after him, I feel obliged to lay on a spread, though he doesn't eat very much at all (is it my cooking?) He's gone out to dinner this evening to the headmaster's – they were in the same regiment in the army but didn't recognise each other at first – and Keith has gone out to play bridge again so, for a change, I can have a bath and lounge around in my nightie without having to worry what people will think (hope I don't get surprised again!).

Keith's mam is in Torquay at the moment and sounds to be having a brilliant time. She has gone on a tour with a woman neighbour and says it's the best holiday she has ever had. They keep stopping at pubs and one of the men on the bus is a bit of a comedian; he can play the spoons and his wife plays the piano so if there's a piano in any of the pubs the tour stops at, they all have a good singsong. I was telling Keith that his dad will be turning in his grave. He thought only the lowest of the low went to pubs drinking – he didn't know what he was missing, poor thing!

It was lovely going out driving by myself this afternoon. I drove miles just to get the feel of the car and at one spot came across a pack of baboons. Keith won't be using the car much now as he mainly drove me to work and back and the round trip to church. Now he can have a lie-in a couple of mornings when he isn't teaching the first period. He's nearly as happy as I am, I can tell you. I prayed to a nun to help me pass. This nun was the founder of an Order in Canada, and there is a Council in Rome set up to decide if she should be beatified. I know it sounds daft (anyway, Keith thinks so) but I promised that I would make a Novena if she helped me and, despite what Keith says, I know she did help me because on this test I didn't do too well as I was so nervous. Anyway, I shall keep my promise whether it's possible for such a thing to happen or not. Maybe it's because I have a feeble mind and need something to grasp, but it certainly helped to have 'something' to rely on.

Hope you are both keeping well. We are looking forward to seeing you again. I found a couple of blondish-brown hairs on one of the cardigans. It's nice to know you won't have changed at all! Not even hair colour.

Bye for now. Lots of love.

K and A xxxx

MY PEARL RING came as a big surprise as I had wanted one for such a long time. When we got my engagement ring six years earlier, I had been undecided whether to choose the solitaire Zircon (we couldn't afford a diamond ring) or whether to get a ring that had a twist of pearl and Zircon (apparently the Zircon is the oldest substance on Earth; the oldest samples are even older than the moon, which formed about 4 billion years ago. It is also 50% denser than diamond). I had often regretted not getting the two-stone ring, particularly as I thought the pearl was my birthstone. But in the end, I had gone for size as the Zircon was large and lovely. So now, at last, I had what I had always wanted. The ring had arrived by post a few weeks earlier in a package addressed to Keith. The packaging was quite large, like a book, which I assumed it was, and that it had something to do with his work. However, on my birthday morning, I recognised this as being the same package that Keith was giving me, and I was puzzled at first, as I hadn't expressed a desire for any particular reading matter. But when I opened the package and started to leaf through the pages of the book, I saw that my present was a ring-sized jewellery box sitting in a square cut-out of pages halfway through the book. It was a lovely present and had been purchased through Jack back at home. Good lad!

Unfortunately, over time, one of the pearls erupted, possibly due to the fact that I never took the ring off my finger for the first few years, whether washing the dishes or gardening. In the 1980's I had the two pearls coated in 9ct gold and continued wearing the ring until my finger got fat and I either had to leave it on or not wear it at all! My granddaughters will have the benefit in the end.

THURSDAY, 8 August 1968

DEAR MAM AND DAD,

Received your letter yesterday and the Batley News today. Things are pretty much the same here, except that we have been without potatoes for eleven days and there's not much hope of us getting any in the near future, so far as I can see. We have had rice, rice, rice until we're sick of the sight of it. In the Southern region, potatoes are probably going bad for want of selling, but no-one seems to think ahead about these things. I heard a rumour yesterday that the supermarket was expecting to get 400 lbs sent up by road transport but no-one seemed to know exactly when the delivery would arrive. So, when I was at the supermarket yesterday, I enquired about them but the staff are so gormless they didn't seem to know what I was talking about, they certainly didn't have any idea the potatoes were coming. So at 1.15 p.m. today, Keith and I went into town to see if they had arrived only to be told that they had arrived in the morning and been sold immediately. I could have cried.

Keith has finished teaching now for three weeks. Next Thursday, we go to the Luangwa Valley for three days; this is the game reserve in Zambia. We are hoping the Luangwa Bridge is now open as a few weeks ago it was blown up by rebels!

It was interesting to read the Letters column in the Batley News about Rhodesia, both for and against. The people against would get a surprise if they visited Rhodesia and saw how they were prospering despite sanctions and, as someone commented in one of the letters, Britain stopped buying tobacco from Rhodesia and now have to pay nearly twice as much from America for the same thing.

Also, you can't buy new British cars anymore. The Japanese now have a sole market and they are making a bomb as their cars are selling like hotcakes. Although our Morris Oxford is a BMC car, it was made in Rhodesia, but this was in 1965. The factory has probably closed down now because of spare parts difficulties.

We received a postcard from Mavis and Bill the other day from Spain. They seem to go every year now, together with the two boys. They must be doing well from their business as I hear the house in Carlinghow Hill is even better than the house in Dewsbury. How are Barbara's neighbours? Hope by now they have either quietened down or moved! Karen should be making her First Holy Communion soon, shouldn't she?

We are making provisional bookings for 30 April to sail back to the UK on the Castle line from Durban. That means we shall drive down to Durban, put the car on board, have our meals on board and sleep there, but while there we are allowed to get off and on as we please. We will use the ship as a hotel but get off during the day to see films, do shopping and general tourist things. Then the ship will travel to Cape Town and anchor there for a few days, so we can do the same.

The only thing that puts us off is the eleven days' journey from Cape Town to Southampton with only one stop and that's only for a few hours. We may cancel the booking at the last minute and fly home, which will only take a couple of days, stopping in Nairobi and possibly in Europe somewhere.

We shall see how we feel nearer the time. It's a pity the Suez Canal is closed, as that would be ideal because that route you make about a dozen stops in all.

Did I tell you about what happened to the prisoner who

stole my spectacles? When he appeared in court he pleaded guilty, so I didn't have to make an appearance. But he was sentenced to one year's imprisonment! I felt very guilty about that afterwards, though I believe they are happy in prison as they get good meals and clothes provided. And everybody convinced me that it served him right!

It's beginning to warm up now, thank goodness, just as you are starting to feel the cold. Hope it's warm in the UK next April/May. At least we shall have a car, although we have no heater in it!

Bye for now.

Love to you all.

Anne and Keith xxx

FRIDAY, 30 August 1968

DEAR MAM AND DAD,

Well, the school holidays are nearly over until Christmas, thank goodness. Keith is absolutely fed up. We get about ten paperbacks from the club library each week and have done so for about a year now, so as you can guess, there's not much left worth reading, and as there's no TV ... boredom.

These past three weeks have been taken up with the Mzuzu tennis championships and it was a prize giving night on Wednesday. Once again, Keith is the Singles Champion, and he and our American friend won the men's Doubles. Each prize was a beautiful copper mug inscribed 'Tennis Champion – Mzuzu – 1968' with either 'Singles' or 'Doubles' added, so at least we shall have something to remember Mzuzu by. Last year Keith won the Singles (he didn't enter the Doubles) and for that, his prize was a Dunlop Maxply tennis racquet. There were quite a lot of people present at the prize giving and you should have heard the reluctant clapping as Keith's name was announced:

95% of Mzuzu would have been extremely pleased had he lost. You can bet they are happy to learn that we shan't be here for the 1969 Championships – thank goodness.

We have a new member of staff this term. She may be lucky as there are many more males than females in Mzuzu, though she is about thirty and doesn't look the marrying type, but one never knows, she's not bad looking. Sue and Ken, the couple I told you about who only met in January/February and who went to the UK two weeks' ago to get married, are due back on Monday. They were going to spend a couple of days in York and I did think at one time of asking them to call in to see you but thought they would be rushing it, so didn't bother. Anyway, according to a short note Sue sent, they didn't have time to visit York and spent most of their time in the south. It must have cost Ken a fortune as he still has two years of his contract to do, therefore didn't have his fare to the UK paid, although Sue was okay as she was due for leave anyway. But with his fare and the expense of the wedding, we reckon he will have gone through £500.

She'll probably make him buy a new car too when they get back, as their present one isn't running too well. Poor Ken. He lived for thirty-nine or forty years without any aggravation or worry; now, look what he's got!

I was looking through an old scrapbook of Keith's last night and I came across a Sunday School Attendance Card for 1949 for Mount Pleasant Methodist Church. He had eight 'stars' in it because his mam had sent him off to Sunday School on four Sundays – mornings and afternoons – but by the fifth Sunday he had figured out a way of not going, so there were no more 'stars'. It never fails to amuse me how many hymns he must have learned in those four Sundays because he sings away with the radio if we ever manage to tune into a Sunday service.

I hear Princess Marina died during the week. She can't have been very old?

How are you all keeping? I understand it is very cold or at

least has been over the past few days. Still, I suppose you can't grumble as you seem to have had a fair share of sunshine. I bet Mike, Barbara and the kiddies are brown (that's if Mike takes his coat and tie off). I thought it was funny to see Michael and my dad in a snapshot Barbara sent, on the beach with their long trousers and coats on. Mind you, I am a bit out of touch with English summers and will probably do the same when we get back, but everyone here (including Keith) wears shorts, even at school to teach in. Can you imagine Keith walking down Briggate in his shorts? The IN thing in southern Africa these days is for men to wear safari suits, linen shorts with matching jacket and long stockings. It's even considered 'dressed up' in the large hotels where men usually have to wear a jacket and tie. I can see we shall have some trouble getting back into English habits again.

Bye for now.

Lots of love.

Keith and Anne xxx

Big PS. By the time you receive this letter, I should be eleven weeks' pregnant. Pray that I'll make the twelfth week (critical time!).

THURSDAY, 12 September 1968

DEAR MAM AND DAD,

Received your letters yesterday. Keith is out playing 'you know what' again across at school, so it's nice and quiet for letter writing.

So far, I'm still okay so far as the baby is concerned. I miscalculated the date, but I shall be three months a week tomorrow and the baby will be due at the end of March – the twenty-fifth-ish. We had planned to go to the Luangwa Valley Game Reserve during the school holidays last month, but four days before we were due to set off (I had an idea at the time that I was pregnant) I thought I was losing the baby again and Keith drove me straight to the hospital. After taking a swab and examining it under the microscope, the doctor told Keith he must take me home straight away. That I should stay in bed for about three weeks otherwise there was a good chance that I could lose the baby again; that in any case it was still a possibility, even with the precautions! We were in shock initially, but are listening to the expert. I had to let my boss know that I wouldn't be in for work and for the last three weeks I have rested. The doctor came to give me injections twice a week and now I go to the hospital for them. She said that I was lacking the hormone progesterone, which is the thing that keeps the foetus attached to the womb (or something like that – she used technical terms I didn't understand), and these injections should do the job for me until I was sufficiently advanced to take over naturally. They are lousy injections as the needle has to go very deep into the muscle to do any good, and they have to be given twice weekly until I am about four months. But it will be worth it if it does the trick.

Because I've been getting bored, I have asked my boss to send me some typing to do at home if they can, and they brought over a typewriter and some copying and odds and sods. Someone collects what I've typed every other day so I'm happy all round.

We have altered our passage booking to 7 May from Durban, mainly to give me an extra week in case I'm late, but also because it's a much better ship. We shall have to leave Mzuzu around 27 April in any case, because the person taking over Keith's job will be wanting to move into our house, as the new term will be starting at the beginning of May. Keith sent his notice to the Education Department the other day, so we have made a start on our homecoming. Even before the baby is born it begins to take precedence. It is funny, isn't it! You have to work out how it will be convenient for the baby before we book passages and how we can fit the luggage in the car to suit the baby – everything centres on it. You'll probably hear Keith cursing in Batley before the nine months are up, though he hasn't started yet! At the moment, he's wallowing in glory as everyone congratulates him. Of course, he says he could have managed without me at a pinch (the bum!).

There's going to be another wedding on the station on 30 November as the Frenchman has decided to take the plunge. The girl he's marrying is of Greek parentage, living in Canada. I can foresee some problems as naturally, she would like to live in Canada, but Jean-Pierre, being French through and through, doesn't relish the thought of speaking English for the rest of his life and his fiancé doesn't speak French! I'm sure he realises the problems he is facing and will overcome them. He says he is dreading this weekend as he has written to tell his parents (and his fiancé in France!) and they should be receiving the glad tidings at the weekend. He says his mother will probably faint – her poor little boy getting snatched up by a foreigner. He's twenty-four, by the way. He hasn't exactly led a sheltered life though, as he lived with his 'fiancé' before coming out here to avoid doing a full two years' National Service – he only did one year. He's an extremely likeable person though, and we all sincerely hope it's a good match.

When we were making the film last year, we met an Asian man in Lilongwe who works for British and American Tobacco Limited, the makers of most of the good cigarettes. He comes to Mzuzu about every two months and plays good tennis, so Keith usually sees him. He does auditing for a branch of his company in Mzuzu. Last week, we asked him to dinner and he brought with him two hundred cigarettes – king-size Benson & Hedges. They are sitting in the wardrobe as Keith doesn't smoke anymore, but it would be pointless sending them to you as they would be dry and battered by the time they reached you. Anyway, we are allowed to bring about three hundred each into the UK, so you may as well wait for fresh ones.

Hope your cold is better now and that Dad is keeping well.

Bye for now
Love,
Keith and Anne xxx

SUNDAY, 29 September 1968

DEAR MAM AND DAD,

Received your letter on Wednesday, although it seems ages since I last wrote to you. Hope you are both keeping well.

I'm still going strong – three and a half months now and, although I have to have the injections until four and a half months, the doctor says she is pretty sure I'm safe.

We may have to cancel our homeward passages again though, as the Head has just returned from a meeting in Blantyre and been told that we may have to stay on for another term as they are having difficulty recruiting another science teacher for April, saying they will stand a better chance of doing so in September. Unfortunately, there's not a thing we can do about it if it does happen as our contract says two to three years, termination to be at the discretion of the ministry concerned. But in August we can tell them to go and jump in the river, as we shall have done thirty-six months by then and aren't allowed to do more than this contract at any one time. It's a bit disappointing as we have made so many plans, but we have heard that the science teacher in Dedza – the secondary school in the Central region – is leaving in April after two and a half years and this will also apply to him. The difference being that since Easter he has had a chart pasted to his living room wall, marked off in half days up to the time he was due to leave, and each lunchtime when he went back to the house, he would mark off another half-day from his total. Can you imagine how he'll feel if they tell us we really must stay on? Poor devil! In our case, it might be a blessing in disguise, as the baby would be five months old in August, which is a better age for travel, I think. As it is, if the baby is on time, it will only be five weeks' old by the time we leave here. Whichever way it turns out, I'm easy as there will be inconveniences no matter what. Keith also feels the same way, but for the sake of face, we have both grumbled. Of course, there'll also be the matter of an extra £200!

I'm busy two evenings a week taking cake icing lessons here at the school – I believe I told you already. It takes an hour to just make up the icing as it has to be beaten with a knife into the white of an egg. You can bet the first thing I get when we get home is an electric mixer. We're concentrating on roses at present and I'm not doing too badly, although some of them do look like cabbages. I should be quite expert by the time we do get back (I hope).

There were a couple of 'baby books' I wanted as there are no prenatal clinics here, so I have no idea what exercises I should do. I don't know of any shops in Batley that might sell them, so I'll try to find out the publisher and send off to Blantyre or direct to the publisher.

We had a reply from the Ministry of Agriculture and Fisheries about quarantine for the cat and got quite a shock. It costs between 35/-d and £2. 10d. per week for six months plus about £15 fare to England, plus between £7 and £20 to pay for an official from the kennels in Harrogate (the only ones in Yorkshire) to be at Southampton to meet the ship – that will make him a £70 cat, and we can't decide whether or not this is worth it. I think not but Keith wants to bring him back. It's shameful to think about spending so much money on an animal when there are people starving in Biafra and places, but I suppose Keith is right as we are much attached to him I'm afraid.

Our boy has been on a week's holiday and returns tomorrow. It's been a devil doing everything myself, especially cooking. I know it sounds lazy, but it takes two to three hours of continuous stoking to get the oven anywhere near 400° (gas mark 5), which means the kitchen is like a blast furnace by the time it's hot enough to start preparing the food. And it's a heck of a job putting polish on stone floors, not to mention washing clothes in the bath! We don't even have the convenience of having bottled milk, which means mixing the powder and water every time we want a drink of tea. Talk about life in the wilderness.

Now I know how Livingstone felt.

Bye for now.

Lots of love to you both.

Keith and Anne xxx

PS. Oh, for some fish and chips!

TUESDAY, 22 October 1968

DEAR MAM AND DAD,

Well, I have good news. We can leave Malawi in April after all, so you can expect us in Batley some time at the end of May. We have changed our leaving date from Mzuzu to 26 or 27 April and will make our way to Durban as arranged. I do hope the baby is not late, but in any case, it should be old enough to travel and not give us too much trouble (fingers crossed). We can start thinking about packing up our things now that we know what is happening. I am still working and will try to stay on until sometime in January. The other European has given her notice to leave at the end of November and it isn't anticipated that there will be replacements for either of us until March/April time and I don't like to leave them in a jam. Besides, it gives me something to do as it is only half days and keeps me out of mischief.

We went to the Luangwa Valley Game Reserve over the weekend from Friday until Sunday. The roads were shocking and it was mostly bush. I was terrified that the car would break down and we would be miles from anywhere, especially as the heat was overpowering. We travelled nearly three hundred miles on Friday and had anticipated being at the camp by two o'clock, having left Mzuzu at eight o'clock in the morning. We took sandwiches and a large flask of orange juice and thought we would have enough with that. By four o'clock, we were still miles and miles from the camp and the heat was over 100°. I didn't think I would last to the end of the journey. It was a nightmare! We finally reached the camp at a few minutes to six, our camp being another forty miles further north, but we were so shattered we couldn't go on that night, and it was dark by this time and very dangerous because of the wild animals. We had paid to stay at the other camp (15/- a day) but instead, we stayed the two days at this first camp, which cost us a further £3 each per day. We were only able to go out between the hours of 4.30 a.m. to 8.30 a.m. and 3.30 p.m. to 6 p.m., because both we and the animals couldn't bear the heat. We then spent the rest of the day lying in a cold bath trying to breathe! The game warden at the camp, whose name is Norman Carr, has written a book about the two lion cubs he reared, similar to the Joy Adamson book Born Free, and we bought a copy of his book and had him autograph it. It will be a nice reminder of a hectic time. There is one thing we learned from our trip, and that is that we wouldn't live and work in Zambia for all the tea in China. At the camp, we had both Malawian and Zambian waiters and the difference was astounding to see. As soon as the Malawians learned that we were from Malawi, they all came up to us and introduced themselves. It was quite touching. They told us they had heard a rumour that Kenneth Kaunda, their prime minister, was going to kick them out of Zambia very soon, which would mean they would have to leave with just the clothing on their backs – no money, possessions, or wives and children. Many of them had married while in Zambia. So they said they were leaving of their own volition within the week, as the camp was due to close for the hot season! I must say we thought it was nice to get back over the border again into Malawi and feel safe.

There is trouble at work as one of the African bosses has

stolen £131-odd police money. When it was discovered he went missing for three days and, when found, he was at the regional minister's office here in Mzuzu, trying to get the Minister to sort the mess out. He was brought back to the police station under guard and spent the night in the police cell. It is quite a shock as he seemed such a nice fellow. You never can tell, can you? Some people seem unable to control their urges – to steal money, to indulge in sex and to drink too much – in that order.

There was also trouble at the school over the weekend concerning the African deputy headmaster. The headmaster, as well as most of the other people on the station, had gone away for the half-term holiday, but Keith and I didn't go until Friday, so we were in on this trouble. The deputy head had been caught on a previous occasion 'entertaining' one of the schoolgirls at his house and warned by Mr Goodwin that it had to stop, though the girl said she was his niece! A few days before the holiday started, this girl had asked for a pass-out to stay with friends in town, or so she said (they need passes as they all board here). She was given the pass-out but was also given fair warning, as was the deputy head, that they were to stay away from each other. Anyway, come Thursday night – 10.20 p.m. – the person who is in charge of the girl's dormitory came knocking on our door to say she had reason to believe this girl was staying the night with this African deputy head and what should she do? Keith and Reverend Jeffreys – the Church of Scotland minister who is based at the school - together with the school matron, went to the house of the deputy head and got the girl out of bed! The next day we were going to Luangwa, so it was not until we came back that we found the girl had been expelled and a report sent to the Ministry of Education about the deputy. The terrifying thing is that when Mr Goodwin leaves Mzuzu in August next (after us T G), this African deputy head is in charge of the whole school. Before Mr Goodwin was posted here the headmaster was an African also and the people in town have told us that he used to have a roster for the girls who would sleep with him each night. It made no difference that he was married. What a world. (Goodness... I'm nearly at the end of the paper.)

Bye for now.

Lots of love

Keith and Anne xxx

PS. We had a letter from Keith's brother Jack the other day, asking us to stay with them when we get back, so you needn't go to lots of trouble getting rooms ready. We shall stay with them for a couple of days and then look out for a house to rent. There are lots in the Reporter every week in the Batley area and it will be better than putting on people.

Xx

THURSDAY, 7 November 1968

DEAR MAM AND DAD,

Sorry it's been a while since I last wrote, and I bet you were wondering if anything was wrong. Things are pretty much the same – even the weather hasn't altered for months. It gets too hot in the afternoons – maybe it's because I'm putting on weight and my clothes are getting a little bit tight! I'm feeling fine in myself, thank goodness, not even a touch of morning sickness.

This time next month the cat should be in quarantine near London. We are sending him early so that he will be nearly due to come out when we arrive in the UK. We made the mistake of not sending him a little bit sooner, as then we could have collected him on our way through; as it is, he will be 'released' about ten days after we dock in Southampton. But at least it will give us ten days or so in which to find a small flat or something. About a month before we arrive in the UK, we shall place an advert in the Batley News for accommodation and ask Jack or someone to go and look at any property from any replies we get.

We are still counting the weeks to our leaving Mzuzu –

twenty-four weeks on Saturday/Sunday. I shall be glad when the baby comes because then, at least, I shall know we will then only have four or five weeks to our leaving on our return journey.

We are still doubtful about our future prospects and have been making tentative enquiries with universities in Canada for Keith to take a degree course. If he can do it in two years of part-time study and if the degree is acceptable in England afterwards, then we would certainly like to go to Canada. But it's still a bit early yet to do anything.

An amusing thing happened at work today. I had to sit in and take notes on a reprimand of one of the African policemen at the station – in fact, he is the policeman who taught me to drive and had been highly recommended at the time! It would seem the policeman had overturned a police Land Rover on the dusty road near his village where he had been visiting on police matters. But it was his mitigating circumstances that creased me up. When the officer-in-charge asked the constable why he thought he had overturned the Land Rover, which was now a write-off, the constable went into a long, drawn-out story saying that, as he was driving back to Mzuzu Police Headquarters, he had looked down at the dashboard and noticed that his petrol was very low. He had put his foot down on the accelerator in order to travel faster as he needed to get back to police headquarters before the petrol ran out completely, and in doing so he hadn't noticed a large stone buried in the road dust which he had hit with the front of the vehicle and turned the Land Rover over. I was staggered to think that someone who had that mindset had actually taught me to drive. Keith says he's ordering some walking boots!

Hope my grandma had a nice birthday, though I doubt if it would be any different from any other day. She must be really cheesed off with life these days, especially if she isn't able to go out of the house.

How is everybody at home? Hope you are all okay. Keith's mam seems to keep okay, thank goodness, apart from the usual colds like yourselves. Gerald and Jack are anxious for us to get back as they want someone to play tennis with. The Thursday nights' out they all used to have before we came out here – which started on the bachelor spree before our wedding day, would you believe? – seem to have fizzled out as we thought it would.

There is a basketball contest this afternoon between staff and students. I must take the cine camera when I go to watch as I'm certain they'll make a spectacle of themselves, especially as Keith and some of the others have never played before. There was a football match – staff versus students - about five weeks ago, and Keith twisted his ankle; it's still swollen, though he says it doesn't hurt.

Will strawberries be in season when we get back in May/June? I could just eat some now, with fresh cream. We haven't seen a strawberry in the eighteen months we've been in Mzuzu. I'll probably go mad when I see the variety of food, especially all those chocolate biscuits from M&S. Also, the sales should be about ready to start, and if Keith is teaching I'll have use of the car during the daytime. We'll be able to live it up occasionally, Mam, especially if you have an odd day off work, or we might even get my dad babysitting then we can go off in the evenings. Keith says he's happy for me to go on a spending spree – he's going to give me £1 to do anything I like with (isn't he generous?).

We're going to try to get a nice suntan before we come back, even though it will be gone in a few weeks, but as we are now, I doubt we'll look any more suntanned than you. When it's hot we just stay indoors, just the reverse to England.

We have another wedding on the site in three weeks; however, the marriage from last August doesn't seem to be doing too well. Maureen had booked a passage to go home at the end of this month, after three months of marriage, leaving her husband to fend for himself but we've talked her out of it, for the time being anyhow. She's already pregnant too, which hasn't helped matters. Still, it's her funeral (I don't mean that literally, of course!).

Bye for now.

Lots of love to you both.

Keith and Anne xxx

PS. Do you have any baby name suggestions?

TUESDAY, 26 November 1968

DEAR MAM AND DAD,

It's been a long time again, hasn't it? I keep putting it off thinking I'll have time to type a letter at work but then I find I'm too busy. Five months from today we'll be leaving Mzuzu for home! Then six months from today, we shall dock in Southampton. We have had confirmation of our sailing so, apart from packing, we are ready. Also, the cat leaves Blantyre a week today. At 5.30 p.m., we shall see the VC10 flying overhead on the way to Nairobi, and know that by six o'clock the following morning, Wednesday, the cat will have landed at London Airport. We have decided to quarantine him at Southampton, so if anyone is visiting London they can pop down to Southampton to see him (some hopes!) It's going to be terrible without him because he's just like a baby. We have a performance putting him to bed every night. Although he is an outdoor cat during the day, he is an indoor cat in the evenings as he doesn't like staying out at night. I only hope he's not too upset at the journey and the change in weather and people. The woman who owns the kennels sounds a nice old dear, though. She has asked for a list of food he likes and said to put any toys he likes in the basket with him. Also, to put an old jumper or something personal belonging to us in the basket, too. I know the kennels are centrally heated so he won't feel the cold too much, but he'll have a fit when he sees the snow. The upsetting thing is he will never be the same cat again and will have to start getting used to us once more when we pick him up.

I've sent off to Mothercare in London for baby clothes. I suppose I could have sent you the money and asked you to buy the things for me, but there aren't many local shops selling baby things in Batley and I imagine Leeds will be the nearest centre. Plus, I know you're working so wouldn't have much time to baby shop. Anyway, we can go to the sales in June/July for the things I've forgotten. I'm not doing too badly for weight. I am still wearing my normal clothes at five and a half months! I suppose I'll put it all on at once in another month or so.

I wrote to Grandma the other day. I doubt if she would be able to read my writing though, and would probably have had to ask someone to read it to her, so I was careful what I put in the letter!

The other afternoon the cat brought a snake into the house. He had killed it by biting the back of its neck. It wasn't a large one, but nevertheless, it could have been quite harmful if it got a bite in first. The cat was all for eating it as usual, but luckily, he always brings his 'catch' into the house to show us first, so Keith took it off him. The last thing I remember about the snake was seeing it lying on the floor in half-inch strips; I think Keith used the panga to decimate it! Our poor cat would probably have been poisoned had he eaten it, he's such a little dope.

I went to the local butchery today for some fillet steak, going to the back door as usual as the Africans were three deep waiting at the small dark open windows. The African in charge asked me into the back and took me over to half a cow hanging from the ceiling which had just been slaughtered (it was still warm), and told me to wait for him to chop its leg off with an axe. The smell of blood was overpowering and I could hardly breathe.

The market butchery is just a very large brick building with a few small openings acting as windows to serve the customers outside. Taking an axe, the African started chopping the ribs off the animal and I finally got my 4lb piece of fillet attached to four ribs. As he was chopping away, the blood was splashing about. At the other side of the passage was the other half of the cow in the company of two more halves of an animal.

It's a good job my stomach doesn't get too upset because you have no idea what the smell was like and I can't describe it either (metallic-y). They slaughter the animal outside the butchery, out in the open, with the African children hanging over the fence watching them. But this only happens after the local vet has inspected the animal, still tied up out in the open, and certified it fit to eat!

As I said in an earlier email, nothing is wasted. Someone buys the head complete, minus body, someone else makes a grab for the stomach lining, which is a colour I've never seen before – I've gone off tripe! Then the four legs disappear, complete with skin and hooves. I imagine someone even soaks up the blood as I'm sure there isn't an inch wasted. But as a mollycoddled and hygiene-conscious European, I find it all revolting.

However, it does make me smile to read the odd letter of complaint in the Birstall News when someone finds their milk sour and insists that, in general, the milkman should be instructed to deliver the milk to the doorstep before six a.m. If only you knew!

We get bottled milk from the supermarket three times a week flown up from Blantyre, and it's always sour or just going off, and at 2/1d a pint, it's quite expensive, don't you think?

Then the people back home complain about postal deliveries. Here, there is no such thing as a postman; everyone has to go to the post office to collect their mail.

It's the BIG wedding on the station on Saturday between Jean-Pierre, the Frenchman, and Evie, the Greek girl. Her dress has come from Paris and has cost a fortune. We're putting Evie's uncle up from Friday until Monday but, of course, being the boring person that I am, I'm not looking forward to it one bit!

Bye for now.

Lots of love to you both.

Keith (the silent partner… keeps saying he'll write!) and Anne xxx

TUESDAY, 3 December 1968

DEAR MAM AND DAD,

By the time you get this, there should be at least part of the Walker family in England. We sent the cat off to Blantyre yesterday, in the company of another cat (separate cages). He was terribly upset on Sunday after the tranquiliser we gave him to calm his nerves, and on Sunday night he slept with me, much to Keith's disgust. We then gave the cat another pill on Monday before Keith took him to the Mzuzu airport, and he seemed to go mad. He broke out of the cage and cried and cried. Luckily, I was at work so didn't know until Keith called in at work on the way back from the airport. He was really choked and too upset to sit down and talk. Of course, this made it worse. It wouldn't be so bad if the plane went straight to the UK. As it is, it lands in Blantyre at two o'clock Monday afternoon and the UK plane doesn't leave Blantyre until 4.50 p.m. Tuesday – it's now 3.15 p.m. Tuesday and I'm counting the minutes. We put some straw on the floor of the cage and an old sweater of Keith's, together with a tin of steak and a saucer. If anyone pinches his food or sweater it will be awful. I keep trying to console myself that he was not alone, as the cat that also went to the UK would be in the same predicament. Keith said the other cat was just as upset as ours. But I'm still worried to death about our cat. I keep putting myself in his shoes and trying to imagine how he must be feeling, as he is an extremely dependent and soft animal. If I went to lay down in the afternoon he would come into the bedroom, jump on the bed, lean against me and go to sleep; he did the same with

Keith. I can't stop crying and feel like I've lost my first baby again. Unfortunately, my imagination is too good as I can feel his suffering. We should be seeing him in about twenty-four weeks (if he hasn't died of a broken heart). (Author's note: Little did I know then!)

We had the big wedding on Saturday and the bride and weather were both beautiful. The bride's uncle stayed with us over the weekend but hardly ate anything. As with a previous guest, perhaps it was my English cooking! He owns a big electrical shop in Salisbury and asked us to go and see him and his wife in April on our way home. We shall certainly try to do so, but I know that we can't palm our bones, all three of us by then, onto someone we hardly know. It's easy with only one or two, but not three.

The 'little one' has bouts of kicking now and again, but doesn't keep me awake at nights – yet. I'm still squeezing into my normal clothes – I wore my coming home crimplene suit on Saturday and no-one could tell I was pregnant. I shall be twenty-four weeks on Friday, so I'm very proud of myself. On my last visit to the hospital my blood pressure was up. I'm surprised it hasn't blown the roof off my head these past three days. I bet I shall have a long thin baby with all the trauma – easier to manipulate on D-Day, so I'm not worried on that score. We're going away for a few days at Christmas to the Nyika Plateau, which is a high plateau further north containing wildlife, even lion we're told, although we're really unlucky where cats are concerned as we haven't seen a wild one yet. I guess we'll have to visit Manchester Bellevue Zoo when we get back as we shan't see any here on their home ground!

Now it's getting near I want to be packing up our things, but the carriers aren't coming to collect the baggage until 1st March. Only twenty more weeks on Saturday, then off we set, but an awful lot has to happen before then. Keith is anxious to get the new term restarted in January – though we only broke up from the autumn term today – because then he can say we're the next to leave. What makes you think we want to get out of here!

It's almost 3.50 p.m. and only one hour to go before the weekly plane from Mzuzu to Blantyre sets off. It passes over our house at 5.30 p.m., though it's usually too high to see, we can only hear it, and it's a bit cloudy today, anyway. This time yesterday Sam, our cat, was flying overhead and it breaks my heart to think that he's probably missing us as much as we are him. I feel as though I'm going through a bereavement at the moment which is stupid when compared with a real loss. Ah, well.

Bye for now.

Hope everyone is well.

Love to you both.

Keith and Anne xxxx

AS SOON AS the autumn school term ended on 3 December, we loaded our car and set off on the trip to the Luangwa Valley Game Reserve in Zambia. I was six months' pregnant. Some friends had recommended a precise route which took us over the usual dirt roads to south Luangwa but which, they assured us, was the shortest route. After travelling more than eight hours over roads that almost shook the skin off our bones, we finally arrived at the recommended crossing over the Zambesi River, only to find that the bridge was closed. If I close my eyes now I can visualise our arrival at this point, some forty-eight years later. It was stinking hot, well above 80° Fahrenheit, and the realisation of our situation was beginning to panic me. We had no air conditioning in the car and, as usual, hadn't prepared ourselves very much for the journey, at this point only having a couple of cans of cola and a bottle of water left to drink. Luckily, we had spare petrol and water for the engine secured in the boot of the car, but very little else.

Keith turned off the engine and got out of the car to stretch his legs, walking over to the sign. I was too spooked to do the same. I could see that apart from the sign telling us that the bridge was closed, there was no indication as to where we could cross. Isn't it strange how we women rely on men to solve these problems? I remember I had flippantly thought 'Keith will be able to sort it out', although I thought we would have to retrace our journey back to Malawi, another eight-hour journey, and this time in the dark. But, of course, Keith had other ideas. Getting into the car once more, he restarted the engine and we headed back along the road we had just travelled, once again rocking my 'internal' baby to sleep (or should I say jolting our baby to sleep). I held on to my stomach for all I was worth as Keith sped over the corrugations and indentations at what I imagined was great speed, but was in fact no more than twenty miles per hour. He had noticed a turn-off which I, in my daydreams, hadn't noticed, and upon reaching this, he headed straight on hoping for the best. Then a miracle happened. We saw a sign indicating that we were once more headed for Luangwa though, fortunately, we didn't know that it would take us another three hours to reach the camp where we had booked to stay the night. By now, the weather had cooled and we were feeling chilled. On our arrival at the camp we quickly unpacked and after taking our evening meal, we retired to bed, very tired but happy. Having been advised that the best time to see wild animals was in the very early morning we set the alarm for 6 a.m., only to find the camp almost deserted, most of the other occupants having awakened at 4.30 a.m.! Ah well, we would investigate the area ourselves. But by 9 a.m., the sun was beginning to glow and we were starting to overheat. Also, the camp was filling up once more with the 'residents' who were raving about the animals they had seen. To say we felt left out would be an understatement.

As the sun began to rise we began to wilt, and without any fans or A/Cs in the huts, like on a previous trip to a game park, we ran a bath of cold water and took turns to lie in it! Luckily, I hadn't put on very much weight at six months so wasn't displacing too much water. This became a ritual for us both twice daily.

SUNDAY, 29 December 1968

DEAR MAM AND DAD,

Hope you both had a nice Christmas. Received a letter and card from Auntie Mary saying you were going to Cleckheaton over the last weekend. Hope you stayed sober. We did, although we were not in Mzuzu. We visited the game park in the northern region of Malawi, which is a beautiful high plateau – 8,000 feet above sea level. There wasn't much game to see, though we saw impala, zebra and a few smaller animals, but no leopard, unfortunately, although some people there had seen leopard twice in the same day and those near the camp cabins we stayed in. We went walking through the woods a couple of times but didn't see anything of note. It is funny how nonchalant one gets after a while about wild animals, as we were asking for trouble walking about in the bush on our own. But we were hoping we would perhaps see a leopard from a distance and not that we would come face-to-face with one, though I understand if you do, you should just lie flat on your face. The 'cat' would probably come sniffing at you and perhaps paw you but, because you were lying still, would think you were dead – I would be from fright! (We often go walking in the bush around the school and there are plenty of snakes, though we're led to believe they would run away if they heard a noise). On Christmas morning, we were thinking about you both. At the time, we were stranded in the car sixteen miles from camp with our African game guard asleep in the back (he was a very helpful chappie, indeed!). We had gone out looking for game in bright sunshine on a 'road' which the game guard had said was a bit rough. What an understatement! It's a good job I'm only six months pregnant and not eight months or I would probably have given birth riding over the first mile.

Anyway, we were travelling along this narrow, ploughed field – sorry, road – stopping occasionally to look at the view which, incidentally, was very beautiful, when it started to rain a little. We were forty-odd miles from camp at this time, so we started to make our way back but, when we were about sixteen miles from camp, we came upon a steep hill, all muddy after the rain, and couldn't get up it. After a few attempts at pushing, which were unsuccessful because it's a big car, we had to turn the engine off as it was overheating. At about this time I was 'taken short', and made the excuse that I was walking to the top to see if there were any more hills. Suddenly, everything was enveloped by wet, cold cloud including me, and I only just made it back to the car. You couldn't see your hand in front of your face. Keith was sitting in the car but the guard had disappeared. I was nearly in tears but Keith was dying laughing – he could see the funny side of it. You were all probably saying 'Well, Keith and Anne will be sitting in the boiling sun drinking Coca-Cola', whereas we were miles from anywhere, it was dinnertime and we had been invited to the game ranger's house for Christmas dinner, and to add insult to injury, we had lost our guard. He eventually came back – I think he had been taken short, too – and promptly fell asleep again in the back seat!

We were there for two hours before the cloud lifted and the rain stopped, and by some miracle, we managed to get up the hill this time. When we arrived back at camp, the ranger had gone looking for us, our dinner was cold and the ranger's cook had eaten all the potatoes! Lovely Christmas Day. Then blow me, if we didn't get stuck again on Boxing Day, but we were only a mile from camp this time and it was all downhill. The ranger had to go out again with a team of five men to lift the car out of the mud. I bet he was glad to see the back of us.

The term here starts a week on Monday, 6 January, and I

finish work at the end of January. We will be leaving Mzuzu sixteen weeks on Wednesday, which isn't very long, really.

Keith has gone into town to help decorate the club's hall in readiness for the New Year's Eve dance, our last one here, thank goodness. I suppose the next weeks will fly. We'll have to put an advert in the Batley News a few weeks before we arrive back to try to get a flat or a furnished house for a while. I need to tell you this, Mam and Dad. We are seriously considering going to Canada if anything comes of the job that Keith has applied for. Then, after a couple of years, we shall have to settle down, I think.

I did read about Shirley Scott's dad dying but didn't know that Shirley was also in Canada. Do you know where? Probably somewhere in British Columbia where we would like to go, or maybe Vancouver.

We had a Christmas card from our pussy cat at the kennels. She must either be a sentimental owner or a good business-woman. Keith thinks the latter, I think the former!

Bye for now again and lots of love and best wishes for the New Year, and wishing you both the very best of health (and wealth, of course).

Love,
Anne and Keith xxxx

SIX

Letters From 1969

FRIDAY, 24 January 1969

DEAR MAM AND DAD,

Gosh, the weeks fly past, don't they? Yet we don't seem to be getting any nearer to our homecoming. We spend all our time wishing our lives away, I'm afraid, as we have our departure time mapped out to the last day.

We have asked the French-Canadian unmarried teacher on the site to be stand-in-godmother at the christening as we thought we should christen the baby before we left Mzuzu. The lady is forty years old and called Louise Toupin, and is a really nice person. Louise is absolutely thrilled to bits to have been asked to be godmother and doesn't stop talking about it. She would have loved children herself but it was not to be. She has had a tragic life as apparently, she was engaged to a Frenchman a few years ago, but had to go into hospital for, she says, a fissure – same as myself. While they were operating, they found that her uterus was stuck to her bowel (that's all I could get from her description) and, while operating, they accidentally cut through from one area to the other, giving her big, big problems. The resulting operations have left her in severe pain and have taken away her chances of ever having children so she called off her engagement allowing the man to marry someone else. So, all in all, she has had a hard time. She tells me that it is because of this trouble in her lower region that she is so fat there. Apart from Bernadette, the African lady and Jean-Pierre, the Frenchman, Louise is the only Catholic we really know on the school site, and knowing that in England we don't make much of christenings, we thought Louise could just stand in for Margaret; however, she is taking it all very seriously. In Canada, she says it's a big day when all the family gather together. They have a special christening gown which is always used for each subsequent baby, and in her particular church, the baby is presented with an enormous candle. Then, on any special religious day, such as First Communion, Confirmation, and even Marriage and finally death, this candle is always burnt, and in fact, is buried with the body, which is a nice idea (if you like that sort of thing!). She is always asking me how her godson or goddaughter is getting on and is making a christening cake for the occasion. I hope she doesn't embarrass us by spending any money on the baby, which she is quite likely to do. We have asked a Scottish White Father to christen the baby – aptly named Father McSherry. He seemed to think it was a great privilege to do so and even suggested we could have the bishop of Malawi christen the baby if we wanted (which we don't!). I know it all sounds very grand but Keith and I have decided that we should just go along with the flow and have a happy day, as Mzuzu is such a small place with not much to do that even a small occasion should be boosted to make a big one. Life gets rather tedious at times and any excuse will do. So, we're not grumbling. I'm still anxiously waiting for the clothes I sent off for from Mothercare in London. They were despatched on 21 November, over two months ago, and yet I haven't heard a thing about them since. There is nearly £20 worth of goods, both for the baby and myself. I'm in a quandary about nappies as I don't want to be bothered washing them on the boat, and yet the disposable ones seem so big for a little baby. I suppose I shall have to play it by ear and see how I get along. I'm not looking forward to nights on the boat as I shall feel very embarrassed if the baby cries because the walls of the cabins are like tissue paper. Sister Pauline, the doctor here, says she will give me some sleeping pills, just in case we do have any trouble. Sleeping pills for the baby – not for me! The purser on the boat is a good friend of one of the boys at the bank here and we are going to get an honourable mention so that if we do have any trouble, if the cabin isn't very good and providing there's a spare one, we might be able to get a change of cabin. But even if we can't, it's always good to know people, even if they are only friends of friends of ours.

We shall start packing our things in about three weeks' time. That I'm looking forward to as it is at least a start to our journey. The carriers are coming to collect our packing cases and trunks on 1st March. By that time, I'll only have just over three weeks to go before the baby is due. Sometimes, I can hardly believe anything is going to happen as I have been absolutely normal the whole of the time. I'm not looking forward to actually having the baby but, of course, it's a necessary evil. At the last check-up I mentioned to the sister/doctor that I hadn't been to any prenatal classes and didn't know what to expect, therefore could she recommend any books for me to read, but she surprised me by telling me in her best Irish accent: 'Now don't ye worry about not knowing what to expect, sure we'll be here to tell ye what to do at the time', which seems a bit scary to me. Jack and Margaret don't have a family yet, though I think Margaret would like a baby – I'll have to ask Keith to give Jack a talking to when we see him – that's if the forthcoming event hasn't put him off!

Bye for now.

Lots of love and looking forward to seeing you soon.

Keith and Anne xxx

TUESDAY, 11 February 1969

DEAR MAM AND DAD,

Received your letter yesterday. As you say, time is passing quickly to our journey home. I am leading a lady's life at present (and disliking it, I can tell you). There is absolutely nothing to do here during the day. Consequently, I'm not tired at bedtime and so don't sleep very much. No doubt things will change rapidly in a few weeks when the baby arrives but at the moment, I'd give anything for my old job back. I worked until the end of January but could have gone on longer. The baby is due five weeks on Friday, around 21st March, but it would be nice if it came on 23 March, which is Mother's Day in the UK, I believe. I've been knitting and making blankets and sheets but we have bought most of the baby clothes. I'm really looking forward to the sales when we get back.

You said you thought the matron at North Bierley Hospital was in the same order as a Dutch nun here in Malawi, but it can't be the same order as the nuns up here in Mzuzu because they are all Irish, from the Medical Missionaries of Mary, Co. Louth, though I believe there is a Dutch order somewhere in Blantyre. Or she may be in one of the out districts – out in the bush – in which case I wouldn't be able to find her, but if you can find her proper name, the one before she became a nun, then that might help. Our sister/doctor here was called Anne Hilliard, now Sister Pauline.

We shall be packing our belongings in a fortnight ready for the Road Services people collecting them on 1st March. I shall feel that we are really on our way once that happens. Keith sent to a film library in South Africa the other week for a film about the Windsor Castle, the ship we are travelling home on, and it arrived last Saturday, so we had a nice preview of things, except that I suspect most of the pictures were of the first-class section! But it is a beautiful ship. And we noticed a nurse attending to some young babies, so we should have an enjoyable passage back without being tied down too much. We anticipate the roads out of Malawi being bad in April but once we get over the border into Rhodesia, it should be plain sailing right through to South Africa. We shall be setting off when the staff here are on their way back to recommence term, and about six people are going to South Africa during the Easter holidays, so if there are any bad stretches of road they will tell us about them. It's just like us to leave during the rainy season! We can't believe how soon we shall be leaving Malawi – at this time, ten weeks' today, we should have been on our way south for about four hours, but it's going to be a nine to ten-hour drive to Blantyre via Lilongwe. From Blantyre to Salisbury, through Portuguese Mozambique is another nine to ten-hour drive, so that's two days of hard driving. I hope we have a 'good' baby, but Sister Pauline is all for giving the baby sleeping pills if we have any bother with it, and I suppose that's one way of having a quiet journey.

We have sold quite a few of our larger possessions – the tape recorder, radio, fridge, carpets etc, – so we won't have too much to pack, but over the years we have accumulated a small collection of copperware, plus two china cats – Siamese, of course. But thanks to slippery fingers Christopher, our boy, we don't have too many glasses or bowls to pack. I'm all for starting packing now but Keith says we should be able to do it all in one evening.

Hope by now you have started working and that you like your job, Mam. Don't you have to produce your birth certificate for superannuation purposes at the hospital before you can start work? Also, hope you both have recovered from your bouts of flu. From the newspapers, it sounds as though you have been having a spot of bad weather in the UK but perhaps it will have quietened down by May. We have had rain, rain, rain for days here and the grass in our garden is like a forest. Once it gets to this time of year it's a full-time job keeping it short even with the lawnmower, but our mower has been out of commission for months now so it has all to be done by hand with a panga – a long-bladed knife. As you can imagine, Christopher is none too happy about this. Still, it gives him something to do.

Keith will be in for lunch in a few minutes so I'd better close now. I usually cook something but it's going to be sandwiches today.

Look after yourselves.

Lots of love to you both. See you soon!

Keith and Anne xxxx

SATURDAY, 1 March 1969

DEAR MAM AND DAD,

Sorry it seems ages since I last wrote to you, but by now I have difficulty leaning over the table to write. We have no air letters left and there's no point buying any more so I'm having to use the normal post, but I shall have to make it fairly short. Wish I had my own typewriter (Keith says he will get me one when we get to the UK).

It will probably be the last letter I'll write for two or three weeks because I have to go into hospital on Wednesday, and on Friday the baby is going to be delivered by Caesarean section. By the time you receive this letter you will have already received a telegram from Keith. We are trying to decide what to put in the telegram and Keith suggests 'Father and baby doing well' – bum! You are not to worry though, as I am most certainly not worrying. In fact, I'm quite looking forward to it, especially as I shall know exactly when the baby is going to be born, whereas normally no-one can say to within a fortnight either way and in this heat, it's quite exhausting. Also, the baby will be almost seven weeks' old by the time we leave here, instead of three or four (if it had been late). It's been in the breech position now for a few weeks and the doctor has tried on a number of occasions to turn the baby although it's been too uncomfortable for me when they have tried as the baby seems to catch somewhere and then to swing back to its original position. It's what they call here a special baby because its allowed to develop normally although I wouldn't have carried it beyond the third month without the intervention of the doctor at the beginning. As the placenta isn't 100% safe it would be dangerous for the baby if they tried a normal delivery. We have a civilian doctor at the hospital now besides Sister Pauline and he is better qualified than she in baby care, so I have no qualms about anything.

By the way, I forgot to mention in my previous letters that the baby clothes from Mothercare arrived safely in January or beginning of February. They will wonder what on earth the matter is when they receive your letter! But don't worry. I doubt they will bother to waste a 9d stamp trying to find out!

It's a pity the baby isn't coming on Thursday, 6 March, as it's Keith's mam's birthday on that day.

We shall start our return journey to the UK seven weeks on Wednesday. We have already sent off our packing cases and trunk in readiness. It's amazing what rubbish one accumulates in three years. Do you remember I mentioned in my last letter that we had two pot Siamese cats that we treasured which we had bought whilst on holiday in Rhodesia? Well, last week, I knocked one down onto the stone floor and smashed its head off. We collected the broken pieces and Keith has provisionally glued them together and we have packed them for the UK. I understand there are places at home that do invisible mending on pottery. What will they think of next! It is a public holiday on Monday – Martyrs Day, Malawi branch. These are the people who fought the colonialists in 1963 and who were killed by the swine Europeans! All very friendly, I must admit, as I'm sure the locals don't know what Martyrs Day means, except that they are entitled to a free day's holiday. In view of the holiday, the mail won't leave Mzuzu now until next Wednesday. Hence the delay in receiving this letter.

Hope you have a nice Mother's Day on the twenty-fourth, Mam. I shall be one myself by then!

Bye for now. Don't you go worrying yourself about me as I'm in the best possible place so far as hospital treatment goes – much preferable to being even a private patient in the UK. In fact, that's exactly what I shall be here in my own little room.

Keith promises and promises to write to you as I write occasionally to his mum, but you know how much writing men do. In your next letter, you will have to call him a few names to buck him up a little – maybe that will get him writing a few choice names back to you! Think of some juicy ones!

Lots of love to you both. Look after yourselves.

Keith and Anne XXX

TUESDAY, 11 March 1969

A COMMUNICATION from Keith at last...

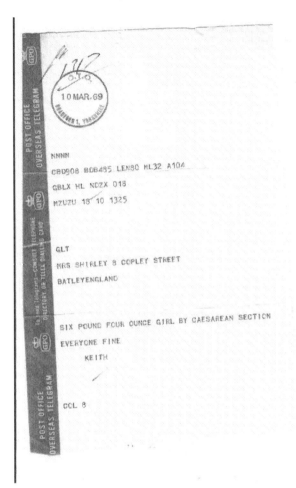

Linda finally arrived!

Dear All!

You should have received my telegram ages ago, so you'll probably know it's a girl. We are calling her Linda – hope you like it. You may know that she wasn't due until around March 21st, but for the last month or so was in breech position. The doctor tried unsuccessfully to invert her, so the Caesarean section was the best way. Anne went into hospital on the fifth to be put under mild sedation so that they could have another go at turning the baby but the new doctor, having discussed Anne's situation with some of the sisters, realised that having had two miscarriages, trying to invert the baby was not the correct thing to do and, therefore, on the tenth, she was given a spinal injection and the baby removed. Anne was conscious the whole time but didn't feel a thing. She saw the baby as soon as it came out, and I was with her as soon as she got back from theatre – no after-effects at all! The baby was 6 lbs 4 oz., which isn't bad for two weeks' premature. Some say she looks like me, some say like Anne, but to me, she looks like any other baby. She was born at 11.10 a.m. and by 4 p.m. the anaesthetic had worn off and Anne was going through hell with pain, but today she is much better and looks very well.

She should be on her feet tomorrow and out of the hospital in another week. She's very lucky to be in that particular hospital, private room, nurses in attendance all the time, etc. They really look after you up there, nothing is too much trouble. The doctor always explains very patiently what is happening and what he intends to do. In England, they just do it and that's your lot whether you like it or not. Anyway, you need have no worries, she's in very capable hands.

Well, that's about it, no doubt she'll be dropping you a line in a few days.

We leave here six weeks tomorrow for our ten-day 'holiday' in Durban before the cruise back – yippee!

Be seeing ya. Keith and Anne and Linda

LINDA WAS the first white baby to be born at the new hospital after its completion as, during the couple of years I had been visiting the hospital for various things, the place had been in upheaval – a complete building site. This was part of my problem – the reason for the Caesarean. Each time I had been to the hospital I had been seen by a different doctor or nurse and, apparently, no-one had made any notes, so the doctor who was now looking after me had no idea that I had previously had two miscarriages. My baby had been in the breech position for a few months and the sister-doctor had tried to 'turn' it during the prenatal visits I had made during the final three months of my pregnancy, but there seemed to be no paper trail to this effect. I went into the hospital on the Wednesday, expecting to have the Caesarean on the Friday, only to be told that the doctor was going to give it one more try to turn the baby but this time under light anaesthetic (presumably, in an effort to afford the easiest birth procedure for them).

However, I was sitting in the room looking out of the window, still in my outdoor clothes, when the doctor came rushing in and, to my surprise, began to reprimand me harshly. He told me he would never have considered turning the baby had he known of my previous miscarriages, that I should have told him and that there could well have been a problem doing the procedure. I was shocked at his lecture, but I pointed out that I had expected him to have seen the notes of my previous visits to the hospital. He said there weren't any!

I had my baby on Monday, 10 March at 11.10 a.m. Once I was on my feet, the lovely Swiss nurse who was looking after me suggested we take Baby Linda over to the African ladies' wards to show her to the new mothers there. It was a wonderful sight to see as they crowded round Linda, holding her little hands and feet and touching her face and hairless head. There were lots of 'oohs' and 'aahs', as well as shy laughter. One lady showed her newly born baby to me and I was surprised to see that her little girl had five fingers and a thumb on one hand. The nurse told me this was not at all unusual and that they would merely tie off the fifth finger at the outside of the hand and it would shrivel up and drop off eventually. Really strange, I thought. The ward itself was like any ward in any NHS hospital, but the difference was mealtimes when the African families would bring their own food to the hospital to feed their sick relatives, sometimes even cooking the meal outside on the veranda of the ward. I can only surmise that for the African, even hospital stay had to be paid for.

I was never able to feed Linda myself as my milk didn't come through immediately and by the time it did, she was already taking the formula well. At the time, I was thankful I wasn't breastfeeding, as I thought I would feel embarrassed nursing in the different locations and situations on our return journey to the UK, but with hindsight, it would have been far better to have been able to feed her myself. I was never sure about the germs in the water or bottles due to the unhygienic travelling conditions. We weren't able to buy a proper baby crib in Mzuzu so we had one made at the local African market. It was based on an old-fashioned laundry basket with a handle at each side and was made from wicker. I lined it inside with green plastic material and found a thin piece of foam at the market which I shaped to the base of the basket and covered in the same plastic. Linda remained in this 'laundry basket' crib until we returned to England two months later when we bought a proper carrycot, though we didn't have this in our possession for long, as can be seen from later letters.

SATURDAY, 5 April 1969

DEAR MICHAEL AND BARBARA,

Thank you for your lovely baby card. I was going to write last week but you know how it is! I seem to spend my entire day making up bottles, feeding the baby and washing Terry towel baby nappies as I don't trust Christopher, our houseboy, to wash them properly. Linda has had a bad nappy rash since she was only a few days old, so I have to be extra careful. She is four weeks' old on Monday and in some ways it has flown by, yet in other ways we always seem to have had her. Touch wood, she is very good, only having occasional spells of irritable crying between the 6 p.m. and 10 p.m. feeds, which I'm sure she will soon grow out of. She doesn't do too badly at night; I can usually get to bed by 11 p.m. and she doesn't often wake before 4.30 a.m. for her next feed. I made the fatal mistake of waking her around about 2 a.m. for the first few days because no-one had told me not to. Here, there is no pre- or post-natal clinic and I have to either rely on my Doctor Spock book or ask other mothers what to do. Keith sometimes gives her a feed at 10 p.m. if I have gone to bed, and the little blighter manages to get through 4 oz. milk in about fifteen minutes for him, yet she can take ages for me – the longest time being one hour ten minutes for the same amount!

We leave Mzuzu two weeks today, so this will be my final letter from here. It's quite sad in some ways, yet in other ways exciting, as we are both looking forward very much to seeing you all again.

We had a final party last Monday and were given a copper plaque of the school badge as a memento. Lots of the staff have now left the school site for their Easter holiday, so we have made our final goodbyes to them. It's impossible to live in a place for this long without getting attached to things and I know I shall be a bit upset on the day we go, though Keith says for him it will be the happiest day for years (other than our lovely baby). At least we have a nice holiday to look forward to, provided the roads out of Malawi and Portuguese East Africa aren't too bad and the car doesn't let us down and Linda doesn't cry too much…

Am I wishing for too much here? I only hope the cabin walls on the ship are soundproof for the baby. But on the other hand, we might get a better cabin if she disturbs enough people. But again, on the other hand still, we might end up swimming back!

I've been caught out this weekend as I hadn't realised it was Easter until it was too late and I have nothing extra in the house to eat – no butter, no bread, no meat and no money! I've been trying to be careful what I bought in the food line, having only a few weeks to go. I didn't want a stack of tinned food when we left but now the cupboard is bare. Oh oh, the monster awakes... it's time for her feed.

Last Sunday, we had Linda christened. She is called Linda Anne as the priest wanted a saint's name, too. Most of the school staff who were still on the site went to church and came back for a cup of tea and some christening cake, which our neighbour had made and iced.

It was a miserable, dark day and we weren't able to get any good shots of the cake on film, but it was designed as a crib with a beautiful lacework of icing all around and a quilt and pillow of organza with the name 'Linda' in icing on the pillow. It must have taken hours and hours to do. I hope there is at least one reasonable shot of it to show you all back home.

The African sisters came to church and sang some hymns which Keith recorded, and even the doctor came for the church ceremony. He was going to come back to the house but never arrived, so we assume he was called away on an emergency. These are the people I shall always remember and even Keith agrees with me. The priests and nuns are so unlike the ones at home. They don't ever try to push religion down your throat and are as ordinary to talk to as anyone. Keith has spent many happy hours playing bridge with the Fathers and Brothers and religion was never even mentioned. In fact, they could hold their own when it came to expressing their feelings at being dealt a bad hand!

Linda should be going on for three months' old by the time

we arrive in the UK – not really a baby anymore. At least she should be taking an interest in things and not just demanding food and sleeping (and crying). It will be nice to see the reactions of the kiddies when they see her. Give my love to them.

Bye for now – see you both about 26 May.

Happy birthday, Karen and Michael.

Love,

Keith, Anne and Linda xxx

LINDA'S CHRISTENING was brilliant and different to anything I could expect in the UK.

Unfortunately, it was a cold, rainy day and therefore we had dressed her in an 'all-in-one' suit before we left the house, with the intention of changing her into her christening gown just before we went into the church.

Louise had given us the christening gown, which was a long white satin dress, the long skirt gathered into six rows of smocking. It had tiny double sleeves and was fastened at the back with tiny satin buttons. It was finished off at the back, near the smocking, with a pretty flat bow.

It was so lovely and so kind of Louise to produce the dress as she had already spent hours and hours making and decorating the christening cake.

About a month before Linda was born, and after I had completed my 'Cake Icing Lessons', Louise had suggested we make a candle (for use as explained in an email above). It was a time-consuming matter, as the candle turned out to be approximately four inches thick and about nine inches high and, when completed, I could see how it could be saved for perpetuity.

[Author's note: we continued travelling for a number of years after this time and sadly, somehow, the candle was lost at some point during our travels.]

The guests to the christening arrived independently and, for a while, we stood outside the church talking quietly, showing off our offspring, then suddenly, without any prior warning, Father McSherry opened the church door and invited us all in.

We hadn't had a chance to change Linda into her beautiful christening gown and sadly, she was in fact christened in her little white 'all-in-one' outfit, much to the amusement of the guests. It was a day I shall always remember.

SUNDAY, 13 April 1969

DEAR MAM AND DAD,

This is probably the last letter you'll receive from us in Mzuzu as we set off on our journey back next Sunday. We shall stay overnight at two stops in Malawi and two nights in Rhodesia (I shall make sure I have a good look at the shops in Salisbury), then perhaps two nights en route to South Africa. We shall have approximately one and a half weeks in Durban before the boat eventually leaves. We have to get to Durban in good time in order to get a garage space on board ship for our car as, if there are no spaces left, the car will have to stay on deck, braving the sea spray for nineteen days, which won't do the paintwork much good. It's already chipped all over from the stones thrown up on these dreadful roads.

Peter and Pat, a young couple from Manchester who we met here at the secondary school while teaching and whose wedding we shall be going to in August in Manchester, set off on their journey back on Thursday last week and though they are flying back, we have planned to meet up with them in Durban for a few days and they can then see us off on our final journey. Our arrangement then is that Chris and Wendy, who became our friends when we were living in the south, are going to meet the boat in Southampton and take us back to their home in Basingstoke for lunch. Although the boat docks early in the morning on 26 May, we don't get off until about eleven o'clock due to the formalities of Customs and Immigration as well as having to wait for the car to be offloaded. We shall try to make Batley on the same day, but it will most likely mean staying overnight somewhere past London if we are delayed too much. We shall keep you posted by postcard anyway, as we make quite a few stops between Durban and Southampton.

I keep thinking it's the last time for this and the last time for that and personally feel very sad that we are leaving after two years in one place. Keith says I'm mad as I have hated it just as much as he has, but there are one or two nice things about the place I shall miss. There are only four of the 'originals' left now and two of them leave next term. There is still no replacement for Keith, or for Peter and Pat, our friends from Manchester who teach maths and biology, so with Keith's chemistry and physics not being taught, I don't know what they will do with four fewer of the sciences. Still, that's their problem.

Did I tell you already? The Ministry of Education here say they have no replacements for leaving staff as they forgot to advertise the posts. Can you imagine the uproar in England if the Ministry of Education admitted that? Somehow, the Africans here seem to have no sense of urgency and just go unperturbedly through life. We have an African living next door now and he spent time in Rhodesia obtaining a degree in economics. He is one of the very few who admit that Africans are not ready yet to take over their countries. He says he has been waiting for his pay from the Ministry of Education here since last October. He can't even afford to buy curtains for the house and he is living on loans from the headmaster. You should hear what he says about his own people. It would turn your ears blue. I wouldn't be surprised to hear that he had been deported before the year is out!

Linda, our offspring, is doing really well with just occasional crying, vomiting, etc. She is steadily putting on weight but hasn't been weighed for over two weeks and I don't make my final visit to the hospital until Friday. But she should be nearly 8 lbs now.

She is five weeks' old tomorrow. Doesn't time fly by? I've bought a baby's cereal for her to try but I'll wait a few more days yet.

We have the president of Malagasy, an ex-French colony in the Indian Ocean, paying a visit to Mzuzu, and Malawi in general. I had to go to seven o'clock Mass today because he was having a special Mass in French at eight o'clock, but this meant I was up at 5.30 a.m. this morning as I needed to give Linda her feed before I left. Keith offered to feed her but it wouldn't have made all that much difference really, although I wish I had taken him up on it as it's now 9.30 a.m. and he's still in bed, lazy devil!

It's strange the habits one gets into because normally, if we are still in bed at 8.30 a.m. and the boy is around, we feel very guilty at appearing so lazy. Mind you, we go to bed at 10 p.m. which helps. No wonder there are eight or nine pregnant European women in Mzuzu at the moment. As Keith says: 'Well, there's no TV here!'

Bye for now. Sending lots of love to you both until we see you on 26 or 27 May.

Happy birthday too, Dad.

Love,

Keith, Anne and Linda xxx

KEITH and I left Mzuzu on Sunday, 20 April 1969.

We docked in Southampton on Monday, 26 May 1969. The car journey from Mzuzu to Durban had lots of glitches, more than we could ever have imagined.

It took hours to load the car before our journey started, the back seat taking up all the baby things, including the baby in her Moses basket. We had to take a large plastic bread box and numerous bottles of the baby-bottle steriliser, as the feeds and sterilisation had to be done on the run. We stayed overnight in Lilongwe, travelling for hours from Mzuzu on dirt roads, but once we left Lilongwe the following morning, we were on tarmacadam – although of course, it was single track tar. Nonetheless, the journey seemed like heaven until we hit the Malawi/Portuguese Mozambique border, where we once again took up the dirt roads. I can't even say the bumps put Linda to sleep as we were either being bumped off our seats over the rocks or being drummed to death on the corrugations.

It was such a euphoric feeling to finally reach the Mozambique/Rhodesian border crossing, but that wasn't without its problems. The Zambezi River crossing which separates Mozambique from Rhodesia via the car ferry was busy by the time we arrived, and we had a long wait while the ferry was being pulled back and forth over the fast flowing river, but eventually, our turn came. Once across, Keith and I took a deep breath as we felt we were finally on our way home.

View of Cecil Square, Salisbury from the Meikles
Hotel. Such beautiful jacaranda trees.

We stayed in Salisbury for two nights catching up on a little retail shopping, then proceeded on our journey south. The car was full to overflowing and it wasn't practical or hygienic to keep soiled nappies in the car, so we disposed of them as and where we found a suitable place. We travelled through scrubland and empty roads and, much to my shame now, we left a trail of detritus that could have been considered a health hazard. Once over the border into South Africa, we heaved a sigh of relief knowing that here at least we would be able to buy most of the necessities that were unavailable in Rhodesia.

Keith and I drove on towards Durban, mile after unrelenting mile of asphalt, recognising that each mile was one mile nearer home, but it was harder than we had anticipated or been led to believe it would be, and each night we were glad to rest our aching bones in a bed before continuing the interminable journey south.

We stayed one night in a town called Newcastle, which was reminiscent of a street scene in one of the popular Roy Rogers western films. During our previous hotel stops, we had found that we were being charged for the baby, for accommodation and hot water for her feeds, which we thought unbelievable, as she had her own travelling cot and surely, warm water was available all the time in a hotel. Feeling we were being fleeced each time we decided that, at this stop, which appeared to be a motel rather than a hotel, we would leave Linda in the car while we checked in. Access was through a reception area but egress was via metal steps at the far side of a long outside corridor (which was presumably a fire escape). Keith checked in, leaving me in the car with Linda and, once we had the room key, I carried the baby into the room via the 'fire' steps. During our evening meal and breakfast, we ordered tea with extra water and then surreptitiously filled two or three feeding bottles with the excess hot water, which we used for Linda's night and morning feeds. After breakfast for both us and our baby, and while Keith went down to reception to settle the bill, I crept out of the room with Linda in her carrying basket and retraced my steps once more down the fire escape steps and into the parked car.

Keith and I quickly drove off feeling proud of ourselves that we had saved a few Rand by not declaring our baby on the bill. That evening, tired and weary once more, we booked into the next hotel on our journey. We showered and readied ourselves to go down to the restaurant for our evening meal. Going to my suitcase to pick out the only good pair of shoes I possessed which, incidentally, I had bought while in Salisbury on our third night, I couldn't find them. It only took a few seconds to realise that, in my hurry to leave the room quickly that morning, I must have left them under the bed in the Newcastle Motel as I knew I had worn them at our evening meal the previous night. We had saved a couple of Rand on water and spent tens of Rand on shoes. Of course, I had to get another pair in Durban. I nearly cried with frustration. Even now, nearly fifty years later, amazingly I can remember what the shoes looked like: they were brown crinkly leather, flat heeled, round- toed and with a flap at the top, and had leather soles and heels.

[Many, many years later, I visited South Africa and the town of Newcastle in particular, but my recollection wasn't good enough to find the Motel again! Memories].

We arrived in Durban as planned a week before the boat was due to arrive and booked into a hotel near the seafront. Unfortunately, Linda's colic had now become an evening nightmare both for her and for us, and the long journey south hadn't helped. We weren't 100 per cent sure it was colic; it was just that Doctor Spock said it was in his book. Poor Linda. She was always affected in the evenings, after her 6 p.m. feed, and usually just as we were getting ready for our own evening meal. I would burp, jog and nurse her, but nothing seemed to take away her pain. I believe we took it in turns to eat that first evening at the hotel but realised we couldn't cope with another three weeks of this. The following morning, feeling the need for expert advice, we took our beautiful, helpless, tiny, new-born baby daughter to a chemist near the hotel where we explained the situation to the dispenser. Without hesitation, he immediately recommended some strong cough medicine (!) which he said would put her to sleep. What did we know? We were inexperienced first-time parents, and I shudder now to think that we actually followed the dispenser's advice.

I tried this medicine that evening when the screaming started, but it didn't appear to make any difference, so we shamefully put our baby daughter into her sleeping basket and sat it just inside the wardrobe with the door partially closed. We could still hear her muffled screams as we hurried down to the restaurant for a quick bite to eat. The same routine continued on and off for the whole of our stay at the hotel, and we were thus prepared for what we were to experience on the ship during our homeward journey.

Once on board and settled into our tiny cabin, we were

introduced to the cabin steward who was a big bear of a man with dark brown wavy hair, aged about thirty and with a strong Geordie accent.

Keith and I got used to the predictable pattern each evening as, almost immediately after Linda had had her evening 'meal', she would start crying just as we were trying to get ready to visit the restaurant for our own meal. I would go through the routine of burping etc, but it never made any difference, there was absolutely nothing I could do to relieve her stomach pains. It was so sad but so frustrating at the same time.

We sailed from Durban making two short stops; the first stop was East London and the second was Port Elizabeth. At neither of these stops did we leave the ship. The next time we stepped onto terra firma we were in Cape Town once more, where we remained for three days before setting sail for home. In Cape Town, we bought a pram-cum-pushchair, which came in useful on board once we were really on our way, and I spent a good part of each day walking around the deck pushing Linda in the pram.

During the long journey back, we befriended our cabin steward who was such a nice guy. Having discussed our evening mealtime problem with him we decided upon an arrangement whereby, as we were leaving the cabin after having made our baby comfortable, we would find the steward and let him know that we were going to the restaurant to eat. He would then keep an eye on the cabin 'in case' Linda started crying though invariably he would be found standing at the door to the restaurant, waving his arms like a banshee to get our attention to inform us that Linda was crying again! At those evenings, Keith and I would take turns to finish our meal, one of us sitting with Linda often until she had fallen asleep. Amazingly, this was almost the only time she ever cried. She was generally an incredibly placid baby.

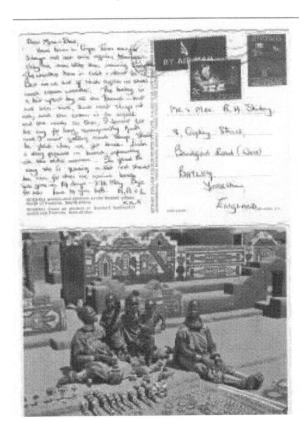

During the day on board, we would wheel Linda around the deck in the pram and people would come up to us asking to look at our new-born baby. She was so young she was almost a celebrity. I only remember one occasion when she cried badly during her daily walk and that day, after wheeling her around trying to lull her to sleep to no avail, we decided to give up and go back to the cabin. Linda was still screaming when we got into the lift, which was already occupied by two elderly ladies. Having tried everything possible to quieten the baby, we just wanted to get back to the cabin where, in the coolness, we hoped she would fall asleep. Above the sound of Linda's screaming, one of the ladies loudly said to her friend: 'If people can't take care of their children properly, then they shouldn't have them.' I felt mortified and very hurt at the time, as anyone with two eyes could see that we were obviously struggling to cope with our new-born daughter. But I must now admit that, before we had Linda, I would have said exactly the same thing.

Early one morning, when we were two days sailing out of Southampton, we returned to our cabin with Linda, after having had our usual speedy breakfast, to find a telegram on the bed advising us that our lovely, adorable, amazing, irreplaceable Siamese cat had just died! Strangely, I feel much more sadness now at losing him, while typing this, all these years later, than I did at that time. Our new baby was using up all our energy and our priority was to keep her safe. Yes, we were sad, but I think we were more worried about Linda; whether she was going to cry at the wrong time, whether she would pick up a bug, whether we would pick up a bug. There was probably too much going on for us to grieve the loss of our lovely cat who, as can be seen in my letters home, I had never, ever, called by his official title, Sam. He was always 'cat' in my letters. We consoled ourselves that we wouldn't now need to break off our homeward journey to go to the cattery in Southampton to pick up Sam, as we wanted to get home as quickly as possible.

We had previously arranged for our two friends from Zomba to meet us at Southampton port, but the arrangement was changed at the last minute and instead, we drove to their home in Basingstoke and had lunch with them, finally arriving in Yorkshire in the late afternoon.

Our first stop was to quickly visit our parents and show them our lovely daughter, then we headed for Jack and Margaret's home, where we stayed with these two wonderful people for a couple of months until we were finally able to sort out our own accommodation.

Linda at 3 months, taken outside Jack and
Margaret's house shortly after return.

Unfortunately, at the time we arrived back in England we
didn't really know what we wanted to do in the near future, but
knew that we needed money to keep us going, although we
didn't want to spend the gratuity we had worked hard for in
Malawi. So, Keith applied for a teaching post at the local high
school near our temporary accommodation with Jack and
Margaret. Thankfully Keith got the job and, because the school
needed someone to fill the post urgently, the local borough
council granted us a housing association flat to rent; thus, we
joined the land of the 'under privileged'. We furnished the flat
with second-hand furniture, making it comfortable, and this was
to be our home for the next six months.

Teaching in the UK was a shock for Keith, both culturally
and intellectually. He had taught overseas for nearly three years
at schools and colleges where most of the time the children all
wanted to learn; they were like sponges soaking up anything you

were willing and able to teach them. However, even in 1969, the rot in the UK was setting in so far as discipline in schools was concerned. Within a month of taking up the position, Keith inadvertently found himself in conflict with a youth at the school and, not getting any support from the Headmaster, he gave his notice to leave at the end of that term, December 1969. We realised this would be our future if we stayed in England and so, after a very short discussion, we decided to try our luck overseas again. I was more than happy to do this, even though I knew I would be taking my daughter away from her grand-parents.

We originally requested to go to Canada, Keith applying for a position in Vancouver, and he even went up to London for an interview for the position. However, we finally settled for Rhode-sia, though, initially Keith had submitted an application to the South African Embassy to work in Cape Town. We had been surprised at the time to receive job application forms to be completed from a school in Bulawayo but, remembering how lovely Rhodesia was, and having decided our lives would surely be better upon returning to Africa, Keith completed the forms and in January 1970 he became a science teacher at Gifford Technical College for boys in Bulawayo, Rhodesia. We realised afterwards that the white South Africans were intent on keeping a buffer between them and black Africa for as long as possible, and were redirecting job applications on to Rhodesia whenever they could.

SEVEN

Rhodesia

We flew out to Salisbury, Rhodesia, from Manchester International Airport on Monday, 19 January 1970, changing flights twice, firstly in Nairobi and then in Johannesburg. Because of Rhodesia's Unilateral Declaration of Independence, the UK government mandate stated that no goods or planes would be allowed to fly into the illegal state of Rhodesia. Consequently, the journey with our baby daughter was long and tiring.

There was no baggage allowance for our baby at the UK airport and the allowances for ourselves weren't enough to cover even our own needs particularly as we were, to all intents and purposes, emigrating. So, trying to outsmart customs at the UK airport, we had packed the base of the baby carrycot with a number of tools we knew we would probably need for the new car which we had purchased in the UK and which was being delivered to South Africa to await collection. We had also packed a good supply of nappies and other bits and pieces for the baby. However, the air carrier weighed every single item of baggage (including the baby and her carrycot) and, in the end, we were so over our weight allowance that not only did we have to leave the contents of the carrycot, but we had to leave the carrycot as well. This meant that, for the next 24 to 36 hours, we had nowhere to lay our baby down, having to physically keep her in our arms even whilst we dozed on the flight. They were all heart!

Then, shortly after we arrived in Rhodesia, we received a letter from Midland Bank in Dewsbury advising that the Bank of England had instructed them to freeze the balance on our account due to our immigration to a country no longer recognised by Great Britain. However, we weren't too worried. Before we left we had withdrawn most of our funds, and the amount being 'frozen' by the Bank of England was precisely £0. 2s. 4d. (11½ p); we thought this was hilarious as it had cost the bank more in postage stamps than the amount frozen.

We had fallen in love with Salisbury on our very first visit that Christmas 1966 when we had holidayed at the Wankie Game Reserve, passing through Salisbury on our way back to Malawi. However, this time on our visit en route to Bulawayo, knowing our stay was possibly permanent, we had found it even more enchanting. The people we met, whether black at the railway station or white at the bank, were equally lovely and, from the moment we arrived, we wished we had been posted to a school in this city rather than Bulawayo. It was such a clean, neat city and was particularly lovely at that time of year (January), with the jacaranda trees lining most of the streets. We truly lost our hearts. I felt that I had already died and gone to heaven and must surely be the luckiest woman alive at that moment.

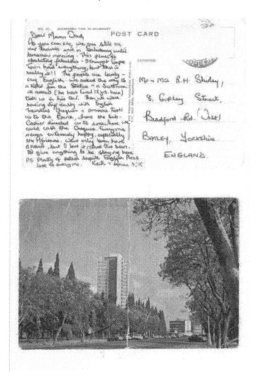

Our first stop - Salisbury en route to Bulawayo

I wrote to my parents:

"As you can see, we are still on our travels and in Salisbury until tomorrow morning. This place is absolutely fabulous– I thought Cape Town had everything, but this is really it!

The people are lovely, very British. We asked the way to a hotel from the station and the Scotsman we asked (he has lived here twelve years) took us in his car. Then we were having difficulty with English traveller's cheques and someone took us to a bank. Everyone seems extremely happy, especially the Africans. We've only been here five hours but I love it (what I've seen of it). I'd give anything to be staying here.

PS. Plenty of petrol, despite the English press."

RHODESIA HAD MADE a Unilateral Declaration of Independence on 11 November 1965 after earlier discussions between Great Britain and Rhodesia had failed on the issue of majority rule in Rhodesia.

Our main concern on deciding to live in Bulawayo was the implication of the economic sanctions that had been imposed on 12 December 1965, after another and final round of discussions between Ian Smith and Harold Wilson had failed to end in a suitable agreement. The cruiser HMS Tiger had been sent to Gibraltar on 1 December 1965, and between 1 and 11 December, the cruiser had sailed through the Mediterranean to ensure the talks between Ian Smith and Harold Wilson would be conducted in the strictest secrecy. But as HMS Tiger cruised through the choppy waters of the Mediterranean, the atmosphere on board turned as turbulent as the weather. Unfortunately, the two men failed to come to an agreement suitable to their respective countries and the British government went to the United Nations for their advice.

Once sanctions had been imposed, Wilson had blustered that UDI would fail in a matter of weeks and not months, but it was clear from the outset that force would never eject Ian Smith. The sanctions only caused inconvenience, as some goods were still being imported and exported to and from Rhodesia. Fortunately, Switzerland and West Germany were not members of the UN, so conducted business as usual.

Iran still provided oil, Portuguese marketed Rhodesian products via false 'Certificates of Origin', and South Africa refused point blank to accept the UN sanctions. However, we didn't notice too many imported goods.

Signed Proclamation of Rhodesia's Unilateral Declaration of
Independence

Translation of Rhodesia's Proclamation of their Unilateral Declaration of Independence

Whereas in the course of human affairs, history has shown that it may become necessary for a people to resolve the political affiliations which have connected them with another people and to assume amongst other nations the separate and equal status to which they are entitled:

And whereas in such event, a respect for the opinions of mankind requires them to declare to other nations the causes which impel them to assume full responsibility for their own affairs:

Now, Therefore, We, The Government of Rhodesia, Do Hereby Declare:

That it is an indisputable and accepted historic fact that since 1923 the government of Rhodesia have exercised the powers of self-government and have been responsible for the progress, development and welfare of their people;

That the people of Rhodesia having demonstrated their loyalty to the Crown and to their kith and kin in the United Kingdom and elsewhere through two world wars, and having been prepared to shed their blood and give of their substance in what they believed to be the mutual interests of freedom-loving people, now see all that they have cherished about to be shattered on the rocks of expediency;

That the people of Rhodesia have witnessed a process which is destructive of those very precepts upon which civilisation in a primitive country has been built, they have seen the principles of Western democracy, responsible government and moral standards crumble elsewhere, nevertheless, they have remained steadfast;

That the people of Rhodesia fully support the requests of their government for sovereign independence but have witnessed the consistent refusal of the government of the United Kingdom to accede to their entreaties;

That the government of the United Kingdom has thus demonstrated that they are not prepared to grant sovereign independence to Rhodesia on terms acceptable to the people of Rhodesia, thereby persisting in maintaining an unwarrantable jurisdiction over Rhodesia, obstructing laws and treaties with other states and the conduct of affairs with other nations and refusing assent to laws necessary for the public good, all this to the detriment of the future peace, prosperity and good government of Rhodesia;

That the government of Rhodesia has for a long period patiently and in good faith negotiated with the government of the United Kingdom for the removal of the remaining limitations placed upon them and for the grant of sovereign independence;

That in the belief that procrastination and delay strike at and injure the very life of the nation, the government of Rhodesia consider it essential that Rhodesia should attain, without delay, sovereign independence, the justice of which is beyond question;

Now Therefore, We, The Government of Rhodesia, in humble submission to Almighty God who controls the destinies of nations, conscious that the people of Rhodesia have always shown unswerving loyalty and devotion to Her Majesty the Queen, and earnestly praying that we and the people of Rhodesia will not be hindered in our determination to continue exercising our undoubted right to demonstrate the same loyalty and devotion, and seeking to promote the common good so that the dignity and freedom of all men may be assured, do, by this Proclamation, adopt, enact and give to the people of Rhodesia the constitution annexed hereto;

God Save The Queen.

Given under our hand at Salisbury, this eleventh day of

November in the year of Our Lord one thousand nine hundred and sixty-five.

Prime Minister (signed by Ian Smith)

Deputy Prime Minister (signed by Clifford Dupont)

Ministers (signed by John Wrathall; Desmond Lardner Burke; Jack Howman; James Graham, 7th Duke of Montrose; George Rudland; William Harper; A. P. Smith; Ian McLean; Jack Mussett; and Phillip van Heerden.

MY FIRST LETTER FROM RHODESIA

THURSDAY, 22 January 1970

C/O Roslington Hotel
   71 Wilson Street
   Bulawayo
   Rhodesia

DEAR MAM AND DAD,

I'll start this letter today, though goodness knows when I'll finish it.

We arrived safely on Tuesday morning after a very tiring flight and an overnight train journey from Salisbury to Bulawayo. Linda didn't sleep much at all on Monday night, only about three hours. Consequently, Keith and I were both tired out on our arrival here. To make matters worse, we were collected from the railway station and taken straight to the hotel to dump our suitcases after which Keith was whisked straight off to school, supposedly to teach. All this after having had approximately five hours sleep in the last forty-eight! The poor thing was tired before we left the UK, so you can imagine what he looked like by this time.

It is now Saturday. It's nigh on impossible to write with Linda around. We are booked into the hotel for two weeks and it is a bit chaotic living in the one room but we have a fair chance of getting a small furnished flat next week. Keith teaches from 7.30 a.m. to 1 p.m. and, apart from two afternoons when he has sport, we have the rest of the days to ourselves. He says it is a fabulous school so far as discipline goes, but we understand the head is a bit of a tartar: he's domineering, bossy and overbearing, though I'm sure Keith will soon cure him of this! Bulawayo itself is all right but not nearly as friendly as Salisbury. We doubt if we shall settle here, but are pleased about the prospective flat. We also have our name down for an unfurnished house which will become vacant in February but that means we have to get second hand furniture – again!

Things are much more expensive here than we at first thought and the shops seem nearly empty of stock. Sanctions really are hitting Rhodesia, even though no-one will admit it.

We are still comparing things with Malawi and now think it would be nice if we could go back, though I bet you never thought you would hear me say that! We are finding the heat very bad here in Bulawayo, the difference being that Mzuzu was on a plateau and the weather was usually lovely. If we wanted the heat we would go down to the Bay. Linda's arms are really red and her little face too, so I shall have to watch her in the sun. She's everyone's favourite here at the hotel and has a grin for everyone. There's one particular woman resident who she just sits and stares at - someone with white hair and glasses, but she's a little bit fatter than you, Mam. However, Linda won't go to her, but she looks and looks!

It's now Monday and I'm determined to finish this letter today. We went to the park yesterday and at the little zoo there was a tame baby deer. Linda loved it but so far as she was concerned, it was still a 'puthy'. Then the peacocks and rabbits came for a stroke and they were 'puthies' also! She absolutely loved the swings and the toy train.

I'll have to go out and buy some more nappies today as we were overweight at the airport and had to leave behind the carrycot and about twenty terry towelling nappies, as well as other things we had 'hidden away'. Even so, we had to pay £14. 15s. extra to take our stuff with us on the plane. Has Jack brought the pram over yet, Mam? We are planning on getting it sent over to us as prams are very expensive here.

We'll write to Jack to explain what to do.

Sorry Mam and Dad, hope you will be able to read this. It's nearly impossible to write in the same room as Linda as she's grabbing the paper and pencil! (My writing must have been worse than usual if I had to apologise for it!)

The couple who own the local garage have asked us to go swimming at their private pool next Sunday. They have a baby six and a half months' old with lots of ginger hair, but she's so tiny that Linda could easily eat her for breakfast!

Sorry we had to leave before you phoned on Monday; they had cancelled all the flights from Yeadon that morning but we didn't know it and, unfortunately, we didn't enquire until after lunch and then we had a mad rush to get ready to catch the 3.45 p.m. train. We even had to leave the three-piece suite in the flat, so don't know what has happened to it after we left. We didn't have a chance to say goodbye to anyone except Keith's mam and Mavis. I apologise for that it's a scrappy letter and will write again as soon as we move into the flat.

Lots of love to you both.

Big special X from Linda.

Keith, Anne and Linda xxx

WEDNESDAY, 4 February 1970

FLAT 13 CASA Di Bella

Grey Street

Bulawayo

DEAR MAM AND DAD,

At last, I'm able to sit down and write a letter in one go! We moved into a one-bedroom furnished flat on Monday and, although it's not brilliant, at least it's better than the hotel. We have an African girl named Belta working for us now, which leaves me free to do my own jobs. She also looks after Linda, taking her for walks, giving me a few peaceful hours during the day to catch up on things. Unfortunately (or fortunately whichever the case may be), Belta doesn't cook, so we only have her come in in the mornings and occasionally at night to babysit. Linda seems to like her but when I'm around she clings to my skirts, not letting me out of her sight for a second, even following me to the toilet! Linda had a nasty bang on the forehead yesterday as she slipped on the polished floor and caught her head on the cot. I was a bit worried for a couple of hours as she had an enormous lump which was turning purple, but she didn't seem to feel any pain after the initial shock of falling. I watched her carefully to make sure she wasn't acting any differently and today the bump is nearly flat, though still discoloured. I'll continue keeping an eye on her for a few more days to be doubly sure.

The people at the hotel were forever complimenting us on having such a happy baby as she always has a grin for everyone (and, you'll be pleased to hear, I think she has a few more hairs on her head).

The weather has cooled down considerably, thank goodness. It's strange how quickly the temperature can drop too, as in Monday's paper it said that Sunday had been the hottest January day since 1933, yet in Tuesday's paper it said that Monday had been the coldest January day since 1942! Sunday's temperature was 90.4°F and Monday's temperature had been 60°F.

I bought a freezer full of meat on Monday for 21/- - I got 2½ lbs pork fillet at 4/6d. lb, 2 lbs T-bone steak at 2/6d. lb, two pork chops at 6d. each and 1 lb bacon at 4/6d. lb. It's all best-grade meat too, not like in Mzuzu.

But cars are terrifyingly expensive. Had we known, we would have kept our Malawi car, which we had taken back to England, and brought it here, together with the new one as cars cost almost double in Rhodesia. Someone at the hotel is bringing a £2,000 Jaguar car over and selling it after six months. He says he has already been offered £4,000 for it. If we're short of cash after having had our car for six months, we are going to sell ours, too. The chap at the local garage said we'd get £1,700 for it, and it will only have cost us £840 alto-gether. The annoying thing is we would have been allowed to bring in two cars duty-free, but we didn't know all this before we set off from England. Cars the same year as our old one are selling for £595 - and we sold ours for £275 cash! There are some really old cars running around Bulawayo but the body-work is still in pristine condition with no rust in sight, but I understand that this is because it is so hot and there is no humidity.

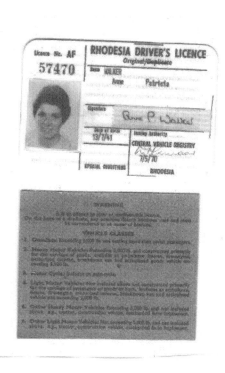

My Rhodesian driving licence.

Keith has just gone to play tennis for the first time since we arrived. He has had difficulty breaking into the cliques at the school as they stay in their various groups and ignore newcomers. In fact, he had been at the school over a week before he knew the names of any members of staff. Today will be the first time he has met anyone outside the school, so things are looking up a bit. He thinks the school is very nice but, compared to Mzuzu, teaching conditions in his laboratory are not so good. I'm afraid there'll never be another Mzuzu Secondary School no matter where we go, although I know we complained constantly while we were there. The devil you know.

I went for a job interview yesterday, mornings only, and the pay is pathetic – only £35 a month. If I'm offered it I will take it as there isn't as much scope here compared to Salisbury where, according to the paper, they are offering £50 to £60 for the same twenty-two hours. We're feeling that Bulawayo isn't for us in any case, and are thinking about asking for a transfer to Salisbury because Keith wants to get out of teaching altogether before he gets too old to train for anything else, and Bulawayo is just a small town so there isn't much scope here for him. If we can transfer to Salisbury, he can begin to look out for something else. We certainly don't intend settling in Bulawayo and if we can't get to Salisbury, who knows? Maybe teaching in Mzuzu again or back to the UK. We've nearly exhausted the possibilities, haven't we?

There are some beautiful houses for sale here, but…!

I'll have to seriously think about a job if Linda and I are going to be visiting you next year. Anyway, that's another day, isn't it? Hope you and Dad are keeping well. Have you got a job yet, Mam?

Bye for now and lots of love to you both.

Also, lots of love to Michael, Babs and the children.

Keith, Anne and Linda xxx

MONDAY, 16 February 1970

DEAR MAM AND DAD,

We were expecting a letter from you before now but I suppose you are waiting to see if Barbara's baby arrives to let us have the good news. I can't remember the date she was expecting, so I don't know if the baby is late or early. Anyway, we're keeping our fingers crossed for a boy this time.

We had to have a passport photo taken of Linda the other day so I'm enclosing a copy. Her mouth is just like Keith's but her eyes and nose are a bit like mine. She was eleven months' old last Tuesday and since then she has started surprising us. She stands alone and has begun taking steps by herself, too. Now my problems will be starting! At least I won't have to scrub her knees every night once she gets onto her feet properly.

Things are settling down here now and we are getting to know people. We had a couple round from school for bridge last night, and in the morning, I shall be visiting a woman I met casually one day last week when I was out walking along the road with Linda. She also has a little girl. We stopped for a talk, and a few days later I saw her in town and she asked me round for coffee tomorrow. She seems a really nice person. Hope I can find her address as I'm still not fully familiarised with Bulawayo! Then the other day we were introduced to a Welshman. We had gone to see him on a business matter and, as we were leaving, he gave Linda some money for her moneybox. It's funny but the casual acquaintances seem by far the best.

A bumper cheque arrived a couple of days ago covering Keith's salaries for January and February, as well as another cheque for £350 covering the cost of our fares out here, so we're going on a spending spree tomorrow - we have seen some fabulous copper table lamps which we would like. We are short of lights in the room, there being only the ceiling light which is in the wrong place for reading. Although it's a furnished apartment, the furniture is sparse and quite well used, though functional. We understand the reason for this as we don't suppose we would put out our best furniture and equipment if we were renting out our own apartment. There isn't a TV, and we were going to rent one, but think it's too expensive here for just the one channel, which opens at 5.15 p.m. and shuts down at 10.35 p.m. For those feeble few hours the licence fee is £6, and the rental charge is £4 a month for a twenty-three inch set. To buy an ordinary twenty-three inch set, you would pay around £125. Besides, all the programmes are American TV shows with canned laughter, which gets on my nerves. As it is, we're reading

Ed McBain, Perry Mason, and any other thrillers we can get hold of. We're back in the routine of going to bed at 9.30 p.m. again and getting up at 6.30 a.m. We push Linda and her cot out into the living room when we go to bed at night. The living room is next door to the only bedroom. The arrangement works quite well, everything considered.

Keith has an interview for a job in Salisbury next week, away from teaching, as I mentioned in an earlier letter. He's really off teaching now and it doesn't help that he has been given the 'slow learner' classes of the school – last comers get the worst, as usual. He hasn't had any trouble at school but he really would like to get out of teaching before he gets any older, so he says he is planning on giving his term's notice at the beginning of next term to leave in August. He will hopefully have something else lined up in Salisbury by then (or Malawi maybe?) but, if not, he says we will return to England as he thinks he has an open offer with a firm in Bradford. We won't have lost any money as we would sell the car (if it ever arrives!), and the money we made from the sale would pay our fares home. But I really hope we get something out here as it is a fabulous place to live and we have seen some lovely houses for £4,000 (some with a swimming pool).

Yesterday, we watched some professional tennis played live. Unfortunately, I didn't have anything on my head and we sat for two hours with the sun blazing down on us. But today, I know about it. I felt sick and headachy all morning and now I have a running tummy. It's nearly bedtime and for the first time all day I don't feel too bad. I've now got a lovely big Greta Garbo hat (closing the stable door comes to mind...).

Trusting you and Dad are all right and that you now have a job, Mam. I keep thinking about you both and miss you.

Big X from Linda.

Bye for now.

Keith and Anne xx

TUESDAY, 19 February 1970

DEAR MAM AND DAD,

Received your letter about Mrs Greenwood yesterday. I don't think I've ever had as big a shock before! She was such a good neighbour to you when we were children and living in Birstall and I can't believe she would end her life in such a tragic way. You say that Kevin was driving the car she was in and his wife driving another car carrying their children. Have you any idea if he was injured in the crash himself, which sounds like it could have been a head-on collision? Poor man, he must be in total shock and feeling really bad about it all but hopefully he doesn't feel he was the cause of his mother's death. The roads here and in South Africa are so wide you could almost drive four ten-ton trucks alongside each other without touching which makes me wonder if they were both overtaking other vehicles when the crash happened. Please God, she wouldn't know what had hit her, but that's no consolation. I'll write to Kevin, but I'll wait a few weeks.

I have another interview today for a morning's only job. Hope I get it as it's quite nearby and, as we still have no transport, I'm getting plenty of exercise. The weather is cooling down a bit these days and the sudden changes have given Linda a cold. On Tuesday, I went to spend the morning with that person I told you about. She looks after a baby of aged fourteen months, a little boy. His parents are teachers. He was a lovely fat baby, though he weighs the same as Linda, but he is quite different from Linda in that he seems to sleep nearly all the time and isn't able to stand yet even though he can give Linda three months! She started pushing him around a bit which we had to stop so then she took his biscuit from him, making him cry. But he was so lazy he didn't try to crawl out of her way, and apparently, he has only just learned to crawl. Linda thought it was lovely poking at his eyes and pulling his hair, until we stopped it, but he just sat there letting her do it. She's certainly merciless. She's becoming a bit more independent now, thank goodness. She goes onto our small balcony – we're on the first floor – and looks down into the yard below. If the little girl from the flat, or their cat – 'puthy' – is there, she has a lovely time chatting away, usually with no response of course – especially from the cat. As we pass people in the street, they often remark about her English rosy cheeks, as most of the kiddies born here appear to have pasty complexions.

Keith has an interview in Salisbury a week tomorrow, but if he is offered the job and the salary is less than £2,000 per annum, he won't accept it.

We're going out to dinner tonight, which will be a nice change. Then it's bridge again.

We hope Barbara is okay and that maybe she has her baby boy by now. She didn't look big enough for twins – I'm hoping the doctor is wrong!

I agree with you that it's a pity about the carrycot having to be left at the airport, but really it wasn't much good as the hood kept falling down and overall it was a bit tatty. However, we also had to leave behind nappies and my electric iron, which had some value. But Keith has now written to BOAC complaining about our treatment and he has received a letter saying his complaints are being looked into. So, we may yet receive some compensation. So far, we have received £6 from the Rhodesian government towards the cost of excess baggage. Who knows, we may come out on top after all, which will be a change for us. Nappies here are expensive and they are like toilet paper.

We told BOAC we had to buy duplicates of everything we had left at the UK airport on our arrival here, including the carrycot (which we haven't actually bothered to replace). The main thing we left back at Jack's was the pram, and in view of the cost of prams here, we were going to have it shipped over. However, Jack has enquired about the cost and we understand the shipping charges will be in the region of £20. So that's out!

Anyway, if we're back in the UK in September/October, I'll probably need it there. We are staying here in the flat anyway and not considering buying now until we know for sure what our future plans are. It's no use going into great expense, is it?

Bye for now. Glad you've got a job, Mam. Lots of love to everyone.

I'll write to everyone else soon.

Love

Keith, Linda and Anne XXX

FRIDAY, 27 February 1970

DEAR MAM AND DAD,

Received your letter today. Still no news about Barbara's baby at the time you wrote your letter, but perhaps she will have her little boy by now, though it would be nice if he was born on Linda's birthday, 10th March. I'm trying to write this with Linda pulling and tugging at me. I've just given her some peanuts to keep her quiet, which I probably shouldn't have done, but I'm watching her and she just sucks them without swallowing, then spits them out.

You must have misunderstood when I said about Jack having some things to bring over to you. They are just things which we had to leave behind and which we would like to put in your spare bedroom. I don't think there's anything of yours as I believe I gave you back your sheets ages ago. These are mainly things we had packed to bring with us, but when we weighed our cases at Jack's, we found we were drastically overweight. We took out what we thought we wouldn't need here but there wasn't much really. We did leave the pram, which is going to cost too much to send out to us. Jack probably just hasn't had a chance to bring these things over to you and we had told him there was no urgency, that they would do sometime when he was passing. We had packed the little plastic chair to come here (just in case we ever have any more children).

Linda is now sitting on the floor with a bag of toffees, biting the silver paper off each one; I'll have to take these off her. She's like a little mouse. She managed to get her hands on the tin of biscuits the other day, and took a bite out of seven or eight, not eating any particular one. Now she's got the telephone (it's not connected) and is bashing the toffees with the receiver. You know, Mam, she still remembers when you phoned us at Jack's because I've made a few phone calls since we've been here and she always tries to get hold of it to hear what's being said!

Last Monday I started working mornings. It's quite nice to get out for a change. I'm getting £40 a month for five mornings, which is a great help. We have a girl each morning to clean up, wash and iron and look after Linda, for which we pay £5. 10s. a month. She also babysits two nights a week, so we can go out. My job is quite interesting but was a bit complicated at first. Also, my brain doesn't want to work after being idle for so long. I have to concentrate really hard to remember things. The firm I work for makes handbags, suitcases, belts etc., as well as clothes. I work for the sister-company which is the financial side, and which deals with the shares of the main company. My new job is to follow the shares through the broker when they are bought and sold. I issue share certificates when they are bought and cancel the certificates when they are sold, but all the information has to be entered into various registers. It's a really nice job with really nice people. I've been told I can buy anything from the wholesale side at cost plus twelve per cent off, which is a fabulous saving as clothes are expensive here. It's a pity I didn't know before, as a few days ago, I had to buy two skirts and a blouse so that I'd have something nice to wear if I got a job. Knowing that part-time jobs are very difficult to get here, I consider myself privileged to be employed, especially as there were two of us for the interview – the other lady being from Scotland, and she needed the job just as much as I did. I'll feel pretty awful if Keith does get a job in Salisbury and I have to give my notice. The managing director's secretary is a lovely Scottish lady and if I have finished what I've been left to do, then I usually walk over to her office and, with her approval of course, pick up things from her tray to type. I prefer being busy and it seems to help her, too.

The weather is really hot at the moment and people say it's even hotter in October. I dread to think what I'll do then.

The school staff seem quite friendly once you get to know them and they get to know you. I suppose, like most things, it takes time and people are always wary at first (especially of the Brits – Harold Wilson and all that!), though nearly everyone we meet says we have lots of courage to come out at times like this, and probably respect us for it.

Anyway, enough of that! How are you all? Hope you and Dad are both well and coping with your cold weather. You ask about the church, Mam. Well, it's very grand and is a cathedral rather than a church. It's called St Mary's Cathedral. I have about a twenty-minute walk from here to get there. I managed to entice Keith as far as the outside the Sunday before last, but he then sat on the wall reading the newspaper. I did take Linda in with me once but she made a lot of much noise. Now we get our girl to come in on Sunday morning to look after her.

Bye for now.

Love to Michael, Barbara and children.

Lots of love also from Linda to you both XXX.

Keith, Linda and Anne xxx

WEDNESDAY, 11 March 1970

DEAR MICHAEL AND BARBARA,

Presumably the baby has arrived by now. We haven't heard from my mam for a good week so are supposing she's waiting to give us the good news. I'm sorry about the little plastic baby chair but as we had a little room left over when packing our cases, we decided to put the chair in. If and when we ever settle down, we'll try for another baby (hopefully a boy) ourselves, so maybe the chair will come in useful.

I started work a few weeks ago, half days, and really enjoy it. It also means I am encouraged to get dressed up each day, whereas before I used to loll around the flat in my oldest clothes. I must say, the money comes in very handy too, as the cost of living, on the whole, is much higher than in the UK. But no matter how much money one has, it still goes, doesn't it? Linda is now walking by herself and there's no holding her back. I only wish we had had the use of the baby walker truck we bought her at Christmas. Instead, we packed it in the trunks with everything else. I'm sure she would have been off sooner if she could have used it. We bought a couple of little coffee tables a few weeks ago, and Linda has been using them to push-walk against over the polished floor, then she started taking a few steps on her own, and on the eve of her birthday, she was walking from the room through the bedroom and out onto the balcony without touching anything. Although this happened on the eve of her birthday, nonetheless, we can always say she was walking at eleven months! But oh dear, she still doesn't have any hair. Her head is just the same as when we last saw you. Will it ever grow?

We still have lovely sunshine here but it should be getting cooler as the weeks go by. In fact, it's chilly at night these days, which is nice, too. But everyone says from May to August it's very cold, even during the day.

Our trunks arrive here at the end of this month, thank goodness as we're badly in need of the things we sent over from UK. I had to buy a pair of sheets and pillowcases as well as a cheap blanket when we first arrived, and they have been washed weekly and put back on the bed the same day ever since. It'll be lovely to have spare bedclothes for a change. It's the same with clothes of course. Because we only had a 44 lbs baggage allowance each for Keith and me, with no allowance for Linda who took up most of the space with all her dresses etc, I only packed four dresses and two suits for myself, so as you can imagine, I'm pretty desperate to get the rest of the things. I've already had to buy a couple of skirts and a jumper, which have cost me a fortune. Our car will be arriving in Cape Town on 24th April, so we will hopefully have that by the middle of May. There's quite a lot to see around about but you do need transport. Fortunately, Keith and I only have a ten-minute walk to get to work and the flat is in town for ease of shopping, but we suffer because of the noise of traffic. It goes on well into the early hours. And there seems to be no law against the sounding of car horns after 11 p.m., unlike U.K., because the noisy fiends here play tunes on their horns as they speed along the road. Unfortunately, we live on the main road from Blantyre to the South African border so the traffic and noise are nonstop day and night. We also have noisy neighbours living below us who often have ferocious arguments well into the early hours, so you can imagine the joy of bedtime! Linda doesn't do too badly though, and only occasionally wakes up because of the noise. The people who row told the previous tenants to knock on the floor if the noise got too bad, and we have been tempted to do this many times, but afraid it would only cause bad feelings. The flat is a bit more sound-proof than the Soothill flat and I believe the only reason we hear anything at all is because we have our windows open due to the heat. We have now bought a TV but I'll never complain about British television again. At least you have a choice of stations! We don't and we also have adverts every ten minutes. For this pleasure we have to buy a £6 TV licence, which has to be produced and the number noted before you are allowed to either buy or rent a TV. And if you take the TV for repair, you have to produce the licence first before they even book the repair in. What a swizz. But it means everyone has a licence if they have a TV, unlike England!

Give our love to the children and to yourselves.
Bye for now and hope you are okay, Barbara.
Love, K, A, and L xxx

WEDNESDAY, 18 March 1970

DEAR MAM AND DAD,

Received your letter and birthday card yesterday. I thought you had probably forgotten the date of Linda's birthday as she came before she was due. But I also thought you would have got a little grandson by now. Maybe by the time you get this letter you will have (though another granddaughter will probably be just as acceptable). There will be great excitement when it does eventually arrive, especially for the kiddies. I wrote to Michael and Barbara last week, but I still have not written to anyone else. I thought you had arranged to meet Auntie Mary and Uncle John the Sunday after we left. What happened?

Keith has gone for a final interview for a job, the job I told you about in my last letter. The director who saw him locally during the first interview seemed very impressed and now the director from Johannesburg has come to Bulawayo to see Keith here and another chap in Salisbury. So, it looks as though it's between the two of them. It's an informal interview as the arrangements were for Keith to have dinner at the hotel in town this evening at seven o'clock. It's now just after 9 p.m. but I expect they are having a talk over a drink. I don't anticipate Keith will know anything when he gets back, as the chappie will want to see the other applicant in Salisbury before making a decision.

Our trunks and packing cases arrive in Portuguese Mozambique on Monday next but it will probably be a fortnight before we get it into Rhodesia. Our car is due at Cape Town on the twenty-fourth of next month, so by the middle of May we should have transport, though we have been negotiating for an old second-hand (probably sixty-second-hand) car. It's over ten years old and needs a Vehicle Inspection Certificate, though the person selling the car isn't very happy about having it tested for some reason! But it has to have a test certificate before we can insure it. So, it looks like a 'no sale'. We've been lost without a car since we came as it's impossible to move without your own transport. Luckily, we both work within walking distance of the flat, but at weekends we could see the sights if we had a car. I'd also go to the small church, which is about three miles away, as I'm sorry to say, I detest intensely going to Mass at the cathedral. The building is beautiful but the people aren't. I have only taken Linda twice but each time have had to come out because of the sour stares I got when she made a noise. I've heard that the priest has been known to interrupt his sermon to tell the 'miscreant' that children should be left at the nursery down the road and not brought into the church. 'Suffer little children to come unto me'! What a laugh. The last time I took Linda she wouldn't stay with me and I eventually had to bring her out. But the door at the back was locked and as I was struggling to open it, an old crone came storming up to me to say I had no right to be disturbing the priest! Even though I was still in the church, I almost gave her a mouthful but thought better of it, of course. Now that Linda is walking I wouldn't even dare to take her. But the little church I could go to instead is mainly for nuns, as there is a Catholic hospital run by them about three miles away, Anyway, we'll see how it goes. I hope you don't have to pay postage on this letter. If so, it's going to cost you a fortune.

Hope you are still all well. Also, that the baby has now arrived.

Love and lots of kisses – a big one X from Linda.

Keith and Anne

xx

FRIDAY, 3 April 1970

DEAR MAM AND DAD,

Received your letter on Wednesday and am really pleased about the baby. I'm sure the children love her just as much as they would a boy. It seems amazing to think they now have four daughters. I daren't suggest that maybe the next one will be a boy. Of course, they could always let us have Michelle and then try again! Michelle is a lovely name but I suspect she would have been a 'Michael' had she been a boy!

Linda seems to change by the day. I caught her expression recently and it was identical to Jacqueline's. I think she is changing into a 'Shirley' after all. I'll never forget what the sister-doctor said to me immediately after Linda had been born. After cleaning her up she brought her over to me and said, 'Oh goodness, she looks just like her father', then she hesitated a second, before saying: 'But never mind. She might change!' I have to add, she did have a smile on her face as she said it, and we all laughed. Linda's hair is now quite frizzy at the back, and if it wasn't so flat to her head she would have some long hairs! But on top she's still sparse. She lays her pillow on the floor now and gets down on her knees and pretends to go to sleep. But she can't pretend for very long as she can't keep her eyes closed. We curl up laughing at her sometimes, she tickles us so much. She's due for a smallpox vaccination in a week or two, which I am dreading and I know I won't be laughing then.

Our baggage still hasn't arrived, though it's in Rhodesia by now. But the nights are getting cold and we really could do with another blanket on the bed. I hope we have enough bedding to make up a bed on the settee as we are expecting a visitor at the weekend, a young chap who came out on the same plane as us and who was posted to a school in Plumtree, a small town on the border between Rhodesia and Botswana. I understand there are plum trees there as well as fig trees, which I think make it sound quite exotic but, according to Bruce, it's even more primitive than Mzuzu. The young lad is coming up to Bulawayo to spend the weekend in the 'big city'!

I'm still working and liking the job very much and life is getting easier as Linda gets on well with the girl who looks after her. At first, there were a few tears when I left in the mornings but now she runs to the girl with open arms. We're still 'legging it' around and normally I wouldn't mind, but it's so hot during the day and I'm usually beggared after an afternoon of food shopping whilst pushing Linda around in the pram. The car is due sometime in May. Yippee.

All being well, we'll be going to Mzuzu the first two weeks in May. Linda's stand-in godmother, Louise, will be away unfortunately, visiting friends in the south I believe, so she won't get to see Linda, but we will have use of her house and her cook-boy. It's going to be a costly holiday for us though, as I'll lose my wages while we are away as I haven't worked for the company long enough to get paid holidays, and the fare from Salisbury will be nearly £50 each return plus ten per cent of our fare for Linda. Quite honestly, I'd rather keep the money but Keith wants to go to see everyone, so I suppose we shall be going.

They have joined a chain letter club at Keith's mam's. All the family have joined. We think they are mad, but they say they've already got their original £4 outlay back and they stand to gain £2,000 if it goes all right. Apparently, it's been well publicised, both in the press and on television.

Well Mam, are you still working? I don't think you said where or what you were doing – was it in the mill? Keith is still slogging on, though still unsettled in his job.

Did you have to pay postage on the last letter? Would it be worthwhile to send to you some of Linda's dresses? If I send them by sea, I don't think you would have to pay too much surcharge. What do you think?

Bye for now. Big X from Linda.

Love from Keith and Anne xxx

SUNDAY, 12 April 1970

DEAR MAM AND DAD,

It was nice to receive your letter last week and glad to hear the baby is getting along fine.

But it was sad to hear about Aunt Jessie, though I don't remember her very much. I was still a child the last time I saw her. They say things happen in threes – Grandma, Mrs Greenwood and now Aunt Jessie. Poor Uncle Cecil, he must wonder what's happened to his world. Will he be staying with one of his daughters? I'm so sorry. If you get chance Dad, please pass on my condolences.

I wish you could see Linda now. She rocks her arms and lifts one foot and stamps down in time to the tune, and sometimes she turns around and around and around. It's the same when we have the TV on. She stands in front of it, dancing and grinning. She occasionally hums too, which makes us laugh even more. She's just too full of beans - she has Keith's nature – so much so that I am determined not to take her to church for another few months. We took a cine film almost exclusively of Linda, which we are contemplating sending to Gerald for you all to see. But it says in our papers that the GPO is charging over twice as much as the price of stamps on letters and cards, so we are afraid either Gerald would not receive the film or it would cost too much in the surcharge. Never mind, there is the chance that we may be back by Christmas, unless things change rapidly here. After all, it isn't our fight so let them get on with it. They had their election on Friday and Ian Smith's party is still in power. But we noticed in their election speeches the parties were all hinting about segregation and separate facilities for Europeans, Coloureds and Blacks – we would have gone to South Africa had we wanted to live under those conditions. When we think of the nice Africans we knew in Malawi we feel embarrassed.

Keith is out playing tennis at the moment. The school allows the courts to be used during the weekend and Keith has managed to find a couple of older boys who are quite good players, so he is in his element at the moment.

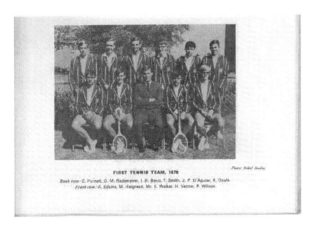

The tennis club

Our packing cases will be arriving here on Monday, so the place should look something like a home instead of a bare flat. It will also be nice to have some different clothes to wear. We are thinking of cancelling our visit to Malawi after all because our car, which should have arrived in Cape Town on 25 April, will not now arrive until 15 May and we would have needed it to travel to Salisbury to catch the plane to Malawi. Without the car, it means we have to fly to Salisbury the previous day and stay overnight in a hotel, which would bring the cost of the holiday to about £200 for a fortnight in fares alone. So, I think we are going to scrub the idea (I'm pleased to say).

We heard the commentary on the match at Wembley between Leeds and Chelsea on the radio yesterday. We were imagining you all sitting round the TV. Did Michael go to Wembley, as I remember Barbara saying he was thinking about going? It was a pity Leeds couldn't keep up their lead, wasn't it? Never mind, maybe second-time lucky.

In view of the amount the GPO are charging on Rhodesian mail and the chance that they will stop delivering letters and parcels, maybe I had better not send any of Linda's clothes for the baby. In fact, the dresses are originally ones worn by Michael's little ones anyway and which Barbara passed over to Linda afterwards. In another couple of months, the postal problems will fizzle out I think, so I'll be able to send the things then.

Bye for now.

Love to you all.

Big X from Linda as always.

Love,

Keith and Anne xx

TUESDAY, 21 April 1970

DEAR MAM AND DAD,

Received your letter last week. I'm pleasantly surprised to hear you are not paying a surcharge on my letters. Some people in the UK are having to pay as much as 3/- on an air letter, according to the newspapers here. How is everyone?

For us, we are all fine – still enjoying the sun. Keith is on a month's holiday and as we are not now going to Malawi, he is bored to tears. Needless to say, I'm working as usual when he's on holiday. Nothing changes! This afternoon, to give me some peace, he took Linda up to school for a walk. He has said never again! It normally takes five minutes, but he said it must have taken half an hour. She stopped at every pebble and cigarette packet she saw and didn't want to walk on the pavement, but either preferred the gutter or the rubble on the side of the pavement. Whenever she came to the end of the pavement, she would lift her little hand so that Keith could help her down, then she would shrug him off and toddle off across the road until she came to the kerb on the other side of the road when she would lift her hand again. All the way to school it was like this. Occasionally, she stopped to look at the Africans passing, probably thinking she could recognise our girl. She was only wearing slippers too, which didn't make Keith too happy as they were bright blue with funny pompoms on. She had a little blister on her heel, so I thought it was better to wear something soft. We bought her the slippers the other day and were surprised to note that she now takes size four. Keith says she can start wearing my slippers when hers wear out – well either that or the shoe boxes the slippers come in! I don't know what size a thirteen-month old should wear, but I'm sure it's not size four.

Jack and Margaret go to Canada on holiday in eleven weeks' time for three weeks. It's funny but Canada doesn't appeal to us at all now as it once did. It's probably something to do with the cold weather there. The temperature here dropped on Sunday and we were walking around (in the house) in jumpers and coats. Then on Monday, we were back to 80° again.

Our girl was ill at the weekend and I didn't expect her to come in on Monday, but she was better by then. Apparently, there's a forty-eight-hour flu going around here though luckily, Linda doesn't seem to have caught it. Maybe I'm tempting providence making such a statement!

I am watching a programme on television about William Shakespeare, which looks as if it's going to be interesting. Some of the programmes are dreadful, especially the ones produced in Rhodesia. The canned stuff isn't too bad, but the old American films get a bit boring. We also get annoyed with the adverts, especially as the TV is only on for five hours a day and, as we have to pay £6 licence fee, we don't expect to have advertisements before the film titles, after the film titles, and then ten minutes later, and so on for the rest of the programme. They even interrupt the news half way through (it's only on for ten minutes) to advertise products or services. The advertisements are so cheesy that they are sometimes quite funny. For instance, the person reading some serious item of news will suddenly stop, lean over to a side table, pick up a product, hold it up to the camera, and excitedly start reciting the blurb to go with the product. Then, still smiling, the newsreader will put the article down, put on a serious expression once more and proceed to read the news where they broke off. But it's amazing how accustomed one can get to these petty annoyances.

We are still without transport, though we had a letter on Monday saying the car arrives in Cape Town on 13 May.

That reminds me, there are lots of birthdays next month, aren't there? I hope I don't forget them. I must write to Aunt Alice soon. I think

I've got her address. I'm writing to everyone slowly but surely, but there isn't really much news to tell everyone and I know they all read your letters too, so it sometimes seems a bit pointless writing separately. Still, I suppose people like something of their own. Glad you saw Aunt Mary and Uncle John the other day. Michelle sounds lovely. On 26 May, you will see her as the same age Linda was when we came back from Malawi last year, except for the hair, which is definitely coming along.

Bye for now. Love to you both.

X from Linda

Keith and Anne xxx

LINDA WAS GROWING fast and at the stage where everything seemed to interest her. By the same measure, her inquisitiveness was becoming interesting to us. She was a lovely baby and could make us laugh so easily.

Living in the town as we did, we tried as often as feasible to go out to the country for fresh air. We would sometimes borrow a car and take the half hour's drive out to the Matopos Hills to get some peace and quiet, which was a welcome change from the bustle of Bulawayo, particularly as, living in an apartment, we never got away from the noise. There was a seating area overlooking the beautiful valley and Linda would play hide and seek between the benches. Occasionally, we would venture up the hill to take a look at the grave of Cecil John Rhodes and marvel at the beautiful place carefully chosen for his remains.

When we could afford to, it was nice to occasionally go out for a meal in the evening leaving Linda with Belta (our girl), and I loved 'inspecting' the houses as we drove past them, silently wishing we could move into those of which I approved.

One evening we decided to have a meal at a restaurant that was highly recommended but the directions were vague, and even Keith, who was an extremely capable person, couldn't find the place. As we slowly drove along a road, we saw a couple walking towards us and Keith asked me to wind down the car window and ask directions.

Aiming my question at the lady I said in my best Yorkshire accent: 'Excuse me, but please could you direct us to the Glass Castle?' The couple looked at each other in bewilderment, silently mouthing my request. Then suddenly the penny dropped. 'Oh! You mean the Glaars Caarsle!' I was advised in snobbish Rhodesian Boarding School nasal tones. Afterwards, Keith and I laughed at their accent and we have often dined on this story over the years.

THURSDAY, 7 May 1970

DEAR MAM AND DAD,

Hope you'll excuse the writing but I have broken a finger on my right hand and have it in a plaster cast at the moment. I'm sorry, but this is the reason I haven't written for a little while. I have the plaster covering my fingers down to my wrist with two fingers fastened down. I foolishly slipped on the polished floor in the flat a week ago yesterday and broke my little finger on the jamb of the door. I went to work the following day because, although it was swollen and very painful, I didn't think it was actually broken. After work, I went to see the doctor and he sent me straight to the hospital for an X-ray where the broken finger was diagnosed. I am still working, though, doing two-finger typing and managing quite well. However, because we aren't eligible for Medical Aid until July, we have to pay for any medical care up to then and it's going to cost almost £10 for the doctor and hospital, Unfortunately, we have to have been paying insurance for three months before we are eligible.

We would have been in Mzuzu this week and next week had we not cancelled the arrangement. I wrote to Louise – Linda's godmother – about three weeks ago to tell her we needed to cancel the holiday and would not, therefore, require her house and cook.

But she didn't reply, which was unusual. I wondered if we had upset her by cancelling the arrangement as she would surely have made preparations for our arrival; or perhaps we had said something in our letters to offend her for some reason, which I doubted. However, this afternoon, Keith and I got the shock of our lives when we received a letter from one of the other teachers at the school in Mzuzu, enclosing my un-opened letter to Louise, and telling us that Louise had died the previous Saturday in hospital in Blantyre. She had cancer of the colon. I was heartbroken. Poor, poor Louise, she was such a nice person. She spent her life helping other people and seeming to get nothing in return. Her one ambition in life was always to get married and have a family, though she was forty years old.

As mentioned previously, she had had an operation about four years previously and had been left with only thin tissue between her womb and her back passage and the doctor had told her if ever she married it would be difficult to have a baby. She cried when she talked about it.

She was absolutely thrilled to bits when we asked her to be

Linda's stand-in godmother and she made an impressive cake for the christening. Had we gone to Mzuzu, as planned, we would probably have been driving through Blantyre on the day she died. She didn't talk about herself very much as she was the kind of person who, rather than hog the conversation, would somehow ask you questions and make you feel important. But one day, when she was having a meal with Keith and me, she told me about the operation and about the daily difficulties she had dealing with her health problem.

I now feel in my heart that she came to Africa to die, as I'm sure she knew she had cancer when she came. I remember her telling me she had a sister at a convent in Blantyre, and I guess she came to Malawi to be near her sister when she died. There were a number of instances where, when I now go over things she said, I realise she was anticipating her future. Had we been travelling through Blantyre I imagine her spirit would have reached out to us. As Keith said when he read the letter, she will know by now whether all her daily Masses have been of any use. Poor Louise. She would have loved to have seen Linda as she took her role of acting-godmother very seriously. It's Ascension Day today, so I said my Mass for her. God bless her.

The boys from the school are amazing, at least in my opinion. If I meet any of the boys while out shopping in town, they always raise their caps and say: 'Good morning, madam' or 'Good afternoon, madam'. At first, I thought they were being sarcastic as no-one has ever greeted me this way before, and I expected the boys to guffaw once they had passed me, but they didn't. And the same happens every time I pass any of the boys. They are so courteous.

I'm pleased Jack and Margaret came to see you with our things. Please keep them because you never know!

Linda is recovering from her smallpox vaccination and is a bit cranky but apart from that is fine. She has just cut two more teeth – sixteen now and weighs just two stone.

Glad to hear that Michelle is getting along fine, too. I bet the other children are thrilled to bits.

Hope you can read my writing. Give our love to everyone.

Big X from you know who and our love to you both.

Keith and Anne xxx

PS. Also happy birthday to everyone. Have posted cards sea mail to save surcharge!

SUNDAY, 7 June 1970

DEAR MAM AND DAD,

You shouldn't have anything to pay on my letters in future as we've managed to get hold of some pre-decimal stamps bearing the Queen's head, though heaven knows what difference it makes. Hope you are both well, as we are. We had a telegram from Jack during the week saying that the car should be here in four weeks, and we've also received the manual for the Capri car from Fords of London giving us the engine number so, at last, things seem to be moving in the right direction.

There has been an awful stink in the papers here about the number of new expatriates leaving, but this week we have letters in the papers complaining about the number of new immigrants taking jobs from locals. Most of the leavers seem to be going to South Africa, though I can't understand why they would do that with the horrendous apartheid down there. We heard that the Minister of Health here is leaving for England, and so is one of the 'big wigs' in the railways. When it really comes down to brass tacks though, we can truthfully say the main reason we want to return to the UK is because we miss everyone. We could get a fabulous house here complete with swimming pool for less than £5,000, but what would be the use? We'd have no-one to show it off to.

We have just received two more accounts for my broken

finger, which brings the bill so far to nearly £35 – (£10 more than we expected.) Had we been eligible for Medical Aid, we wouldn't have had anything to pay, but that's the luck of the draw. We're eligible from the first of July, so we're pretty safe from now on.

We had a Jehovah's Witness round last week, someone who knew Derrick and Margaret in Gwelo. She left a Bible for Keith to read and criticise, but he has been too busy reading a book he has bought from the Christian Bookshop in town titled 30 Years a Watchtower Slave. It's written by an ex-Jehovah's Witness and is really an eye-opener. He initially bought it to send to Derrick but I don't think it'll do any good. We had a letter from Derrick last week saying that Margaret was waiting to go into hospital again, so maybe she has had a change of heart. Jack and Margaret go for their visit to Canada in July. They should be getting quite excited by now. Hope they don't like it so much they want to stay, especially when we are planning to return to the UK. We heard about Harold Wilson's egg-throwing mishaps. You'd think he could take the hint by now. The polls seem to be swaying quite a lot, though. I presume you'll be voting Conservative this time. I certainly would be anyway.

We've been having trouble with our girl, or rather her 'husband'. Initially we were introduced to her by one of the waiters at the hotel we stayed in when we first arrived, who said she was his wife. During the last few months we have grown to know him quite well as, on Saturday nights if we go out, Belta will babysit. We normally get back by 10 p.m. and Belta's husband comes to pick her up on his motorbike. She came today and told Keith that George, her husband, was ill-treating her and that she wanted to leave him and stay with her sister in the township. However, she said he won't let her go. It transpires, so she says, that she's not his wife at all in the legal sense, but is just living with him; that he already has two wives back at the village. I know it sounds shocking to us but the Africans have different tribal laws allowing certain things. Anyway, when George came to collect Belta, Keith told him that she didn't want to go with him. This started an argument and Keith told George he would throw him out if he didn't go. However, after some heated discussion, they left together, hopefully to try to sort things out themselves. I'm assuming Belta will be all right! You have to be marriage guidance counsellor, doctor, employer, provider of clothes and food and a thousand other things rolled into one. What a carry on!

I seem to owe everyone a letter again – still haven't written to Auntie Alice. The only chance I seem to get is when Linda has her nap in the afternoon, which is getting shorter and shorter. I'll get down to it very soon, I hope.

You can stop calling at the GPO from now on as we have about sixty 9d. stamps to use up.

Lots of love to everyone.

X from Linda.

Keith and Anne xxx

MONDAY, 22 June 1970

DEAR MAM AND DAD,

Received your letter today. You are right, I had better be careful what I say in my letters if you think they are being tampered with before you get them. If they are, it will probably be from your UK end. Isn't it stupid, the cops and robbers stuff? (I hope someone opens this and reads what I think of them!) Pity they have nothing better to do.

Linda now goes to the nursery every morning while I'm working. I had to let Belta go as she was becoming unreliable, either being late or not turning up at all. She just didn't turn up one day and I had a mad dash to get Linda ready and to find somewhere to leave her. They accepted her at the nursery without any trouble, but I was half an hour late for work and had to take a taxi on top of everything else, which was costly. They charge five guineas a month for Linda at the nursery for the mornings and this includes her breakfast and dinner, which works out at just over 4/- a day, which isn't bad at all as I was paying the girl £6. 12s. 6d. each month and having to buy jars of food for Linda as the girl didn't know how to cook. I now have an older woman to come in three mornings to do the washing and clean up. If it wasn't for the fact that the washing has to be done by hand, in the bath, I wouldn't bother with anyone at all, though this lady also babysits for us on Saturday nights, which is nice. At the nursery, Linda is normally crying when I leave her, which always upsets me, and usually, when I arrive to pick her up she's still crying.

At first, I was worried and spoke with one of the girls about this, but she assured me that, as soon as I am out of sight, Linda stops crying and plays with the other children. It's only when she sees me in the distance walking towards the nursery that she starts crying again! I really hope this is the case!

Linda has already picked up odd words or near words, her favourite being 'no, no, no' with great emphasis. She also says 'ta', when she's giving you something, and 'what's at' meaning 'I want that'. Of course, she still says 'g'bye, g'bye' and 'puthy', and clicks her tongue when she sees a dog. In fact, she seems to do well in every way, except that she just will not sit on her potty. Since she was born, she has had three potties and has never used any of them. But she will sit on the toilet if I hold her, so tomorrow I'm going to see if I can get a baby seat to fasten onto the toilet seat.

We have borrowed a still camera and started taking snaps. Initially, we were going to have Linda's photo professionally taken at the photographers but when I enquired the cost I was told that each photo, half the size of a postcard, would be 12/6d. I nearly fell through the floor! When the snaps have been processed, we'll have one enlarged for yourselves and Keith's mam. I was looking at a photo of Janet when she was about nine months' old, sitting with Karen and Jacqueline, and she has far more hair than Linda had even now at fifteen months. In fact, her head on top is almost the same as the photo of her at six months. She does have some long wisps at the back, but it is taking so long! By the time we get back, maybe she'll have some semblance of being a girl (I still get asked what his name is occasionally, even though she's wearing a pink dress and fancy knickers).

The business about the car seems to be settled now, so we are just waiting to hear from our end. I sincerely hope that the last two or three previous letters haven't been opened, as I'm sure I said things that could have repercussions, especially about the transport!

I imagine it will be a good idea to all live in a big house if you all agree about it, but it's no good if you don't. In fact, it would also be nice for me, especially if you did stop working, to look after the children as

I could also 'palm' Linda off on to you while I got a job. But it's no good taking any old house. It's best to wait until you find one you all like. The house you mentioned sounded ideal for converting into flats. Derrick and Margaret have a nice big house in Oxford Road, Dewsbury and they only paid £2,500 for it. It has four floors and at least five bedrooms. They managed to stop the dry rot before it got too bad (if you remember, the house they bought before this in Heckmondwike was falling down with dry rot).

Bye for now and big X from Linda (who is sleeping – it's now 9.20 p.m. Lots of love to everyone.

Keith and Anne xxx

SUNDAY, 5 July 1970

DEAR MAM AND DAD,

It seems ages since I last wrote but time flies past in the afternoons when I'm not working, and before I get turned around it's bedtime (ten o'clock as we're up at 6.30 a.m. – Keith starts teaching at 7.30 a.m. and I start at 8 a.m.).

Good news about the car. It arrived in Cape Town last Wednesday, 1 July. The AA in South Africa are doing the necessary for us and we should have it by next weekend (my birthday and a public holiday, as well!). We are getting very excited about it now as we have never had a brand-new car before. It's ironic that we have been here six months and not had transport and will only have it a few months if we return at Christmas (we may get back sooner depending on whether we can sell the car earlier or not). It's going to be such a precious car so much so that I won't dare to drive it as, if we have an accident, it will delay our return. The spare parts would have to be brought up from South Africa.

I received your birthday card last week, thank you. Twenty-nine – isn't it horrible! But I keep forgetting, Michael's already thirty-one! And Keith is thirty in December. Even Linda's age seems a shock sometimes – nearly sixteen months, yet it doesn't seem two minutes since she was born. I'm enclosing a few photos we have taken of Linda. She doesn't look much different, does she? And I'm not really as fat as I look in one of the photos either as I had just pulled my blouse out to make it baggy as it was warm work pushing the pram. We have shared the photos out between Keith's mam and you and I'm enclosing the ones for you. I've numbered them for something better to do, so I'll explain them:

1. You can see for yourselves. She likes biscuits.

2. This was taken in the flat with the flash gun. Linda loves climbing, and as you can imagine, she turns her feeding chair onto its back and stands on it.

3. We bought her a big, black, hairy toy dog for her birthday and she loves to tickle her face (ignore the mop and washing).

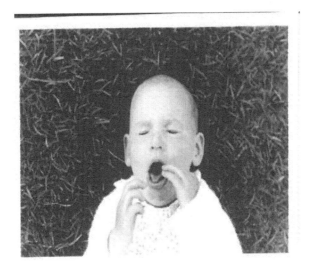

4. She was in a mood and dropped down on the grass to have a good cry (no, she's not choking).

5. Picking flowers!

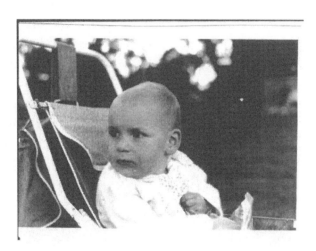

6. Anything to keep her quiet. Crisps, this time.Her
face is dirty; hence, the darkness around her
mouth.

DOESN'T she look like Keith?

Don't know why it takes me two days to write a couple of paragraphs, but it's now Monday. Yesterday (Sunday), they had

328

a big walk at school. The boys were sponsored to walk twenty miles and left at 6.30 a.m. Keith had to be at school to see some of his form starting and as we didn't get to bed until midnight the night before you can imagine how tired he was. He came back at 8.30 a.m., had some breakfast, and then left again at 9.30 a.m. He arrived back at just after one o'clock, left again at 2.30 p.m. and finally arrived back at the flat at about 5.15 p.m. This happened on Sunday, supposed to be his day off! Then the film of the Cup Final – Brazil versus Italy – didn't arrive in time to be shown on TV at 5.30 p.m. as it was supposed to be shown, and instead, it was shown at 10.15 p.m., finishing around midnight. Of course, Keith had to stay up to watch it but he could hardly keep his eyes open. Then he is up again at 6.30 a.m. today, Monday. You can imagine what he's like tonight, can't you? He said he's having an early night – or so he says – it's already 8.30 p.m.! Some of the kids did very well in the sponsored walk, though. One lad ran the twenty-mile course and did it in three hours fifteen minutes. Yet some of the kids still hadn't arrived back by teatime last night. Keith says there are some boys limping around the school today. They raised £2,000, which is very good.

We have all had the flu these past few days and Linda has had a cold and cough ever since she started the crèche in June. I suppose it's to be expected as the children pass the bugs on to each other.

The weather here seems very unhealthy though as, at present, the day temperature is 75°F and the night temperature is 34°F. It's not surprising we all have colds and coughs, is it?

We'd better start putting our things back into the packing cases again, for the umpteenth time. We're old hands at it now though, so it won't take long as soon as we know what's happening. In fact, we're tentatively booked on a flight to leave here on 24 August, seven weeks yesterday, but it's doubtful if we'll have settled the car by then. The arrangements will have to be different this time as Linda is too big to expect Jack and

Margaret to take all three of us. So, if perhaps we can make some arrangements for Linda and me to stay with you and Keith to stay at Jack's until we can find somewhere, we'd be very grateful. We'll be putting Linda into a bed as soon as we're settled, so we'll buy a single bed straight away and I'll use it and we can borrow a cot from Jack. This is all assuming we arrive back together. Alternatively, we could wait until nearer Christmas and I can come back with Linda a few weeks before Keith and try at least to find a house, so that when Keith arrives it will be just to decorate and move into. But it's a long time off yet, so I can't say anything definite. If the car arrives in a few days' time we'll spend a week or so going around the garages to see what arrangements can be made to sell it, and I'll let you know as soon as possible what's happening.

We heard on the news here about some men from Pakistan getting to Bradford illegally. Fancy Bradford being on the world news?

I've nearly got writer's cramp so I'll close now. Bye and lots of love to you and everyone.

X from Linda.

Keith and Anne xxx

WEDNESDAY, 15 July 1970

DEAR MAM AND DAD,

Received your letter today. The house that Michael and Barbara have in Dark Lane sounds fabulous. They were lucky to get it for the price. By the time we get back they will be settled in.

We have decided to wait until December after all. The car arrived a week ago and it's smashing. We have decided to wait because, legally, we cannot sell the car until we've had it for six months and, although a dealer had offered us a deal, it was on his terms, which means we'd only just break even on the price. However, if we stay until December, we can legally get a good price. We are going to try to get a bigger engine fitted, which will make the car quite a bit more valuable as it is a GT Capri and in Bulawayo there are only three altogether. This is because they are British cars and sanctions cut Ford dealers off from dealing in Rhodesia. Some of the cars one sees running on the roads out here are so old, if they had been driven in the UK, they would have been on the scrapheap years ago. Someone at school is selling a 1952 Austin for £125 but you would never see a car advertised in England so old. We only got £275 for our 1965 Morris Oxford, so you can see how valuable cars are here. It's really extraordinary driving the car, as people do turn their heads to see what it is, and when we park outside the supermarket inevitably, when we get back to the car, there is a crowd of people around it, giving it an inspection. I must say, it's nice having transport again and the car came just in time for the long weekend, as Monday and Tuesday were public holidays.

Unfortunately, Linda had the flu and still has. I took her to the doctors this afternoon as, for the past three nights, we've none of us had any sleep with her continuous coughing. She has had a cold for about five weeks now and I'm blaming the crèche as she started it the first week she went. There have been so many advantages to her going, especially as she had other children to play with, but they were telling me last week that she was crying all morning after I'd left her, and only stopped if they gave her a bottle of milk. I was furious, especially as I'd cut the bottle feed out completely and she was doing fine from an ordinary cup. Also, the bottle obviously belonged to someone else's child, as you have to take your own cups and nappies, and that's probably why her cold never got better. Keith said I had to keep Linda at home, so we've arranged for the 'girl' to come in each morning. I wasn't too keen on the idea myself because she's new and quite old by African standards, and I was afraid Linda wouldn't take to her. However, today, being the first day we've left them, they seem to have managed quite well. But we must try to get another flat to take us up to December, as it's no joke having to lug the cot out into the sitting room each night. Also, the bathroom and toilet are through the bedroom and we have to creep about so as not to wake Linda. She's all right with continuous noise such as TV as, being next door to the bedroom, she's had to get used to it. But every door creaks and being dark in the bedroom, we are stumbling about, knocking our shins on the bed legs. If we have any male visitors, they have to go down the fire escape to water the back yard! This has been an even bigger bugbear as we have three flights of stairs to climb. Linda is now pretty good at climbing stairs, as she has had plenty of practice! She is getting quite a lot of hair on top too now, especially at the back, but it's incredibly fine hair. By Christmas, I expect she will look like a little girl at last.

You seem to be having good weather again, according to the papers here. We also get the news about the troubles in Belfast, which sounds pretty bad.

Linda thinks the birthday card you sent is lovely. She recognises the pussy and turns the card upside down and inside out, trying to find the cat.

Better close now as it's almost bedtime – ten o'clock again.

Lots of love to you all and big X from Linda.

Keith and Anne xxx

WEDNESDAY, 23 July 1970

DEAR MAM AND DAD,

For the first time since I started working I have nothing to do, so my boss has said I can write letters if I like. I normally ask the Scottish lady if she needs any help but she's worked up to date also.

Received your letter yesterday. I'm glad you liked the

photographs of Linda. Yes, she is big, especially when you have to carry her. The other day I took her to the doctors as she had had a cold for so long. Unfortunately, we had left the pram in the boot of our car and Keith had gone to school in it. It was almost time to go to the doctors when I realised I had no transport for Linda. They have the same system here as they have in Cleckheaton: one has to phone to make an appointment to see the doctor or nurse. In the end, I had to carry Linda the half mile. I could have let her walk some of the way, but we would surely have been late for the appointment, as she still stops to pick up every piece of paper she sees, together with tab-ends. By the time I arrived there, I was almost on my knees! The doctor said Linda had the flu and to keep her indoors for a time. As I said in my last letter, I had stopped sending her to the crèche and now, as I'm writing this letter, her cold is much better. She is also less possessive!

Someone at work gave me the enclosed copy of England, My England to read and I thought it so good that I made another copy of it. Hope you can read it.

By now, you will have received my other letter saying we would be staying until December. It was very nice of Barbara to suggest we stay with them. If they get the house and if we don't find accommodation for all of us, then maybe if Keith can stay with Jack and Margaret, perhaps we can take them up on their offer. Linda has outgrown two pairs of shoes since we arrived here in January and as I had to pay a fortune for the last pair, I decided to get her some pumps this time. But I couldn't believe my eyes when I saw that size three didn't go near her foot as I always thought pumps were made roomy. I know I had to buy size four slippers recently but I can understand that as slippers need to be less snug. Anyway, I needed to get her size four shoes - Miniature battleships, Keith says.

Her vocabulary has increased a little recently. She now says: 'No – no – no' and 'No, don't.', and if I'm calling to Keith when he's in the bathroom or kitchen, she mimics me and shouts

'Kees.' She occasionally has tantrums too, particularly if we take something from her. Then she runs away, pulling an awful face, and if she thinks we are looking at her, falls onto her knees and starts rolling on the floor. The other day when I was in the kitchen, she started playing up and it went on for ages, then she suddenly came in to see me as if nothing had happened and started 'talking' to me. But I was so cross with her that I just said to her: 'No, I don't want to talk with you, you're a naughty little girl,' and her face just crumpled up and she ran onto the balcony crying. When I went to her, she wouldn't look at me at all. I had really hurt her feelings. She was quiet for ages afterwards. I felt so guilty that I won't ever say that to her again (at least not until she's a teenager!)

We were in dire straits for money the other day and I had to get an advance from my boss. The trouble arose from when the car arrived. We had had the AA in South Africa deal with everything and the AA in Bulawayo took over. Then we had to licence, insure and tax the car before we could use it. That wouldn't have been so bad but a friend of ours (Mike) borrowed £105. 0s. 0d from us a few weeks earlier so that his wife could go down to Cape Town to collect their car which had arrived from the UK. Then we had a threatening letter from the people who own the flat we live in, so we thought it time we asked Mike for some of our money back. But it turned out he was worse off than us. It just goes to show that the cost of living is much higher in this country than in the UK, as Mike is a graduate and gets three or four hundred pounds more in salary than Keith, yet he can't manage either. At first, we thought we wouldn't do anything about the flat payment as, after all, the flat is in Mike's name – we had taken it over from him – but we had second thoughts about it. So, I borrowed money from work and went in to pay the rent. Without even giving my name, the woman wrote down Mrs Dinham. Poor Mike, his credit rating will have gone down badly and I bet they won't get another flat again so easily as their name will be on the debtor's list as bad payers!

Anyway, now that Mike's wife has been able to get a job, we should start getting some cash in the bank again. Mike's wife, Lyn, is a nurse and she has been trying to get employment ever since they arrived. They came in January just before we did. Now she has managed to get a job – one which no-one else wants, though – that of night nurse at the local hospital. She has to work a twelve-hour shift for ten nights in succession – 120 hours in total, for which she is paid the princely sum of £70. I suppose the money isn't too bad, but the girls in the office here working as clerks only work about thirty-nine hours a week for which they are paid £75 (which I must admit is more hours than office workers in the UK). I wouldn't want to do Lyn's job anyway, as apparently, she is looking after a woman who is dying and cannot be left for a minute.

The Africans where I work went on strike yesterday and got sacked into the bargain. They start work in the factory at 7 a.m. and work through with a ten-minute break until 12 noon. They commence working again at 12.30 p.m. and work through without a break until 5.30 p.m. I don't know their salary but, knowing African wages, it will be very small.

The reason for the strike is that apparently the overlooker – a European – had told them they must stay inside the factory at lunchtime and they were not being allowed to go to their homes, which are nearby. The Africans said they had not brought any food with them and must go to their homes for lunch. What seems to have been happening is that some garments – we make dresses, cardigans, and men's shirts, as well as handbags and babies clothes – were being stolen and it was thought they were being taken out by the Africans when they went outside at lunchtime. The overlooker decided that, if he kept them inside, they could be searched just the once each day and that at going home time; this would make it much easier for him.

However, all the Africans said they would not accept this new rule and would go on strike and, true to their word, en masse, they walked out of the factory. The management gave them an ultimatum: either they all came back or they would be fired. I understand approximately forty came back, but the rest stayed outside the factory gates. So, the management told them all to go! They were leaving the premises in droves. Today, when we came to work, there were hundreds of Africans waiting outside the gates, looking for work. In the nearby villages, they soon hear when there are jobs going.

The news in Rhodesia at present seems to be all about the dock strike in the UK. Keith and I were saying the other night that we would seem to be jumping out of the frying pan into the fire! It will sort itself out, no doubt. By Christmas, there will probably be another group of people striking for more pay. As we intend flying back, fortunately, the dock strike won't affect us, even if it is still going on.

Keith has had a letter from the firm in the UK who offered him a job just before we came out here. Although they can't promise him a job just now, they have said they will be pleased to see him when we get back and will find out what can be done then. I suppose he can always go into teaching for the time being and look out for something in the meantime.

The Halifax Building Society have written saying they can give us a mortgage, so that's okay. The house in Grosvenor Road sounded nice, but probably too large for us, anyway. You will keep the bed base you mentioned, won't you? I remember the one – it is quite low, so Linda won't have far to fall if she falls out of bed. I can buy a new mattress to fit it.

The government sent a memorandum around all the government departments the other day – they sent a copy to school, giving information about government houses to let from around 1 August. There were four. So, on Sunday, Keith and I went around to have a look at them. We thought it would be cheaper to rent a government house for £3. 10s. a week than to pay £7 a week for the flat. We would have to buy furniture for the house, of course, but figured we would be able to get some rubbish to suit the house fairly cheaply to last until December, then sell it on. But having seen the houses, we have decided to stay where we are. Pigsties would have been better. I've never seen such a load of rubbish in my life. They were very large, dirty old houses that people hadn't taken care of, with huge 'gardens' which were merely empty spaces of dirt. Also, each of them was about four miles from town, so we would be spending the difference in petrol.

There isn't any more news about this place. I owe several letters to people – I'd better get cracking or we'll already be home!

Bye for now.

Lots of love to you all.

Big X from Linda.

Keith and Anne xxx

FRIDAY, 7 August 1970

DEAR MAM AND DAD,

Received your letter on Wednesday.

Keith has only two weeks left of this term, then about a month's holiday, after which only twelve weeks of the next term. It may be that Linda and I will come back a couple of weeks before Keith, but we'll see. We could travel back by ship if we liked, but it would be a nightmare with Linda now. We'd have to watch her every second as she could easily climb through the railings and there would be nothing to stop her falling into the water. It would be too much worry so we are planning to fly back. Also, it will be much quicker, of course.

We have been receiving the Readers' Digest since about March. Sometimes we get two copies. They didn't send a copy in February so I wrote to Readers' Digest in South Africa and explained I had informed the UK office we were moving to Rhodesia and they arranged it from South Africa. The subscription will have run out by the time we leave here so they won't have to arrange another transfer. The flu is still in the throes here but, touch wood, we have only had it slightly. A great number of people have died from pneumonia caused by the flu, particularly the European population. The problem is that Europeans go to work when they first get a cold but the African doesn't; therefore, the African doesn't spread the virus about like we do.

We measure Linda's height every now and again and put a mark on the wall together with the date, and between 9 June and 8 August, she has grown one and a quarter inches. She's now thirty-five inches tall, which is amazing when we think she used to stand on tiptoe to try to reach the end of the safety chain on the door when we first moved in here in February, yet the other day she was trying to headbutt it like a football. She's not particularly fat though, as the last time I weighed her she was only about 26 lbs. Unfortunately, she seems to be getting Michael's bad habits too as, on Friday night, I caught her 'wowing' with her arms around her little pillow. She still doesn't use her potty, at least, not to do what she should be doing. She wears it, stands in it, carries her toys in it and sits on it after she has turned it upside down, but will she, the little devil, do anything in it? We've now bought her a baby's toilet seat to see if that does the trick. When I'm on the toilet, she takes great delight in banging the toilet lid onto my back, then backwards again onto the wall, and if I'm not watching her, she throws everything in sight down it and has even been caught washing her hands in the bowl. She's a real terror sometimes.

But poor little thing, the other day she trapped all the fingers of her left hand in the door when she closed it and forgot to take her hand away. We had just gotten over that when, as I was closing a cupboard door, she pushed her thumb into the opening without me noticing and I trapped that. Fortunately, nothing was broken and apparently, she's not hurting now either and seems fine.

Keith and I went to see the film Bonnie and Clyde on Saturday and were very disappointed as it had been cut to blazes by the censors. Yet even with this travesty, there was an age limit to see it of twenty-one... so we just about made it!! It's unbelievable, isn't it? The censors say they are keeping the youth clean-minded, not like the status quo in UK and America. Big laugh! In today's paper three twelve-year old girls have been expelled from a public school in Salisbury for taking liquor into their dormitories. There's also another paragraph about the number of people in Rhodesia taking drugs and dealing in black magic. Almost every other issue of Playboy is banned, yet there's a 'Tassel Tosser' with 44-24-36 measurements advertising her appearance at the strip club in town, where teenagers are admitted without any problems. They're all such pure-minded goody-goodies here that it makes me sick.

Keith is handing in his notice on Monday. Not before time too! He had a bust-up with the headmaster today and it ended in a slanging match. It was initially about some instructions the Head had given about tennis balls, and then, a matter of weeks later, he gave exactly the opposite instructions. When Keith tried to point out what he had said originally, the Head told Keith to: 'Get out of my office and don't tell me what I said before. This is what I say now. So get out!' Keith blew up and told him he didn't know what he bloody well said from one minute to the next. In his aggravation, Keith then went up to the staff room, collected all the boxes of tennis balls he could find, opened the Head's office door, and threw the lot in saying: 'You can bloody do what you want with them now, as I'm having nothing more to do with tennis at this school.' Keith said the Head was purple with rage. He'll get a further shock on Monday when Keith resigns. All in a day's work, I suppose! Bye for now.

X from Linda and love from us.

Keith and Anne xxx

SUNDAY, 23 August 1970

DEAR MAM AND DAD,

Received your letter on Thursday. As you say, our letters must be crossing. You sound to be having nice weather in the UK. It's just beginning to warm up here and I understand October is the hottest month. Usually, we find it a bit too warm to sunbathe, not that we have anywhere to sunbathe except on our little balcony, which is open to everyone to see from the road.

We met some very nice people last week – about our own age – and had them to dinner last Wednesday. They have been married almost as long as we have but they have no children, as it seems they are both infertile after being involved in a serious car accident a couple of years ago. Needless to say, they thought Linda was wonderful. They have just put their names down to adopt a baby but there is a two-year waiting list in Rhodesia, which is a shame. Last Friday, they invited us back to dinner, together with some other people we had never met before and got on with quite well. We had to take Linda with us as our 'girl' was ill, which pleased Nora no end. She nursed Linda for ages before she'd let me put her to bed in their bedroom. The adopted baby is going to be so spoilt, in a nice way, as Nora and her husband have everything ready for when it comes, from the cot and clothes right down to baby toys. She's much better equipped than I am. They are trying hard to talk us out of returning to the UK at the end of the year, telling us that, on their arrival from South Africa – their birthplace, they felt exactly the same as we do, but that things have changed now. They blame our disappointment with the country on the fact that we are three people living in a two-roomed flat, which I must admit is getting on our nerves now. They suggested Keith get back into African education as the promotion prospects are really good because not many Europeans want to teach Africans in Rhodesia. It's a thought and Keith has promised he'll consider it, but whatever the outcome, he says Linda and I can go to the UK for a holiday around Christmas if he gets a suitable offer. But I'm certainly not banking on it. The regional education officer is on leave for two weeks, so nothing can be done just yet anyway. Nonetheless, Keith is definitely resigning at the beginning of the term in September. He's just started four weeks' holiday.

Linda's new word is 'milk'. But one morning this week, as Keith was going out of the door, she ran up to him waving, and said: 'G'bye, Daddy!' We were both surprised as she doesn't usually say two different words together.

I'm taking a week's holiday in September but don't think we're going anywhere special. It is disappointing about Michael's new house. It sounded ideal for them. But I agree it's better to buy a house than rent one, although the big item is always the deposit. Just think of all the rent you've been paying all these years with not a thing to show for it. Hope they are soon lucky. We had a letter from Derrick last week. He said that Jack and Margaret had returned from Canada and thought it a fabulous place and that they were seriously thinking of emigrating there. Jack had also interested Derrick in Canada, as he's not settling in the UK at all. So, in Derrick's letter, he asked us if we would also be interested. But Keith has written back saying no, Canada didn't appeal at all. For one thing, it's far too cold. Jack and Margaret haven't been there when it's 20° below zero. They've only seen it at its best. Still, they have someone there already, which does help a lot. The main problem with emigrating is always the housing and making friends is often difficult. I don't blame them really if they can get there, as in UK Jack is already as high as he'll be able to get with his present job. Also, I understand his pay isn't brilliant – even worse than a teacher's! They sent us a card and seemed to be having a ball of a time, and Margaret's mam and dad who were with them in Canada also seemed to be enjoying their holiday. It will have been really something for them all to holiday together and I envy them as this is something I'll always regret if we return to the UK; that you'll never have had a chance to see Africa, and Salisbury in particular, and once we're back, that'll be it. We really hope that Jack and Derrick don't decide to go to Canada, as there'll only be Gerald left to continue the Thursday nights out they all used to have and which Keith is hoping to continue when we get back.

I don't know what the grease marks are on this air letter – sorry, no doubt Linda has had her dirty dorks on it! Keith and I had a lie down this afternoon and accidentally fell asleep for half an hour. Linda wakened me by banging on the bedside table with a serrated knife! The next thing I knew, she was pushing a mashed-up cigar into my mouth – she had found Keith's cigars on the table. I jumped up with panic; the place looked as though a tornado had swept through. There wasn't a pan in the cupboard and Linda had opened one of the kitchen drawers and pulled everything out onto the floor. Newspapers were strewn all over the floor and she must have thought the place was dirty because she had brought the filthy mop in from the balcony and dumped it on an armchair after making a few attempts to clean the table. She had even reached onto the kitchen worktop and found Keith's nearly empty dinner plate and eaten the remains, except for an odd piece of meat here and there. I was shocked to think we had left her alone, even for a few minutes, and was glad at this moment we weren't living in England, as we would have been prosecuted for child neglect! As I cleaned everything up, she just followed me around, gabbling away, quite unconcerned.

Love from us.

xx

Big kiss from Linda.

Xx

WEDNESDAY, 9 September 1970

DEAR MICHAEL AND BARBARA,

Sorry I have not written for such a long time, I don't know how you manage with four children, as it takes me all my time to get anything done with only one!

You will probably know by now that we are thinking of coming back. I say 'thinking' because Keith has applied for a post at the Gwelo Teacher Training College, although we doubt very much he will get it, or even that he particularly wants to get it. We have just heard that this college is some twenty miles from Gwelo and out in the bush. Actually, Gwelo is rather a nice place to live – that is where Keith's brother, Derrick, and family lived for about eleven years. We had a look around the town some months ago and quite liked what we saw, as it is much smaller than Bulawayo, which really is just like any other big city except that it is very clean and white. Now I come to think of it, we visited Gwelo in 1966 when we were living in Malawi, visiting the Wankie Game Reserve in December that year as we passed through Gwelo en route. We even called to see the house Derrick used to live in and took some film at the time. You probably saw the film at some point as it was one of the first ones we sent back.

I'm on holiday next week – Keith is on school holiday until the week after next – and we had thought about visiting the game reserve again and going to see the Victoria Falls, which we have never seen. But I have had second thoughts about it as it would mean that Linda would have to sleep in the same room as us, and on the few occasions she has done that, I have hardly slept a wink – I hear her every groan and turn. We only have one bedroom here and each night we carry Linda and her cot out into the living room to sleep.

At the moment, Keith is in South Africa having the car attended to and I'm finding it a bit difficult dragging the cot out at night by myself. I nearly always get it stuck in the doorway between the rooms. Fortunately, she never wakes up, no matter how much I bang her about. Re the car, there is nothing wrong with it except that the manufacturers have fitted the wrong brake drums. On one side, they have fitted the Capri brake which is the right one, but on the other side, they have fitted an Escort brake which is much smaller and not suitable for the Capri. Keith couldn't understand why it kept pulling to one side when he braked (I must confess, I never noticed until he mentioned it!), so he took it to the garage in town and they discovered the problem. It's still under guarantee but this guarantee doesn't apply in Rhodesia, of course; hence, Keith has had to take the car down to South Africa. He's been gone since Monday and should be back tomorrow, thank goodness.

By now, the dusky days will be closing in on you in the UK and it will be getting darker, both in the mornings and at night, whereas here the temperature is warming up though we can occasionally still get cold days. Being an apartment, there is no fireplace, which is unfortunate as a log fire always looks so nice.

When we get back, Linda will love playing with the children as, even though she doesn't play with any here, whenever she meets a small child she instinctively puts her arms around it. We took her to a motel a few miles from town last Sunday where they had a beer garden, as well as a playground for children. There was one child there about Linda's age and, as soon as Linda saw her, she ran up to her and put her arms around her shoulders and started playing with her hair. Linda still hasn't too much growth, especially at the top where she is almost completely bald and she seems to have a fascination with other people's hair. The child mustn't have been too keen on this as she started crying and ran off to her mother. Fortunately, her mother hadn't been watching the tableau and the child was too young to tell her. Fortunately, Linda didn't try her new bad habit just now which is biting – usually my chin when she gets hold of me. Of course I was watching to make sure that didn't happen.

Bye for now and see you all soon.

Lots of love,

Linda, Keith and Anne (with a sore chin!) xxxx

TUESDAY, 29 September 1970

DEAR MAM AND DAD,

Just a quick letter. I have given my notice here at work. It is really quite sad because I did like the job very much. As my boss said, never mind, you may decide to come back when you have been back in the UK for a while – Job's comforter!

Linda and I are booked on a flight arriving at Leeds Yeadon Airport on 6 November. We leave here on 5 November, Grandma's birthday. We have to fly down to Johannesburg, then on to Brussels, from Brussels to London and from London to Yeadon – twenty-four hours flying time. I'm not looking forward to this at all, especially with Linda, but it has to be done, one way or another. I think Keith is going to ask Jack or Mavis to pick us up from the airport on 6 November, but I'm not sure of the arrival time so there is no point coming to meet us. We shall ask Jack to loan us the cot again for Linda and if you could maybe get a mattress for the bed from the Co-op Club then, when I get back, I'll pay you for the amount in cash as I shall be bringing some money with me. Keith will be arriving back six weeks later as term doesn't end until 11 December, but in the meantime, I hope I can find a furnished house somewhere for when he gets back. I did look locally when we returned from Malawi but didn't see anything suitable then though maybe we'll be lucky this time. If I were to wait until Keith finished for the Christmas term at school, it would mean we should have to split up anyway as there are too many of us, but if I can find accommodation before he arrives that will be much better. About your suggestion of a house at some seaside resort – sadly, it really wouldn't work, as Keith won't want a teaching position when we get back and there is very little scope, except in a large city, for anything outside teaching.

I can't wait to get settled into a nice little house of our own, with a lovely kitchen (which is something I've never had), as soon as possible. We seem to have been renting accommodation all our married lives – though I'm forgetting our three years in Leeds, aren't I? I think this is possibly the reason we weren't settled in England when we came back from Malawi as the rented flat in Soothill wasn't exactly luxury, was it? You never know, if we're careful we may have a little money left to lend you and Dad to buy a small house of your own nearby. Because we are immigrants in Rhodesia, and as we aren't staying the full three years, unfortunately we shall have to pay this government back the money they lent us for our fares out – that is £300, plus the £300 for our own fares back to the UK. It is a bit rotten really, but of course we knew this before we came out. It's just one of those things. Keith's mam is looking to buy a larger house at the back of the one where she is living at present. I wonder how much she will want for the house she's leaving as she has made it really nice, having had a bathroom fitted by taking a portion off the larger one of the two bedrooms. There is just one large room downstairs with the sink near the window. There is also a dry cellar for storage. I bet it would be ideal for you. However, I imagine she would want around £700 for it. I could always ask, if you are interested.

Apart from Jack and Margaret, no-one on Keith's side knows about us returning. They will get quite a shock when they see us.

Linda's hair is coming on now, especially at the back. It looks a bit curly too, which is nice. She also seems quite intelligent as, if I start to clean up, she takes the brush or duster off me and finishes the job. But I could choke her sometimes! The other day she came into the room and started washing the small coffee tables we have littered around the flat. However, on closer inspection, I saw she was using our face cloth! She had left a trail of water leading from the bathroom and as I followed it, I saw wet patches on the wardrobe doors where she had been washing; also, she had mopped up the bedcover. When I went into the bathroom, I found the floor soddened, and the toilet seat and cover were spotless where she had 'washed' them, all with the face cloth. And by now, you'll have guessed where she got the water from – yes, the lavatory! She knew she had done wrong because when she heard me shout, she couldn't get rid of the cloth fast enough. But her favourite occupation is pulling the pegs off the low clothes line on the balcony and 'dedicating' them to the flat below. She even emptied my purse once but fortunately, there was only about 9d in change. Every few weeks, the people below send their house girl up with a pile of things Linda has pushed through the railings. I'm staggered sometimes when I see just what she has had hold of. I caught her in the act of trying to reach over the top once while holding one of Keith's pumps, which our girl had just washed and left on the balcony to dry. I would have loved to have had a camera on Saturday in the park. Linda had climbed onto a bench with three little African children and was having a lovely time copying them. When they swung their legs, she did the same. Then she threw silver paper balls for them to retrieve and they kindly did as she wanted just to make her laugh. She would have been there till now but for the two European children who came and started playing rough. She loves Africans so much that she's happy to go to any African nanny to be picked up, and usually says 'g'bye g'bye' to me as if to say: 'Get lost now, I've got what I want.' As soon as we are settled back in UK, we will have to get a Siamese cat as she is animal mad; she has absolutely no fear whatsoever, even with dogs, although she was knocked down by one once.

We haven't many 'legal' stamps left so I'll only be able to write a couple more times. Also, we had better keep some back for when I leave so that Keith can drop me a line.

Bye for now.

Give our love to everyone.

See you soon.

K. A. L xxx

MONDAY, 12 October 1970

DEAR MAM AND DAD,

Received your letter today. We leave here three weeks on Thursday, which seems amazing as I can't really visualise leaving here. It's like a dream. Not a bad one I don't suppose, and I'm sure we'll have bittersweet memories of our time in Rhodesia. But to think we'll be leaving here at 11.30 a.m. Thursday and at the hottest part of the year (during the last fortnight, the temperature has generally been 95° in the shade – even 97° one day) and will arrive back to UK at almost the coldest part of the year, on the following day. I believe we arrive at Yeadon airport at about noon on Friday. But we haven't asked anyone to meet us, as I can easily catch the air terminal bus into Leeds and probably a taxi to Batley. It'll be hard managing Linda by myself, but Keith has a harder job doing the packing and trying to get a good price for the car. We have ordered a new engine for the car, one about two and a half times the size of the present one, and if everything turns out all right we should make quite a profit when Keith sells it. The problem is that there isn't much time left now as Keith will be due back around five weeks after us.

Mam, I think it would be better to leave the matter of the bed until we get back as, when we buy a bed, we will want a king-size one, as the ordinary 4' 6" isn't really big enough. The bed I mentioned was really for Linda and I was going to use it until we had our own house, then Linda was going to use it. She is getting a bit big for the cot now as she is already trying to climb out of it – and occasionally gets her foot caught fast between the cot and the wall. She can, however, climb on and off the bed without any trouble and it will be so much safer when she progresses to one. I suppose it's better to leave babies in their cots as long as possible, as you (usually!) know where they are.

You certainly won't recognise Linda as she's quite a little girl now; she seems so even to me. When we give her a banana, after peeling it, she has to have the skin as well and she then toddles off to the pedal bin in the kitchen, lifts the lid and carefully puts the skin inside. I thought she was being very clever and helpful yesterday when she picked up my purse and opened the wallet part - she hasn't got the hang of opening the change compartment yet − and took out a $1 note. She has done this before and usually brings it over to me saying 'Ta.' But this time, she went into the kitchen and came out a few minutes later minus the $1 note. I went to look in the pedal bin, and sure enough, there it was. Today, after I'd finished reading your letter, I left it on the side table and, shortly afterwards, I heard the lid go on the bin. When I looked inside, there was your letter, beautifully screwed into a little ball. The knob is missing off the TV and I have a sneaking feeling it's been 'dumped' you know where by you know who, but I'll be blowed if I'll go searching through the rubbish to try to find it (it's a hired TV though, which doesn't help).

We heard from our American friends about two weeks ago that they now have a baby girl. They have been married for almost ten years, so you can imagine how thrilled they are. They have named her Liesel which is rather an unusual name, but lovely.

I'm working afternoons as well as mornings for the next three weeks − we have to pay for our fares somehow. I'll write again before we leave. Please Mam, don't go rushing about for us as we'll fit in where we can.

Bye for now. See ya soon!

K. L. A xxxx

THURSDAY, 29 October 1970

DEAR MAM AND DAD,

This will probably be the last letter I'll have time to write before we leave here, so here goes.

I finish working tomorrow, the 30th, but there is still so much to do that I shall need the next few days to get organised. Linda and I leave Bulawayo on Thursday next, a week today. We have to change planes four times unfortunately, so it's going to be hard. We are lucky with the connections, as I believe we only have an hour's wait at the longest point. Keith will fly out five weeks later so he won't be much behind, and he has so much to do - selling the car and arranging for the money we get for the car to be transferred out of the country. We have stopped planning for the future as our plans never seem to work out and you must be bored to death with our indecision. But we shall certainly be buying a house when we get back. If we decide sometime next year to go back to Malawi, then we will always have a house to come back to after our two and a half years contract. That is the main thing.

As I mentioned before, the only people on Keith's side we have told we are returning are Jack and Margaret, so the rest of the family will all get a big surprise. As Keith generally writes to his mam for the whole family, he has had to be careful not to give the show away. In his last letter during this week, he had to write in coded messages, which took a lot of doing. When the boys were teenagers Keith and Jack perfected a 'secret code', which I think is called pig Latin, and Keith was able to add a few words at the end of the letter to his mam which only Jack would understand.

Our plane will arrive at Leeds Airport at about 11.45 a.m. on the Friday morning, but as it's such an awkward time, especially as it's so near lunchtime, as mentioned before, we'll manage by ourselves. There is a bus to bring us from the airport into Leeds city centre and we can get a taxi back to Batley, as there will be quite a lot of luggage. If you have already started working, don't take the day off. You can leave the key in the lavatory window (like you used to), or maybe we can go straight to Michaels as I'm sure he has a spare key to your house. I reckon it will be after two o'clock by the time we get to Batley.

I have been working full days for the past three weeks to get a bit of extra money but it has nearly killed me. Maybe it's the heat as it's nearly always in the middle nineties at the moment. I must admit that I haven't had the energy to do a thing when I get back from work. The hours are also very long, as I have been leaving the flat at 7.40 a.m. and not getting back until 5.20 p.m. which has been such a long time to be away from Linda, poor thing, and she has noticed that I haven't been here. Consequently, each day I've arrived home, she has been nagging at me to make sure I don't leave her again. Unfortunately, this time I didn't get a cook-boy so I've had to make the meals on top of everything else. It doesn't help either that Linda won't do without her bath. At around 6.15 p.m. each evening she comes to me and starts tugging at me saying 'bat, bat'. Fortunately, she will stay in the bath by herself, usually without water as, almost as soon as she gets in, she pulls the plug and turns on the cold tap. If I'm unlucky, she'll lean over and wash the lavatory lid for me – of course, usually with one of the face cloths. Oh Mam, she will make you laugh as she is getting to be such a cheeky little thing. She often comes up to me when I'm not expecting it and lifts my dress up saying 'cheeky' – she also does it to herself and, although I know I should try not to take any notice, I can't help laughing. Of course, that makes her do it all the more! She will get to know you both very quickly, I'm sure. In fact, she will go to anyone without exception. We had a visitor the other week who Linda met for the first time. But when she was going, Linda went after her, wanting to be picked up. When Pat pretended to take her along the balcony to go down the steps, Linda merely waved to us bye bye. If we hadn't said anything, I wonder if she would have been content to have left us!

I'll have to go shopping on Saturday morning to get her a coat and shoes. She has outgrown so many pairs of shoes that at the moment she has only one pair of green pumps with holes in the toes where she has outgrown them. I have knitted a cardigan with a hood as I expect it will be cold when we get back. I can't remember what November was like last year. Anyway, not to worry. Everything seems to be happening so quickly now that I can't really think that this time next week, we'll be on our way (or almost). Keith will eat most of his meals at the school, which is only a few minutes' walk up the road. Our next-door neighbour has asked to take over the flat for a friend, so fortunately Keith won't have to pay the rent for the whole of December.

I'm using an old typewriter so please forgive the missed keys. My replacement at the office started working two weeks ago and she now has use of my nice typewriter.

I'll say bye for now. See you all next Friday sometime.

Lots of love to everyone.

Anne xxx

LINDA and I arrived back in England on 6 November 1970 but the return journey was far from uneventful. Due to Rhodesia's continued Unilateral Declaration of Independence, airlines were not allowed to fly to/from Rhodesia, flights having to be made via South Africa or a North African country. My flight had been booked on the route Bulawayo to Johannesburg to Brussels to London Heathrow to Leeds/Bradford Airport, almost a twenty-four-hour journey. I had no idea, as I was setting out from the flat that morning, what a problem I would have over the next 24 hours. Besides having to take care of a twenty-month-old baby and all the associated equipment to deal with her, I also had my own luggage of one very large suitcase, together with a full-size black 'Scottie' dog toy belonging to Linda, which I somehow had to carry under one arm, the other arm often carrying my daughter, and with two strained fingers dragging my suitcase along the floor.

Unfortunately, the flight leaving Bulawayo was delayed about half an hour and, even though we seemed to make up most of the time, when we arrived in Johannesburg, the Brussels flight was on the tarmac with the engines running. Fortunately, someone had advised the airport that my daughter and I were booked on the last flight to Brussels that day, and we were met at the Johannesburg Arrivals by an official who rushed us along corridors and onto the aircraft with literally minutes to spare. Trying to ignore the glares of the first-class passengers, I shame-facedly followed the official through the curtains to the aircraft's economy class and was then led down the plane and shown to my seat, whilst a member of the cabin crew following closely behind with Linda. As the plane taxied down the runway for take-off into the sunset, I breathed a sigh of relief, though sadly, didn't know then that this was to be the last time I would ever step onto soil in Central Africa.

Linda and I settled down for the thirteen plus hour flight to Brussels and both managed to get a few hours' sleep on the plane. We arrived in Brussels at the ungodly time of 2.30 a.m. and our next flight wasn't due to leave Brussels until 6.30 a.m., which meant a four hour wait with absolutely nothing to do. On disembarking the plane at Brussels and making my way to the transfer lounge, I was shocked to find that, even though it was patently obvious I was struggling to cope with a crying, tired baby in my arms, as well as carrying heavy hand luggage and a large toy, absolutely everyone ignored me. People walked beside me and even pushed in front of me in order to get onto the escalator first, presumably concerned that I might hold them up. No-one looked at me or asked if they could help. I am still disgusted all these years later when I think about it.

We eventually arrived at the airport transfer concourse and

found seats on which to rest. I had hoped that Linda would go to sleep on my knee, thus giving me a chance to close my own eyes which, by this time, were almost closed anyway with exhaustion, but Linda was so tired she had become irritated; this is how we spent the last few hours of our trip. It was to be a long, long night.

At 6.00 a.m., I picked up my 'katundu' and headed once more for the departure lounge, walking slowly so that Linda could keep up with me. This flight was short but at least I could rest and there were things happening to keep Linda interested. We arrived at London Heathrow at 8.00 a.m. on Friday, 6 November and soon were on our onward final flight to Yorkshire. I didn't know what to expect on arrival at Leeds/Bradford Airport and was prepared to 'slum' it for the remainder of the journey, knowing it would be hard. But as I was walking down the airport steps, I saw my father and Jack waiting there on the tarmac. It was a lovely surprise and so unexpected. Jack's first words to me were: 'I didn't pick you out at first. It was only when I saw your legs that I realised it was you!' I had forgotten to warn my family that I had dyed my dark hair to a (what I had thought) subtle red shade, but apparently, it had changed my appearance dramatically.

Keith arrived back just before Christmas and we spent the next three months looking for and finding a suitable house, where we remained for the next two years, leaving England once again, for the Middle East this time. But that's another story!

Sadly, we never saw the finished film of our portrayal of a newly married couple in Malawi. When we enquired many years later, we were told it had never been completed and it is now lost forever.

EIGHT

Endings

Unfortunately, as with a lot of couples who marry very young, our marriage didn't last, and by 1973 we had decided to go our separate ways. However, we always remained good friends and spoke, either by phone or in person, on a regular basis.

In 1983, I met my present partner, a wonderful man. By this time, my daughter was in her early teens and it was finally time for me, cerebrally, to move on. The last thirty-three years have been wonderful with Ken and I could never imagine my life without him. Happily, he too came to know Keith over these years, through their mutual love of the game of bridge.

Keith also moved on with his life after our divorce. I was always interested in his ventures, one of them being the time he brought the first British Airways Concorde flight to Leeds/Bradford airport in Yorkshire in April 1987, fulfilling a lifelong dream. This venture proved so popular that he retired early from the teaching profession and formed his own company, running four times yearly Concorde flights from Yorkshire for the next thirteen years, ironically, retiring in 2000 just before the Paris Concorde crash in which all 109 people aboard were killed. I used to think that his feet were guided by the angels, as he constantly trod a safe path.

Sadly, while I was preparing this book for editing, Keith was diagnosed with terminal lung cancer. Our daughter, Linda, became his main carer during those final, heartbreaking weeks and, just three months after diagnosis, he died on 28 October 2016, at home, as he had wished. I spent a number of days with him during those last weeks, sometimes talking about old times, but I realised that he had moved on quite a lot since he and I had been married. He did read the first draft of the book before he was diagnosed with cancer and showed some interest in the letters, but I knew my memories of those times were very different to his and I couldn't compete with what he had done since we had gone our separate ways.

I will miss Keith's regular phone calls in which he mostly talked about the holiday he had just had and where he planned to go next. He had retired quite early and been given the chance to do all the things he always wanted to do as he grew older. In those final weeks of his life, he had confirmed this many times, saying he had no regrets at all and was ready to die.

But he was a scientist to the end and, in one of our last conversations before he became too weak to speak, he told Linda and me that he was convinced there was a planet out there, somewhere, (possibly Planet Nine?), where life did exist though not necessarily life as we know it, and that he intended to find it. I wish him speed on this next great venture and hope, should he find that planet, that he comes back to let us know.

Safe journey, Keith, and God bless you.

August 2017

Acknowledgments

I would like to thank my editor, Laura Dowers, without whose valuable advice this book would still be sitting in Word. She made it happen.

I also thank Angie Phillips for creating the artwork I could never have conveyed.

25658814R00206

Printed in Poland
by Amazon Fulfillment
Poland Sp. z o.o., Wrocław